TROUBLING THE FAMILY

Difference Incorporated

Roderick A. Ferguson *and* Grace Kyungwon Hong

SERIES EDITORS

Troubling the Family

. . . .

The Promise of Personhood and the Rise of Multiracialism

Habiba Ibrahim

Difference Incorporated

University of Minnesota Press
Minneapolis
London

An earlier version of the Introduction was previously published as "Toward Black and Multiracial Kinship after 1997, or How a Race Man Became Cablinasian," special issue, "The Politics of Biracialism," *Black Scholar* 39, no. 3–4 (2009): 23–31. Reprinted by permission of *Black Scholar*.

Published by the University of Minnesota Press
111 Third Avenue South, Suite 290
Minneapolis, MN 55401-2520
http://www.upress.umn.edu

Library of Congress Cataloging-in-Publication Data
Ibrahim, Habiba.
Troubling the family : the promise of personhood and the rise of multiracialism / Habiba Ibrahim.
(Difference incorporated)
Includes bibliographical references and index.
ISBN 978-0-8166-7917-1 (hc : alk. paper)
ISBN 978-0-8166-7918-8 (pb : alk. paper)
1. Racially mixed children—United States. 2. Racially mixed people—United States. 3. Families—United States. I. Title.
HQ777.9.I27 2012
306.850973—dc23
2012008204

The University of Minnesota is an equal-opportunity educator and employer.

Contents

The Rising Son of Multiracialism

ELDRICK "TIGER" WOODS'S RISE TO CELEBRITY in 1997 was accompanied by a debate about his racial identity—black or multiracial—that offers a few paradigmatic examples of the multiracial phenomenon. The multiracial movement was conceptualized and mobilized by stakeholders who were interested in the well-being of multiracial families. Primarily, the multiracial child became an icon that represented the social and political horizon, a future in which the full recognition of personhood—selfhood unfettered by taxonomic restraints—would be fulfilled. But beyond its iconic role in the movement, the multiracial child itself also became the strategic focus of multiracial family organizations. Protecting the multiracial child became the central strategy for adult stakeholders, who chose to suppress a variety of political differences among them in order to keep their safe, welcoming communities of families intact. Focusing on multiracial children became a key approach for maintaining a semblance of collective coherence, even as it simultaneously signaled the narrow limits of such a unifying project. So one particular paradigm of multiracialism—investment in the family and the centrality of children—depended on the interfacing of blackness and multiracialism. Historically, blackness and multiracialism were family: the rule of hypodescent, also know as the one-drop rule, set the parameters of blackness wide enough to encompass racial mixedness.

The year 1997 marked a moment when the two identities strikingly ran up and against each other. The rise of Tiger Woods, which correlates historically with the rise of multiracialism as a salient cultural and political designation, calls our attention to another sort of family feud. In 1997, the future of multiracialism, and the legacy of blackness, both were defined by the same horizon of a rising *son*. In other words, the multiracial phenomenon produced discourses about race that tacitly situated blackness as outmoded and multiracialism as emergent. However, despite this representation of temporal succession, both forms of racialization shared a symbolic interest in the perpetuation of male progeny and in masculinity more generally. Both black and multiracial cultural politics shared an interest in upholding manhood as the central category around which subjects developed a normative sense of social kinship. For this reason, the iconic status of Tiger Woods during the late 1990s reveals what discourses about racialized kinship—or social belonging—emerged when the temporal logic or race was shifting, while the status of masculinity in racialized communities maintained its centrality.

This temporal narrative of succession signals a discourse in which blackness and multiracialism make troubled encounters with each other. If 1997 indicates the trouble between conventional black community and emergent multiracialism, then what might this problem (within the family) tell us? What are the potential outcomes of troubling the line between multiracial and black political ends? Finally, how might a new kinship between blackness and mixedness lead us away from the conflating binds of community and toward a partnership in cultural production, social justice, or a mutual future? If after 1997 it no longer seems adequate to imagine our racial blood as the essential ties that bind, then what will become the passageway into the family? The problem of conceptualizing racial belonging as kinship reveals the simultaneously obscured and obvious presence of womanhood. In other words, the temporal passageway through which black and multiracial subjects imagine the achievement of personhood in public takes up the grammar of gender.

Troubling the Family: The Promise of Personhood and the Rise of Multiracialism attempts to reveal a feminist genealogy of the multiracial movement and focuses on the movement's political and cultural logics between 1997 and 2007. There are many excellent scholarly accounts of the multiracial movement. Much of the recent work spans a wide spectrum of disciplines, with primary concerns that include the U.S. Census and demography, policy, statistical analysis, and popular culture.[1] The aforementioned studies fortify this book by developing a discussion on the intersections of black racial politics and multiracialism. This book participates in this wider conversation about multiracialism and treats materials including memoirs, legal case studies, popular fiction, and journalism that have been treated by others. However, I attempt to build on this thoroughgoing discussion by attending to the manner in which multiracialism gains clarity through gender and providing an analysis of the gendered politics of the movement.

Ultimately, *Troubling the Family* considers whether another version of multiracial temporality—one that incorporated the unfinished historical narratives of second-wave feminism and black nationalism—could have produced a more richly interracial, antielitist, and gender- and sexuality-conscious social sphere. This expanded social dimension would have been "mixed" in the sense of being intellectually and politically conjunctional. From out of entrenched public engagement, it would have produced an array of new knowledge projects.

Troubling the Family argues that the popular emergence of multiracialism during the end of the twentieth century was highly determined by an underlying, normatively gendered discourse. However, gender was rarely acknowledged as providing the foundational logic for what seemed like a strictly racial dissidence between blackness and multiracialism. In this book, I consider the manner in which gender—as a cultural formation and a basis for political analysis—breaks apart the coherence of what an emergent multiracialism became throughout the 1990s and 2000s. In this way, I open with 1997 as a seminal moment for multiracialism that suppressed its own gendered foundations. Understanding this 1990s-era suppression requires a look across historical moments and arguments, first reaching back to the 1960s, when miscegenation laws were struck down. Such a historical glance reveals that the notion of gender was the starting point of an analytics that made categorical multiracialism, and multiracial politics, possible. Once a genealogy of how multiracialism's gendered origins comes into view, it then becomes possible to focus on a range of stakeholders whose interests often ran against the grain of what the dominant multiracial movement of the 1990s, which often privileged the sanctity of the heteronormative family, the labor of child rearing, and more precise forms of racial tabulation. This book begins with an extended anecdote about Tiger Woods, the first 1990s multiracial race man, and concludes with a consideration of Barack Obama, who in this study represents a resurrection of the promise that multiracialism extended into the 2000s: a version of personhood with no memory of its own gendered legacy, and with no self-account of how it became so masculine.

Training a Tiger and a Lineage of Race Men

The case of golfer Tiger Woods illustrates two key conditions of racial heroism. First, as a star athlete whose celebrity status was partially derived from his racial identity, Woods was instrumental in exposing a rift between black and multiracial communities that was particularly acute at the site of cultural race representatives. Second, the very status of a racial representative or hero—someone who figures an idealized version of a racial community—implicitly functions through an account of masculinity. On April 13, 1997, Woods galvanized the public after winning the Masters Tournament, a major PGA title. At twenty-one years old, Woods was the youngest winner of the Masters, having played professional golf for only a year. He had won the PGA title with a record-breaking victory margin of twelve strokes, second only to a lead established in the 1862 British Open.[2] Although his youth and outstanding performance were heavily remarked by the press immediately after his win, the greatest amount of attention was paid to his historic status as the first person of color to win the tournament. The event was marked by the appearance and encouragement of Lee Elder, the first black man to play in the Masters in 1975. Woods understood Elder's support as that which "really reinforced what I had to accomplish. . . . He was the first."[3] As Elder stated with regard to Woods's imminent victory, "I am just so elated. . . . Here we're going to have a black champion, and that's something that certainly makes my heart feel very warm."[4] During his victory speech, Woods was deferential to Elder, Charlie Sifford, and Ted Rhodes as those black golf professionals who "paved the way."[5] Also significant was that Woods's historic win coincided with the fiftieth anniversary of Jackie Robinson's entry as the first black man into major league baseball. News coverage bound the two athletes together within a single genealogy, with Robinson paving the way for Woods, and with Woods breaking the racial barrier in much the same way that Robinson had fifty years earlier. Demonstrating a wider extension of this genealogy, one editorialist wrote, "Had there been no Jackie Robinson, could there have ever been a Henry Aaron, a Bob Gibson, a Frank Thomas or a Ken Griffey Jr.? . . . A Bill Russell or a Michael Jordan? A Lee Elder or a Tiger Woods"?[6] In this way, the immediate impact of Woods's victory was a national acknowledgment of historical, discriminatory practices that subordinated black Americans, as well as an ameliorating celebration of black achievement and racial progress.

It should be noted that Woods's multiracial heritage was in no way hidden from the press at the time of his Masters win. Several journalists alluded to his mixedness, citing both his black and Thai heritages. However, Woods's blackness was made prominently legible in a narrative that contextualized his achievement in genealogical terms—not simply in terms of a racial history, but also in terms of a history of family. In the days immediately after Woods's Masters win, the sort of history reported often resembled a venerable lineage of race men. The precocious, newly adult Woods was part of a line of descent that had begun with Robinson and Elder; this familial narrative gained its emphasis from the inclusion of Woods's biological black father, Earl Woods, who was frequently cited as the person who groomed Tiger for success. For instance, in 1997, Earl Woods published and promoted *Training a Tiger: A Father's Guide to Raising a Winner in Both Golf and Life,* a guide book on golf and parenting.

This genealogical framework is not exceptional when it comes to narrating a trajectory of black achievement. Although the particular case of Tiger Woods posits a black genealogy within the domain of athleticism, similarly imagined genealogies have structured intellectual histories in the academy. For instance, Hazel Carby argues that W. E. B. Du Bois's 1903 meditation on black Americanism, *The Souls of Black Folk,* typifies a masculinist ideology that underlies those "texts which have been regarded as *founding* texts written by the *founding fathers* of black American history and culture."[7] In the study of black culture, *Souls* as a founding text and Du Bois as a founding father pave the way for imagining black American community "through the intellectual and political work of identifying intellectual ancestors."[8] Although Carby deliberately avoids repeating an often-told narrative of black America's genealogy of race leaders— Frederick Douglass, Booker T. Washington, Martin Luther King Jr., Malcolm X—such genealogies of exceptional men allow us to analyze the process through which specific agents, histories, literatures, and traditions come to identify the black community or the family.

Clearly, such a paradigm for delineating which athletic and intellectual properties belong to the family must also produce outsiders. Recognition of kin, therefore, simultaneously requires a consensual recognition of those with whom "we" don't identity. Cathy Cohen's study of black political responses to the AIDS crisis usefully demonstrates this dynamic between an often-perpetuated, dominant communal narrative, and cross-cutting subissues that are either marginalized or omitted from it. As Cohen notes, black Americans have a long shared history of subjection to racist practices and ideologies, and therefore have a shared interest in resistance and struggle. This "shared consciousness, linked fate" has shaped "consensus issues," political agendas meant to address the plight of black community as a whole.[9] However, consensus issues currently are being challenged by cross-cutting issues, which often reveal the diverging lines of interest and influence within the community. She notes that cross-cutting issues "such as AIDS and drug use in black communities, as well as the extreme, isolated poverty disproportionately experienced by black women—all issues which disproportionately and directly affect poor, less empowered, and 'morally wanting' segments of black communities—fall into this category of political issues."[10] I raise the matter of the AIDS crisis in black communities here because it pinpoints a process through which black Americans have constructed a domain of belonging, and it reveals the contingencies of this construction. Fashioning black politics according to consensus often has the effect of scripting vulnerable, queer, or subaltern subjects as somewhere outside of the central discourse.

It therefore becomes difficult to register these outsider experiences as those that can influence our political mandates, our cultural and historical narratives, and our communal identities. In a sense, Woods—by virtue of his class status, masculinity, and, once again, his place in an esteemed genealogy—was not only legibly black; he also stood as a sign of our consensual public image. If, implicitly, it is an image that we give our consent to, then as a matter of function, it must render illegible, moot, or strange those identities that do not assimilate. As a Thai American woman and mother of 1997's favorite son, Kultida Woods's cultural and gendered influence is minimized in a manner that implies her illegibility within a popular account of black American achievement. However, this reduction also reveals a broader phenomenon of how other family members—race women, the morally wanting—are scripted out of black genealogies and consensual concerns. Indeed, consent plays a large role in how we become family and how we decide which ancestors are kin.

Perhaps the exclusion of Kultida Woods, Tiger Woods's Thai American mother, from this narrative usefully demonstrates how the paradigm of racial family forecloses the range of subjects who count, and the range of legitimate concerns within our community. Once the identity of this community is taken for granted, it becomes possible to create markets for the community by exploiting its exceptional representatives. In a seminal piece that reads the social and political significance of Tiger Woods, Henry Yu describes a process in which histories of migration and of international contact within the United States have been obscured by commercial multiculturalism, which takes on the appearance of cultural difference. Woods lost his stripes of ethnic, racial, transnational complexity to become an overly simplified emblem of individuated cultural difference—a multicultural symbol—that ultimately can serve the marketing ends of multinational corporations. Yu writes, "Like Nike's earlier slogan for basketball icon Michael Jordan, 'I want to be like Mike,' the phrase 'I am Tiger Woods' could be translated by consumers as 'My body is black and I am up and coming just like him,' but more likely it meant 'I want to wear what Tiger wears.'"[11]

Both of these possible interpretations—"I am black and up and coming, like Mike and Tiger," and "the clothing that Tiger wears matters"—actually follow a similarly gendered logic, if in ostensibly different nationalistic contexts. In other words, the emphasis on multicultural unity for the purpose of getting everyone to purchase the same stuff can have varying racialized outcomes that nonetheless labor the same way in terms of gender politics. I'll begin here with an explanation of the divergence between racializing consumership and kinship. In a short piece published in the *Chicago Tribune* the day after Woods's first interview with Oprah Winfrey, Ed Sherman describes the new friendship between Jordan and Woods as "made in Nike marketing heaven." Woods is the "up and coming" star next to the more seasoned Jordan, and the piece describes a weekend in which the two icons relate around the conditions of succession. As quoted in the piece, Woods explains: "Mike is in a position where my life is going. . . . I didn't know how to handle certain situations. Like all the visability [*sic*], the press, privacy. Mike has helped me out. He's been there. What better person to relate to me than an athlete relating to another athlete. Mike's almost like my big brother."[12] In this sense, Tiger Woods has a strikingly intimate claim to the declaration "I want to be like Mike" in a way that resembles the less likely interpretation in Yu's analysis of Nike slogans. Indeed, Woods is acknowledging that he is like Mike, and the two share a likeness in the way that brothers do.

Although the short piece makes no mention of the linked racial similarities between the men, Woods himself alludes to a kinship of condition in the overtly biological terms of brotherhood. With Jordan resembling a "big brother," Woods reifies a narrative that requires racial production to resemble a genealogy of succession. If the claim "I'm black, and I want to gain prominence like Mike or Tiger" is salient for consumers, I would argue that it is also salient for those of us who understand our social and political fates to be inextricably linked to Brother Mike and Brother Tiger. In other words, to a public who would form the interpretation, "My body is black and I am up and coming just like him," there is a context for understanding such affinity as the condition for reproducing blackness. "His black body" does the work of representing and connecting "my body, which is black" (and, perhaps, female, queer, morally wanting, trapped in extreme poverty) to a global marketplace most recently as consumers, but also as objects; it connects us to an imagined community that secures our existence at all. One might think of how a pair of Air Jordans, or a baseball cap embroidered with the Nike swoosh, or—if the swoosh too closely resembles our slave name—a black baseball cap marked simply with an X[13]—conflates black bodies and black clothing with the perpetuation of social and political futures.

In addition to the varying registers in which one interprets an affinity with Jordan or Woods, in Sherman's piece, it seems that a common condition between Jordan and Woods—besides iconic status and relationships with Nike—is the way that labor is implicitly represented. Although the piece focuses on a weekend of laid-back bonding, it is also clear that such an occasion is an exception for men who are perpetually under extremely unusual pressures. The road to fame is a rough one: "Jordan already has embarked on the manic road that Woods is about to travel."[14] Paving the way, as we know, is a particular sort of work that involves an intense level of publicity; if for Woods the hardest part about fame is laboring for the media, becoming a representative for the public, then we must also realize that such labor is most socially and politically strategic for counterbalancing the public discourse of black masculinity under siege.

One context for understanding the publicity and popularity of Tiger Woods is the crisis discourse of black manhood. The Million Man March of 1995, and a 1994 roundtable discussion in the *New York Times Magazine* entitled "The Black Man Is in Terrible Trouble. Whose Problem Is That?" are two manifestations of a longer historical phenomenon in which black manhood is publicly pronounced and fetishized, simultaneously hypervisible and undervisible.[15] Yet while the labor of being Mike or Tiger is as much representative as athletic, neither modality accounts for the connected labor in Southeast Asian countries at this time. Yu writes, "Of course, it's not the women and children being paid thirteen cents an hour [to produce Nike apparel] in Indonesia who will be able to play golf and buy Nike shoes."[16] Black masculine visibility as work—and the sort one does when marching with a band of brothers or wearing an affinity with Mike or Tiger—obscures the comparatively hidden labor of women and children in Southeast Asia. As Hiram Perez points out in his constructive essay, "How to Rehabilitate a Mulatto," "the transnational labor of export manufacture is by design both racialized and feminized . . . a guarantor of American multiculturalism. . . . [Woods] cannot publicly acknowledge his mother's body—the body of feminized, Third World labor—without compromising his own mobility."[17]

I would point out that Woods made a point of publicly acknowledging his mother—something he did repeatedly. However, his public acknowledgment did not grant her public visibility. In a sense, this scheme is reproduced in the representation of parenting as labor. The labor of parenthood for Kultida is figuratively more private—perhaps taken for granted—than the markedly (and marketable) public nature of Earl's parental labor. Perhaps the question of labor in this case, and the question of its gendering, bring into focus the vicissitudes of family in terms of privacy, public engagement, and struggle within the terms of intimacy. While blackness and muliracialism have traditionally shared a kinship of condition (which allows us to imagine Mike and Tiger as brothers), this family tradition repeatedly presents an open secret. Kultida Woods is herself present and not present. In a sense, one might speculate here about another kinship of condition—this time, between black men and Asian American women, who, according to Maurice Wallace, are always already caught between being either phantasmal or overly embodied. If Earl is present, it is because of an American strategy that has been put into place over time to render black manhood present and accounted for: genealogy makes his body appear in a narrative that allows us to recognize ourselves.

Perez argues that the iconography of Tiger Woods ostensibly masks the inequitable conditions of miscegenation. He refers to the concomitant ends of legalism with regard to miscegenation for black/white biracial children and for Amerasian children of Asian women and American servicemen. For instance, Perez points out that Earl met Kultida as a Green Beret in Vietnam.[18] He argues that Woods's public persona obscures a prevalent legal condition regarding such a union: "far from being celebrated as America's sons and daughters, most of those children of U.S. servicemen and Asian women are in actuality denied U.S. citizenship."[19] Clearly, this renders Woods's status as progeny a bit ironic, but from Walter White's blue eyes to Malcolm's red hair, we know how the family has made use of irony. Both Yu and Perez compellingly address the problem of the public persona of Tiger Woods, which is to open a space for deliberation on the varying sorts of historical and ongoing violence that produce legible racial/ethnic formations in the globalized modalities of capitalism or imperialism. Building on but departing from their work, I argue that in 1997, African American community may attempt to fore- close this space for reasons other than the pursuit of a life of "production and consumption."[20] The question this raises is: what happens to us— whoever we are—when we contribute to and make conducive a site where historical tensions and contestations lead to multiple narratives that do not cohere into the community we thought ourselves to be?

Robert Reid-Pharr addresses this problem by arguing for an acknowl- edgment of choice. In a study that traces the intellectual production of James Baldwin, Ralph Ellison, Huey Newton, and other public thinkers of the postwar era, he investigates the ways in which black (male) sub- jects demonstrate the possibility of agency in the historical construction of what black is and black ain't: "If blackness is to have any future at all, then so-called black intellectuals must create modes of black articula- tion that do not turn on the erroneous assumption of profound racial dis- tinction."[21] One might imagine that such an articulation would be able to account for Kultida Woods, women and children in Indonesia (and Thai- land, for that matter), for those outside kids who may not legitimately belong to us but who share resemblances nonetheless. Yet what are the modalities for such articulation? If we take the metaphorical space of home seriously—the space where family members decide who they are— then it might be worth taking another look at the most prominent staging for the persona of Tiger Woods: the domestic intimacy of the publicly inclusive *Oprah Winfrey Show*.

Bringing Race Home: Oprah and the Performance of Family

One reason that Kultida Woods did not disrupt Tiger's blackness around the time of his Masters victory was because those masculinist genealogies that lend blackness its coherence also render women marginal or invisible. It is thus fitting that the turning point in the racialization of Tiger Woods— from black to what Woods calls Cablinasian—occurred on Oprah Win- frey's televised neo–parlor meetings that frequently addressed women's concerns. By 1995, as Sujata Moorti recounts, *The Oprah Winfrey Show* "attracted a greater number of female viewers than news programs, night- time talk shows, morning network programs, nighttime talk shows, morning network programs, and any single daytime soap opera."[22] Moorti notes that daytime shows such as *The Oprah Winfrey Show* "are associated with intimacy primarily because of their degraded status as a 'female' genre."[23] But Moorti is particularly attentive to how such a genre, and Winfrey's show in particular, consistently allows narratives of sexual violence to expand from personalized experience to public dialogues. She writes, "The emphasis on discussion make[s] it possible to conceptualize daytime talk shows as sites of an emancipated public sphere that highlights marginalized women's voices."[24]

In addition to the program's popularity at the time and its format, which emphasized intimate expression and conversation, Janice Peck also notes in 1994 that "three quarters of the predominately white audience are women aged 18–54."[25] In the larger context of how Winfrey's show negotiated with prevalent racial discourses in a series of programs, "Racism in 1992," Peck mentions that "Winfrey has been described as a comforting, nonthreatening bridge between black and white cultures."[26] Indeed, in what I infer as an extension of this observation of Winfrey's bridgelike role, Peck explains that "as a woman hosting a genre directed at a female audience, Winfrey is expected to frame the 'topic' of racism in terms of its emotional, interpersonal dimensions, thereby reducing the potential for political conflict."[27] I here argue that this conflict control can just as viably serve an imagined black community as it can placate an overwhelmingly white viewership. Both Moorti and Peck deliberate on Winfrey's show as a space that strategically deploys communicative modes for publicizing racialized, gendered, and sexualized topics. My interest here is in how this space treats a prominent figure of black genealogical potential like Woods, and ultimately how Winfrey's bridgelike status literally makes the difference between black manhood and white femininity.

On April 21, 1997, just days after winning the Masters, Woods sat down with Winfrey on a set that perhaps was meant not only to reflect the stylistic sensibilities of its largely female audience, but also to replicate a living room—a domestic space where women might gather to chat in the middle of the day. The set consisted of two beige sofa chairs, each adorned with a decorative throw blanket. Between the two chairs sat a glass coffee table topped with an arrangement of pink roses. Woods and Winfrey sat across from one another, and behind them was a large screen that at first presented a still image of the moment when Woods was presented with the green blazer of the Augusta National Golf Club, which traditionally is put onto the present winner of the Masters by the previous winner. Then the image was put into motion; as the tape rolled, showing a ceremony of men inducting its newest member, Winfrey asked, "Was the green jacket the moment—that we saw you getting the green jacket? What did that mean or was it a surreal moment"?[28] In a sense, this is a fairly intimate question, one that requires Woods to reflect on the event in ways that can supplement or undercut the imagery of men inducting men into an exclusive club. Winfrey's question implies that the event as we witnessed it—a narrative of succession, albeit an interracial one in which the older, white club members induct the one exceptional male of color—can be interpreted in a manner that disrupts its reality, or the commonsense of how masculinist genealogies are produced. To speculate on whether the moment is surreal creates the potential to separate the observable narrative of succession from another and yet-unexpressed narrative of experience. The potential of this inquiry is the opportunity to emphasize that the moment was indeed a shared occasion. It was one that included the privileged men in the footage passing a symbol of elite achievement from one generation to another, but also the men and women sitting in Winfrey's parlor room of a TV studio, the predominately female viewership in actual homes, and Winfrey herself. The question grants Woods the permission to imagine a way outside of a dominant narrative that inscribes him as the progeny of publicly distinguished manhood by describing for and along with us other interpretations of what that moment means.

Much could have been revealed in Woods's response. Unfortunately, Winfrey herself foreclosed the opportunity for Woods to answer the question. No sooner did Winfrey ask the question than she continued to make a declaration, referring to her longtime black male partner, Steadman Graham: "I thought Steadman was going to fall out of his chair when you thanked all the golfers who'd—all the African-American golfers who'd come before you. He goes, 'That's my boy!' [Audience laughs.] 'That's the man!' Yes."[29] As Winfrey pronounces these last words, she raises her arms for triumphant emphasis. Then she continues to refer to Steadman: "So he's on the phone with Bob and they're yelling, 'Yes! He thanked the elders!' That was a good moment." As the opportunity to provide an imaginative answer had clearly passed, Woods smiled and a bit lazily followed Winfrey's lead with, "That was a good moment," to which Winfrey rejoined, "Yes. Uh-huh."

In this short sequence within the longer conversation, one might recognize the manner in which a feminized space such as the one Winfrey painstakingly created can affirm the inscription of blackness through masculine progeny. Indeed, at the point in which a spontaneous deliberation can occur about the nature of our kinship, Winfrey forecloses this possibility with a substitution of Graham's voice for her own, replicating the proper approach to racializing the occasion. In this case, the tendency toward ventriloquism implies that the labor of reifying consensus often is produced elsewhere. Graham makes the familiar pronouncement that Woods is progeny, just as we're made to accept that being (like) Mike or Tiger is desirable, and just as sneakers and baseball caps with swooshes or Xs are ubiquitous in American markets although they actually come from elsewhere. At the same time, the reification appears to occur as if it were natural for all of us. In a sense, Winfrey's declaration of "That's my boy! That's the man!" is not that far afield from the Nike campaign that had various avatars—people of varying races, ethnicities, ages, and genders—declare that they *are* Tiger Woods. Perhaps it is also not that far afield from what we know very well about who we are: we may not be Frederick Douglass, W. E. B. Du Bois, or Malcolm X, but at the very least, they are ours. When Winfrey evoked Graham, everyone followed suit in a simulation of a shared experience, rendering a process of reimagining community to more adequately address the multitude of concerns we have impossible. Hence, the question of why Winfrey or her audience would be invested in this process of identifying which man is *the* man is obscured by the manner in which we understand ourselves as community. Perhaps a key irony of Winfrey's ventriloquism here is that, in popular consciousness, Graham's presence is utterly subordinated by Winfrey's overwhelming fame. For instance, during a CNN interview with Graham in 2002, Daryn Kagan noted, "You're a very successful businessman and author, and yet most people know you . . . as Oprah's boy friend."[30] While Graham's interview marks Winfrey's much greater success at creating a brand for herself—to be recognizable as a distinctive persona—she trades this distinctiveness of personhood to participate in a theater that is ostensibly one of linked fate, where the authority, ironically for Winfrey, hails from elsewhere.

How a Race Man Becomes Cablinasian

But isn't this the nature of family? No man is an island; rather, one is the outcome of a series of events that occurred at some point elsewhere. Here

I want to explore how the transformation of Woods from our best hope in a line of race men to a Cablinasian crisis is the mechanism for another, gendered transformation. In a sense, Winfrey's interview mediates a moment between the masculinist, black progeny Tiger Woods, and the version of Tiger Woods that becomes so suited for the feminized discourse of the multiracial movement. Oprah Winfrey is profoundly suitable for this task of mediation, if we recall Peck's account of Winfrey as a bridging figure. A bridge is most clearly a spatial metaphor, but at this point I evoke it to speak of temporality, or the manner in which historical linkages are discernible. In this way, one is reminded of Hortense Spillers's important assessment of the role the black female body plays in providing the new world order its coherence. In "Mama's Baby, Papa's Maybe," Spillers begins with the observation that black womanhood bears the excessive burden of signifying a multitude of investments, which are indicated in a number of cultural markers, if not exactly brands: "Brown Sugar," "Sapphire," "Earth Mother," and so on.[31] However, this present-day confounding of meaning at the site of black womanhood speculatively has its roots in the captivity of African bodies, which as property were reduced from subjects in a particular social and historical context to flesh, the profound unmaking of humanized, gendered, and kinship relations. Referring to the processes of reducing the body to its basest level of flesh, Spillers writes,

> these lacerations, woundings, fissures, tears, scars, openings, ruptures, lesions, rendings, punctures of the flesh create the distance between what I would designate a cultural vestibularity and the culture, whose state apparatus, including judges, attorneys, "owners," "soul-drivers," "overseers," and "men of God," apparently colludes with a protocol of "search and destroy."[32]

Although the sort of brutality described here is often imagined as a homosocial event—acts inflicted on black male bodies by other men— Spillers wants to interrogate the manner in which flesh is the passageway through which a logic of gender is produced. Imagine the female black body in captivity torn apart—"female flesh 'ungendered'"—to become the vestibule or passageway through which an "American grammar," or the new world meaning of gender, kinship, and labor reproduction, are given their rationality.[33] In this way, the production of what is American depends on the captive black female, but also, "in this order of things, [she] breaks in upon the imagination with a forcefulness that marks both a denial and an 'illegitimacy,'" or as a disruption.[34]

I reiterate Spillers's famous formulation here to consider how the space of *The Oprah Winfrey Show* acts as a type of vestibularity. Perhaps the set of Winfrey's program, when one takes a second look, does not in fact resemble a living room but rather a vestibule—that temporal space through which processes of identification are produced. Even more specifically, Winfrey herself, as a bridge or passageway, is positioned as Sapphires, Earth Mothers, or Aunties often are.[35] What if the overwhelmingly successful, wealthy, and famous Winfrey was more than a little aware of how potentially threatening this empowerment is to black masculinity? What if her overly enthusiastic claiming of her boyfriend's rhetoric was indicative of her own emasculating potential? One might think of the more recent example of black male hip-hop artists such as 50 Cent, Ludacris, and Ice Cube publicly denouncing Winfrey for her apparent bias against black men. As Boyce Watkins speculated in a 2006 conversation with radio show host Wendy Williams and Paula Zahn on CNN, "If you have a Nobel Prize next to your Oscar, next to your Grammy, you are in good with Oprah. But after that, you have to be on the down low, beat your wife or do something terrible to get her attention. Rank and file black men doing positive things in their communities tend to be ignored."[36] In the psychic order, black women are the conduit through which black masculinity loses its patriarchal authority, through which blackness itself is pathologized, and through which, by its distinction, white femininity is made to feel comfortable, protected, and unthreatened.

Winfrey's interview with Woods demonstrates the persistence of a particular form of racializing discourse. However, the more famous—or infamous—moment in the interview occurred during a profound failure of this form, which was Woods's attempt at explaining his racial and ethnic complexity. Infamously, Woods explained to Winfrey that "Cablinasian," a term encompassing his Caucasian, black, Indian, and Asian heritages, was preferable to the inaccurate label "African American." Here is Kerry Ann Rockquemore's account of the conversation:

It was in an interview on the Oprah Winfrey show that he set off a racial firestorm that brought a narrowly defined multiracial message to the American public and enshrined him as the symbol of the Multiracial Movement. Winfrey asked Woods if it bothered him, the only child of a black American father and a Thai mother, to be labeled "African American." He replied, "Yeah it does. Growing up, I came up with this name: I'm a 'Cablinasian.'" Tiger Woods went on to explain that "Cablinasian" was an acronym, created to reflect the fact that his background is actually one-fourth Thai, and one-fourth Chinese.[37]

After this moment, Woods's symbolism for proponents of the multiracial movement had particular power since Congress was holding hearings in 1997 on how to categorize race and ethnicity in the 2000 U.S. Census. If his status as a son of black genealogical achievement had been undercut with this self-designation, then in the same moment, Woods had been instantly transformed into another sort of progeny. Again, here is Rockquemore: "Representative Tom Petri's bill (H.R. 830) mandating that a freestanding multiracial category be added to the 2000 census became known [as] the 'Tiger Woods Bill,' using the symbol and celebrity of Tiger Woods to move the multiracial agenda into public discourse."[38] The ironic turn here is how this emergent racial politics follows a logic that parallels that of the black family.

However, what has been left out of yet another familial narrative in which progenies are inevitable is the personalized nature of Woods's exchange with Winfrey. In a sense, Cablinasian is personal expression, or a personal event that can be publicized through deliberation rather than declaration. Yu refers to this moment as a failure, insofar as Cablinasian cannot adequately encapsulate transnational, migratory experiences in terms of a shared national condition, and manages to isolate Woods as a branded icon. He writes, "Since the power of racial categories comes from their work of tying a number of people together under a single description, a label such as Cablinasian that serves only to describe Woods's own individual admixture has little use . . . he might as well have used his own name 'Tiger' to label what was in the end a virtually singular racial description."[39] Rockquemore also refers to how strikingly idiosyncratic the term "Cablinasian" is: "Cablinasian has not become a universal category of identification. Instead, it is a term specific to Tiger Woods."[40] However, I argue that Cablinasian, in the particular context of the interview with Winfrey, indicates a breakdown of one particular strategy for rhetorically tying a number of people together. The appearance of Cablinasian at this precise moment performs a failure that is akin to what Spillers describes with regard to black women: it "breaks in upon the imagination with a force-fulness that marks both a denial and an 'illegitimacy.'" It marks a failure to maintain a coherence that depends on the suppression not only of inter-ethnic histories, but also of gender hierarchies and class positioning.

In a sense, Cablinasian is Woods's own private island, a term that hails from nowhere other than his own powers of invention, and as an idiosyn-crasy, it rhetorically cuts him off from the tradition of black ancestral accomplishment that makes him ours. Hence, it is not simply that Cablin-asian disrupts a narrative of black (masculinist) genealogies, but in doing so, the term is not easily gendered. In a sense, as Winfrey gets Woods to participate in the feminized genre of chatty confession, there appears to be little of use to be shared, appropriated, or even revealed in "Cablin-asian" as a term in and of itself. Instead, for the black community, the term signaled a refusal and unmaking of a race man that was, implicitly, the out-come of appearing in the space Winfrey created. In this way, Winfrey becomes instrumental in the unmanning of a racial progeny, which is the sort of national function that black womanhood was made for. Wood's new backstory evokes miscegenation in a way that the homosocial scene at the Augusta Golf Club—white men inducting a black man into a privi-leged space—did not. For evoking this break, Woods himself takes on something of the ungendered body, the undifferentiated space where male and female bodies are torn apart (ca/bl/in/asian) to be made into whatever the dominant culture needs.

The fallout of the Cablinasian confession was just as famous—or infa-mous—as the utterance itself. Examples of the backlash from the black community and state of communal crisis are too numerous to account for adequately here, but one might think of Winfrey's follow-up program, "The Tiger Woods Race Controversy,"[41] or a summer 1997 edition of *Essence* magazine that attended to the crisis within the black/multiracial family by providing a conversation among various famous black Ameri-cans with a range of attitudes about the open recognition of mixedness. In that issue, what exacerbated the sense of disappointment for men like Jesse Jackson, and then-president of the NAACP, Kweisi Mfume, was a highly publicized event that occurred before Woods's interview with Winfrey—indeed, before Woods had officially won the Masters—but that was still in the popular consciousness at the same time as the Cablinasian event:

golfer Fuzzy Zoeller's racist remarks about Woods to the press. Reasons for why these events seem to have occurred simultaneously is partly due to the delayed network airing and reportage of Zoeller's remarks and perhaps also to Woods's late reconciliation with Zoeller.[42] The two did not meet until approximately a month after Zoeller's comments.[43]

In a sense, two dramas occupied the same temporal space of public awareness, a dramatic encounter between blackness and multiracialism that seemed to dismantle the semblance of family. On the one hand, Woods makes a striking refusal of blackness and at the same time is emasculated as a black man on *The Oprah Winfrey Show*. On the other hand, Woods is the target of a highly recognizable form of homosocial white-on-black racism that solidifies the feeling of family. Toward the end of the Masters Tournament, Zoeller said of Woods to the press: "That little boy is driving well and he's putting well. He's doing everything it takes to win. You pat him on the back and say congratulations and enjoy it and tell him not to serve fried chicken next year, got it. . . . Or collard greens or whatever the hell they serve."[44] This was a form of racism that previous generations have experienced—the stereotypical representations of black culinary culture, and the rhetorical reduction of black men to boyhood status. Zoeller's remarks not only affirmed the prevalent attitudes of antiblackness, but they also enacted a confirmation of Wood's lineage. This was a sort of racialized moment that Woods's proximity to Winfrey could not adequately counter. Because Woods's daytime chat with Winfrey was so overdetermined by what seemed like a commentary against the black family, it also foreclosed a space for negotiating between consensually masculine responses to racism and to intimate publics where the political is personalized. In the vestibule between a public consciousness of chickeneating, infantilized blackness and a new cultural assumption that race is personal and even idiosyncratic, what could have been revealed about our approach to formulating responses to race at all?

On Multiracial Motherhood's Claim to Black Futures

Perhaps one of the greatest ironies is that in the outcome of the late 1990s, Tiger Woods was never relieved of his progeny status. Once the descendent of Jackie Robinson, Woods eventually became the representative of multiracial children everywhere. This time, the narrative was not coming from an imagined community of blackness but from proponents of multiracialism who were predominately white. Rockquemore points out that Woods's exchange of blackness for Cablinasianness "lodged the essence of the Multiracial Movement in the public's, especially the white public's, consciousness."[45] And as Kim Williams notes, "white, liberal, suburban-based middle-class women" played a prominent role in driving the agenda of multiracial identity politics, which is perhaps surprising because many "are not typically agitating around racial issues."[46] Winfrey's role, in popular consciousness, was more than casually poised to mediate this transformation of Tiger Woods from black race man to a multiracial child for white mothers and policy makers to make use of politically. If anything, the multiracial movement helped to clarify that the narrative logic of blackness as kinship could serve a set of racialized initiatives that, ironically, are not necessarily concerned with reproducing the black family. The logic that has produced a narrative of blackness—genealogies— is unstable in ways that render it suitable for a range of arguments.

Ultimately, the Census Bureau conceded the claims of a burgeoning multiracial movement by changing its racial and ethnic classification policy: in 1997, individuals were given the unprecedented option to mark multiple boxes on the 2000 Census, signaling the recognition of multiracial and multiethnic identities. Immediately, traditionally black political organizations understood the eroding impact this might have on the family. The NAACP's Hilary Shelton claimed in 2000, "We went through the process where the country referred to us as all sorts of things, and we wanted to identify for ourselves what we are. We decided that we're African-Americans."[47] This is to say that we African Americans know that sometimes our mothers are white; we know that some of us are multiracial or perhaps more accurately Cablinasian, but we also know that our political future—any future at all, as Reid-Pharr has put it—is at stake when we don't choose blackness. I understand Shelton's allusion to consensus as a plea to come home. Yet perhaps the lessons of 1997 are most meaningful when taken askew, rather than viewed toward the racial ends that provide us with either family or nothing at all. The outcome of the encounter between Winfrey and Woods, or the encounter between blackness and multiracialism, is that the crisis within black/multiracial family must attend to how womanhood is posited as an antithesis to the familial narrative. It must attend to the varying kinds of labor that go into producing the myth of genealogy or into reifying consensus around such a myth. At stake is the production of an enduring gender analysis that can lead us toward a yet-unexpressed promised land. Such an analysis must ask why women—and particularly which women—can't be family, and what, exactly, family is, rather than perpetuating a process of determining who our favorite sons are.

A decade later, in 2007, the multiracial senator from Illinois, Barack Obama, emerged as a strong candidate with the potential to become the first black president of the United States. The viability of multiracialism had become mainstream since Woods's pronouncement in 1997, and this allowed Obama to recognize his white mother while simultaneously identifying—and being identified—as black. In *Troubling the Family,* I argue that the multiracial movement took the attainment of personhood as a primary pursuit. However, the multiracial movement of the 1990s seemed to lack an explicit explanation for why personhood was its central goal. Further, the movement is not fully comprehensible without an examination of its feminist foundations. The central problem, then, is why the movement in general either failed or refused to recognize its own political preconditions.

Framing Multiracialism Historically

Although this book seems to focus squarely on the events of a single decade, and more specifically on the development of the multiracial movement at the end of the twentieth century and the beginning of the twenty-first, it actually traces a broader historical arc. The dominance of the multiracial movement in U.S. popular culture in the 1990s is a consequence of the vitality of the logics that organize multiracialism for the general shift to a neoliberal or individualist theory of racial justice. This rupture that gets narrated as simply a historical transition or as an ongoing progressive advancement of U.S. antiracism is a profoundly complicated process that depends on a distinct structure of what I call racial time.

Temporality is especially useful heuristically because of the striking manner in which the movement appeared to operate without a clear approach to how to situate itself within its own historical moment. This movement seemed to take historical presumptions for granted. It also seemed to take for granted that the state is neutral, that citizens seek neutrality as an ideal, and that the ideal of neutrality is the only available theory of justice. The 1980s (or what some have called a neoliberal era of antiracism), the moment that initiates the decade that brackets this study, break from the hegemonic norms for the state that developed in the era of civil rights. In that period, the state was conceived as a representation of the American body politic. Far from neutral, the state was conceived as a representation of the moral structure of U.S. society. Far from being a neutral measure, the modern nation centrally constitutes social consciousness, producing the condition for unifying diverse social worlds into a homogenous social world of national citizens. By the term *racial time,* I wish to suggest that modernity's unifying temporality—which entailed the restrictions of social consciousness and the homogeneity of social life—is not to be taken for granted as a neutral reality that constitutes the meaning of race and embodiment. Racial time is an approach to theorizing temporality and to tracing the ruptures in state logics and norms that multiracialism is a part of and advances.

The primary discourses about interracial sexuality, marriage, and reproduction were in large part determined by a long history of cultural and legal prohibitions that have been legislatively overturned fairly recently, at the end of the 1960s. The multiracial movement recognized late 1960s-era judicial redress as the foundational logic for future activism: the civil right to have multiracial families was the impetus for the movement's development into the 1990s. However, this acknowledgment of 1960s-era legal expansion as the foundation for 1990s-era multiracialism eclipsed the memory how other events, at other temporal moments, also laid the groundwork for multiracial cultural and political analytics. The primary timeline of multiracialism—family time—cast a dark shadow on the alternative modes of temporality that nonetheless underpinned the movement's development. Discourse about the health of the multiracial family, its legal legitimization, and a cultural politics of its recognition indicates a rupture between the appearance of state neutrality regarding the development of multiracial families on the one hand and overt statist interest in the racialization of the black family on the other. Statist recognition of functional multiracial families entailed a legally color-blind marriage market, which implicitly constitutes heterosexuality as antiracist. At the same time, blackness—or how subjects had been constituted as black through varying discourses on race—determined the manner in which the black family, and particularly black motherhood, was always already antithetical to the neutral ideal of national belonging. The appearance of neutrality is required to produce particular forms of racial visibility. More specifically, blackness and black sexuality, and their naturalized location in the city, are underattended to in theorizations of the multiracial family. From the 1960s to the 1980s, legal and policy decisions normalize family by rhetorically naturalizing several of its components: patriarchy, color-blindness or racial neutrality, and heteronormativity.

This revelation indicates that an emphasis on legitimizing the family is not only couched in the civil rights–era antiracist dismantlement of antimiscegenation laws throughout the country, but also that the seeming inevitability of racial equity was in tandem with a decidedly insidious and paradoxical attempt by the state to alleviate its obligation toward racial, sexualized, and economic redress by privatizing these responsibilities through a new national focus on the family. My purpose in emphasizing the contributions of 1960s- and 1970s-era feminist movements is to trouble the implicit timeline of multiracialism. In general terms, feminist activists waged their antagonisms toward the temporality of nationalism, including black nationalisms, because the unifying time of nation enervated the possibilities of creating diverse social worlds in which to inhabit. As a movement, multiracialism did not overtly seek to see beyond the horizon of an ideally neutral personhood; if anything, it reconstituted racial embodiment as that which moved toward the horizon of neutrality. My intention, however, is to inquire about what was often operating within 1990s-era multiracial discourse but seldom acknowledged by the participants of this discourse. This includes the exploitation and curious conversion of the analytic "the personal is political," which rendered "the political as private."

Chapter Summaries

It is for this reason that my first chapter takes up feminist intellectual and political logics that recognize the inextricability of public and private lives. Such logics describe how social relationships, collaboration, and behaviors became occasions through which to elaborate on the operations of power within the lives of women. Chapter 1 argues that this feminist contribution to political life is a precondition of the 1990s-era multiracial movement. However, while the projects developed by white and black women's movements of the 1960s and 1970s aimed to expand social engagement in public in order to redress inequity writ large, the subsequent multiracial movement took a far narrower view of social engagement. Proponents of the multiracial movement often alluded to the outcomes of previous feminist activism, which included the predominant participation of women and an understanding that personal experiences bore political implications; the multiracial movement in general did not overtly recognize its indebtedness to a foundational feminist analytics. It is for this reason that the first chapter traces various analytics of time in order to investigate how the general multiracial movement understood its own temporal situation. The movement appeared to operate without a clear approach to how to situate itself within its own historical moment. The primary discourses about interracial sexuality, marriage, and reproduction were in large part determined by a long history of cultural and legal prohibitions that have been legislatively overturned fairly recently, at the end of the 1960s. Insofar as the multiracial movement recognized a moment of its own inception, this time of judicial redress was figured as the foundational logic for future activism: the civil right to have multiracial families became the impetus for the movement's development into the 1990s.

The second chapter situates the landmark *Loving v. Virginia* (1967) court case as the self-proclaimed origin of the multiracial movement that emerges with full force decades later. First, *Loving* is the originating text that spawns the multiracial movement. Second, *Loving* marks a key turning point, one that reveals the contradictions that produce black feminist antagonisms to statist epistemologies. The current legacy of *Loving* requires an enduring consideration of the legitimization of deviant family formations, which not only include multiracial families but also same-sex marriage and parenthood. The legislation actually shared a concomitant logic with the antiblack discourse of the Moynihan Report, published in 1965. Thus, while the 1967 Supreme Court decision marks the beginning of legitimacy for interracial marriage and multiracial family, and therefore the beginning of a discourse on mixed racialism, this chapter suggests that by remembering *Loving* with the Moynihan Report in mind, we can begin to reveal how both texts normalize the American family by rhetorically naturalizing several of its components: patriarchy, racial neutrality, heteronormativity, and middle-class suburbanization. This revelation indicates that an emphasis on legitimizing the family is not only couched in the civil rights–era antiracist dismantlement of antimiscegenation laws throughout the country, but that the forgone conclusion of racial equity was concomitant with a decidedly insidious and paradoxical attempt by the state to alleviate its obligation toward racial, sexualized, and economic redress by privatizing these responsibilities through a new national focus on the family. This privatization becomes the requisite for multiracial personhood.

Chapter 3 builds on the second chapter by engaging with two examples of an important genre of multiracial personhood, the maternal memoir: Maureen Reddy's *Crossing the Line: Race Parenting and Culture* (1994) and Jane Lazarre's *Beyond the Whiteness of Whiteness* (1997). Although the matter of adult participation within a racially integrated marriage market is an ostensible component of *Loving*, Reddy and Lazarre each narrate the legacy of this legislation in differing ways through a consideration of the legitimacy of multiracial children. Therefore, this chapter treats the politicization of multiracial children as an aftereffect of a problematic condition: while the multiracial family has gained legal, rational legitimatization, these memoirs pinpoint political business left unfinished by *Loving*, which is an attendance to how, precisely, one makes the crossover from the legal unfettering of affective (heterosexual) relations irrespective of racial differences to actually producing a trend of interracial intimacy. *Loving* extends the private, contractual arrangement of marriage and demonstrates a color-blind approach toward achieving racial equity, and it provides legal legitimacy for the children of interracial marriages. However, white maternal subjects describe their interracial partnerships and multiracial children as a sign of de facto illegitimacy, which can no longer be addressed by the rule of law. It is for this reason that they attempt to devise a new logic of racialization through culture and, in this case, memoir, which renders personal experience as political.

Chapter 4 focuses on the modernist literary convention of racial passing, which is appropriated at the end of the twentieth century, to access the genealogical turn that resulted in a neutral politics of personhood. James McBride's bestselling 1996 memoir *The Color of Water: A Black Man's Tribute to His White Mother* and Philip Roth's novel *The Human Stain* (2000) together demonstrate the ambivalent outcomes of a multiracialism that only ostensibly leads to the transcendence of racial consciousness. This chapter reads *The Color of Water* against the grain by asserting that McBride demonstrates how a continued engagement with racial and ethnic difference is facilitated by racial passing, or the very silences and forms of amalgamation that would deem race and ethnicity neutral. He does this by reflecting on the racial politics of his own white mother. This chapter explains how McBride's text recognizes that the irresolvable, ambiguous qualities of racial appearance, kinship, and affect can be effective starting points for imagining racial justice projects in the new century. Conversely, *The Human Stain* conflates contemporary color-blindness and the late twentieth-century opposition to political correctness with the pre–civil rights racial passing: current forms of race neutrality are akin to early African American passing practices. The conclusion Roth draws from this analogy is that 1990s-era attempts to dismantle the leftist reforms of the 1960s and 1970s—through the discursive claims about color-blindness and political correctness—will be understood historically in much the same way that we understand the phenomenon of racial passing: as a justifiable counterbalance to an era's political inequities and excesses.

Troubling the Family closes by discussing the persona of multiracial personhood ostensibly attained during the ascendance of Barack Obama as a presidential candidate in 2007. Whereas Tiger Woods's negotiation with race became a lightning rod for proponents of mixed-racial designation, Obama's negotiation, including the constant references to his white mother, became a sign of the unprecedented advances of black citizenship. Obama's candidacy and Obama as a representative of racial politics produced celebrations of black advancement and of multiracial identity. However, *Troubling the Family* concludes that what was actually being celebrated was the seeming realization of a long-standing dream: to have the idiosyncrasies of our personhood overcome the normative epistemologies that still determine which sort of individuality can appear in public. If Obama signals the promise of personhood we've been dreaming of, then the question that remains is what potentials are lost when we dream our antagonisms to both public and personal logics away, rather than attending to what exactly produced them.

CHAPTER 1

Multiracial Timelines

A Genealogy of Personhood

I try to use the concept of queer time to make clear how respectability, and notions of the normal on which it depends, may be upheld by a middle-class logic of reproductive temporality. And so, in Western cultures, we chart the emergence of the adult from the dangerous and unruly period of adolescence as a desired process of maturation

—Judith Halberstam, *In a Queer Time and Place*

Despite a sizable number of Black feminists who have contributed much to the leadership of the women's movement, there is still no Black women's movement, and it appears there won't be for some time to come. It is conceivable that the level of consciousness feminism would demand in Black women wouldn't lead to any sort of separatist movement, anyway—despite our very separate problems. Perhaps a multicultural women's movement is somewhere in the future.

—Michele Wallace, "A Black Feminist's Search for Sisterhood"

THIS IS A STUDY OF U.S. MULTIRACIALISM. The multiracial movement may be said to have culminated in political efforts to change the racial categories of the 2000 U.S. Census to include multiracial identity, but the movement's impact was much more far-reaching in both direct and indirect ways. The range of the movement's impact is provocative: why did multiracialism emerge at the end of the twentieth century as a new form of U.S. racial identity, and how did Americans come to experience the virtual normalization of multiracial identity between 1997 and 2007? What was the particular result of the multiracial movement's focus on the story of the multiracial child as the script of a new racial era, one that both promised and succeeded in changing perceptions of the political, legal, social, and cultural meaning of race in the aftermath of the formal civil rights era? How did the movement's focus on familial love as the sexual–racial difference of multiracial culture take up and modify earlier feminist criticism in ways we have yet to fully understand?[1] Beyond its creation of a new racial category, this movement has affected popular understandings of the connections between race and gender, family and history, and sex and love.

In particular, it has shaped those cultural narratives that help make connections between different social movements in the making of post–civil rights personhood. The pursuit of a post–civil rights form of personhood forged new connections between unexpected allies: white mothers and neoconservative politicians, multiracial activists and black nationalists, and white feminists and black feminists all provided the voices and legacies that led to the multiracial movement's constructions of personhood. While it promoted a few highly prominent themes and concerns, the multiracial movement in general had no singular identity, and this was because the movement was informed by an amalgamation of political forces. Some of these were the neoconservative efforts to dismantle affirmative action and implement color-blind public policies. Some were the multiracial activists who challenged black nationalism in order to produce a multiracial version of nationalist masculinity. Finally, some were the predominantly female proponents of multiracialism who were looking for public forums in which to express their personal stories, experiences, and aspirations without necessarily relegating these expressions of personhood to legal or nationalist frameworks. However, the overarching picture one gets of the 1990s-era multiracial politics is that some proponents were invested in the promise of personhood, which they imagined as a potential guarantee of racial neutrality, a way into national hegemony, or the liberty of self-expression. Because the temporality of multiracialism is generative of certain naturalized yet historically contingent cultural figures, the promise of neutral personhood—ultimately unfettered by a racial past or identitarian divisions—was the temporal horizon toward which the multiracial movement moved.

This promise of neutrality as a temporal shift from earlier investments in identitarian politics relied on a complicated version of racial time. Racial time is an approach to engaging temporality as a central domain for theorizing and understanding the continued reality of race in everyday life. Further, we need to think of time as an embodying process. To understand temporality as always already racial time and to understand racial time as constitutive of embodiment and the boundaries of personhood is to recognize that racial time powerfully structures both the social realization of personhood and the social delegitimizing of other forms of embodied life. Judith Halberstam refers to alternative embodying processes and an alternative temporality as *queer time,* in which there is no investment in a temporality that privileges the outcome of a disciplined adulthood over an incipient and unruly adolescence, for example, or any normal investment in maturity, inheritance, or longevity, in order to critically assess a fuller and richer range of cultural practices, social arrangements, and modes of identification. The queer subcultures that Halberstam considers are demonstrative of the manner in which timelines can be emplotted in alternative ways. I engage this queer analytic of time to offer a concerted investigation of how the general multiracial movement understood its own temporal situation. Indeed, the multiracial movement expanded a mode of temporality that reconstituted racial embodiment and the truth of race—a mode that, in advancing new forms of human embodiment, seemed to reinvent personhood. Therefore, the movement appeared to operate without a clear approach to how to situate itself within its own historical moment.

The multiracial movement's ostensible structure of time—a version of temporality that accounted for the legitimacy of interracial couples and subsequent multiracial progeny—is that of the heteronormative family. The primary discourses about interracial sexuality, marriage, and reproduction were in large part determined by a long history of cultural and legal prohibitions that have been legislatively overturned fairly recently, at the end of the 1960s. The multiracial movement recognized this moment of judicial redress as the foundational logic for future activism: the civil right to have multiracial families was the impetus for the movement's development into the 1990s. However, this acknowledgment of 1960s-era legal expansion as the foundation for later multiracialism eclipsed the memory of how other events, at other temporal moments, also laid the groundwork for multiracial cultural and political analytics. The primary timeline of multiracialism—family time—cast a dark shadow on the alternative modes of temporality that nonetheless underpinned the movement's development.

Because multiracial politics in general were overwhelmingly identified with a normal timeline of familial affect and succession—even if individual proponents were agnostic about the time of family—it becomes difficult to imagine a queer multiracialism. Perhaps less expectedly, it becomes difficult to reveal the manner in which the multiracial movement unwittingly depended on the contributions of previous social movements, which did not produce analytics that supported the normal time of family. To a large degree, multiracial politics did not provide self-conscious accounts of how its emergence relied on racial or gendered analytics that were developed previously. For the most part, the multiracial movement ironically avoided racial politics in order to steer clear of racially based divisions within a burgeoning multiracial constituency. However, these efforts to maintain unity led to a supplemental avoidance of the foundational analyses upon which political multiracialism depended. Previously developed analytics of race were foundational to multiracialism, but gender politics were foundational to the manner in which multiracialism developed as a racial politics. Yet the movement's proponents seemed generally unaware or unconcerned with the racial/gender analytics that made up its foundations. Because the movement was either unable or unwilling to unlock its own history or to capture the wider scope of conditions that made its emergence possible, the multiracial movement was ultimately at a loss for how to account for its own place in history. It was therefore at a loss for providing an account of its own temporal mobility. By the 1990s, antiracist movements that once been politically and culturally forceful in previous decades—black nationalism, white and black feminisms—had significantly waned in momentum and influence. The central problem for the multiracial movement—a problem that the movement itself failed to recognize—was that it emerged at a time when the very possibility of sustaining a post–civil rights, neoliberal antiracist movement was uncertain.

Perhaps the movement's own lack of self-consciousness with regard to its place within history—its continuities and elaborations of previous historical moments, its greater significance within the context of the 1990s—is the reason why it became so self-identified with the ostensibly neutral discourse of familial love. In a sense, if affect did not conquer all, then it certainly eclipsed a set of underlying political tensions and the manner in which multiracial politics could expand the possibilities for alternative conceptualizations for social relationships, behavior, and personal expression. Although there might possibly be a number of historical moments or events that one could explore in connection to the emergence of 1990s-era multiracialism, it is my contention that the contributions of the 1960s- and 1970s-era feminist movements are particularly useful to remember.

Feminist analytical contributions are poised to trouble the privileged time-line of multiracialism: that of the heteronormative family.

By capturing and explaining this legacy, this chapter reveals an alterna-tive genealogy of racial personhood dependent on feminist explication of how the very possibility of this designation relies on recognition of gen-der formation. Genealogies of racial movements uncover the subjectivi-ties that dominant historical accounts do not recognize. For example, in the second epigraph, Michele Wallace describes the vacuity of a black feminist movement at the end of the 1970s and early 1980s; the essay was published in the seminal women's studies collection *All The Women Are White, All the Blacks Are Men, Yet Some of Us Are Brave* (1982). She points out that black women were heavily involved in the (white) women's movement, which is a revelation that counters dominant accounts of the racial composition of feminism. From the eclipse of a dominant historical narrative, she uncovers black women with a feminist consciousness. This consciousness is not part of an essentialist womanhood; rather, Wallace is referring to the conditions in which political analytics of identity for-mation develop. What such a genealogical uncovering reveals is that the 1960s- and 1970s-era white feminist movement was in fact multiracial. However, in the wake of this implicit multiracialism, black feminism has been captured by the normative timeline of the women's moment, in which white women are the seminal and primary agents of gender analy-sis and black women are either politically belated or absent altogether. Wallace's choice is to offer an alternative timeline of feminist develop-ment: she insists that both black and white women were simultaneously present as agents—and perhaps friends, allies, and intimate partners. She also makes the decidedly more provocative point that "a level of con-sciousness" as a precondition of feminism would not be relegated to any privileged subject. Such consciousness, as she imagines, is not about avoiding the public disagreements between black and white women with "very separate problems." Rather, she imagines a multicultural—and mul-tiracial—future in which the potential for adult collaboration and engage-ment is facilitated through a degree of self-awareness that accounts for the inextricability of gender and racial formations, in addition to the inequi-ties of these formations. Such a future is contingent, nondependent on foreclosing the range of potential outcomes.

In one sense, what emerged as a prominent characteristic of the 1990s-era multiracial movement—the concern of white mothers over cross-racial kinship—is a remnant of a troubled and unfinished history of activist collaboration between black and white feminists during the 1960s and 1970s. The multiracial movement of the 1990s was shaped by the large presence and perspectives of white women, and white mothers in particular, who did not openly reference the difficulties of interracial feminist relationships. Nonetheless, they created communities through which to discuss and mobilize around their experiences as white mothers of racialized children. In addition, the salient character of the movement was to acquiesce that an activist public sphere, so weakened by the 1990s, limited its transformative potential socially and politically. In this way, the temporality of multiracialism was a strikingly conflated one: the public was already diminished as a site for transformative social action, and this condition was projected into a future where all social meaning would be relegated to a neutral, private terrain. This would be the terrain of private family life and affective relationships. However, the limits of this timeline are recoverable when we consider who—that is, which subjects, perhaps lacking designations like *mother* or *child* that come with the logic of family— are out of time, so to speak. If black women are perpetually burdened with a history of nonpersonhood—as the bodily vehicles for reproduction during slavery, or as the objects of public policy discourse—then this signals the complication of racial time embedded in discourses of multiracial family and, especially, multiracial maternity. Reading the multiracial movement with the feminist legacy of racial/gender analysis in mind, it becomes possible to consider why the concept of black maternity in multiracialism indicates a curious absence. The lost legacy is not only black women as objects of gendered analysis, but also, and more precisely, as the agents of analytics of how race and gender are intersectional, and how this condition has material effects. Without capturing what has been lost, the multiracial movement itself remains incomprehensible.

The Political Is Private: Toward a Feminist Genealogy

Among the enduring contributions that the feminist movement of the 1960s and 1970s made to American cultural politics is the now-commonplace concept that what happens in our personal lives is inextricably linked to the public, political world. Activist Carol Hanisch is credited for naming the famous synecdoche of second-wave feminism, "the personal is political," in 1968.[2] This slogan signals a rejection of the categorical separation of the public realm—where political engagement occurs—from the private realm of intimacy and family, which supposedly would have something other than a public function. As an epistemological intervention, the declaration that "the personal is political" also reveals that that our private lives are conditioned by relations of power and by discourses that are generated in social and public spaces. As Nancy Isenberg succinctly puts it, "The public and private are interdependent and defined in relation to each other and neither represents universal nor value-free conditions."[3] Isenberg's summation borrows from philosopher Louis Althusser's theory of the state, in which he argues that there is no neutral, empirical difference between public and private institutions—specifically, various religious organizations, school systems, the family, the legal system, and high and low culture—because they all have ideological functions that make the ideals and status of the ruling classes appear as if they were natural and facilitate the reproduction of dominance.[4] In this way, feminists of the late 1960s and 1970s offered a strategy for women to see the underlying value systems that were operative in their everyday lives and to wage their resistance within institutions of patriarchal power.

The recognition that our behavior as private individuals is inextricably linked to relations of power was a significant precondition for the emergence of the multiracial movement of the 1990s, decades after the second wave of feminism. In a real sense, "the personal is political" was the common sense that enabled proponents of multiracialism to challenge racial orthodoxy by publicizing their intimate experiences. These proponents also made use of popular modes of communication as a site for challenging racial conventions. To some degree, efforts to raise awareness through personal, lived experience did the work of developing a knowledge project that bore political implications. As SanSan Kwan and Kenneth Speirs explain in their introduction to a collection of autobiographical essays entitled *Mixing It Up: Multiracial Subjects,* "Abstract discourses on race, which attempt to define and to fix, cannot fully apprehend multiraciality. Thus, we propose that the personal is the best avenue to understanding that which is necessarily unclassifiable. It is only through the individual lived experiences of mixed-race people that we can understand the plural nature of multiracialit*ies*."[5] This account implies that the ideologies that make race seem classifiable universally have a repressive function on multiracial subjects in particular. Multiracial individuals should resist "abstract discourses" that mystify how strict classifications of race serve some sort of subjugating function by fixing and therefore limiting the possibilities of racial identification. Personal expression is therefore not an apolitical form of self-indulgence. Rather, it provides a starting point for critical analyses of how some individuals are denied agency, self-determination, and the opportunity to wrest control over the meaning of their lives by race as a concept. As Rachel Moran explains with regard to the multiracial movement's central political project to reclassify race on the U.S. Census, "The offspring of interracial marriages . . . have successfully challenged this classification scheme [of single racial identification] because it denies them full personhood."[6] In this way, the personal leads to a political multiracialism predicated on the demand for full personhood.

Multiracial scholars, theorists, and activists took advantage of "the personal is political" as an analytic tool. However, the multiracial movement took a narrower approach to social activity than the black and white feminist movements of the 1960s and 1970s. The previous generation of feminists explained how social or behavioral norms at the workplace and at home have political implications. They were concerned with public funding for social services. The expansion of social collaboration and activity—through heightened concern over behavioral norms and the distribution of public resources—was a goal of feminist gender politics. More to the point, the feminist expansion of the social realm, where the development of new and emancipatory social relationships was key, was an approach toward a richer recognition of personhood. During the 1960s and 1970s, feminists such as Hanisch chose consciousness raising as a key approach to emphasizing how personal existence was political as a matter of course. As Johnnetta Cole and Beverly Guy-Sheftall describe them, consciousness-raising sessions occurred when "small groups of radical women involved in the development of feminist organizations gathered together in meetings and shared their personal stories of being female and oppressed. . . . the details of one's particular story were echoed in the story of another woman, and another, and another."[7] Women of color extended this practice in order to explain how the experiences of racial identity were inextricable from those of gender and class.[8] Although black feminism in general is an outgrowth of the limits and submarginalization produced by the civil rights movement and black nationalism, the movement contains a wide range of ideological differences, including radical opposition, state hegemony, and liberal compliance with statism.[9] The development of 1970s-era black feminism posed a formidable challenge to the hegemonic and essential foundations of both black nationalism and white feminism by denaturalizing the rhetorical linkages between race, gender, sexuality, and class. In this context, fostering political consciousness within the general public required activists to explain how oppression took on a variety of forms and was felt in a number of ways. Activists yoked together a number of issues: domestic violence, labor organization, better health care in black neighborhoods.[10] For black feminism in particular, the enrichment of personhood meant revealing the intersections of identity and oppression, and demanding that the health, safety, and liberty of socially underprivileged persons be made a public priority.

If the expansion of the social was integral to 1960s- and 1970s-era feminisms, then the twilight of the social was a part of multiracialism's emergence.[11] This is not an easy temporal assessment because as a movement, multiracial activism sought the expansion of politicized communities. However, while earlier feminists did not look to the state primarily to validate personal lives in public through legal or civil reform, multiracial activists rallied around the central issue of classifying multiracial identity on state forms—the 2000 Census in particular. The tacit ending of social life in this sense is marked by diminished expectations of what such a life could be. Taxonomical recognition—being counted as multiracial on the Census, for instance—seemed commensurate with public and social recognition of personhood. Taxonomy and personhood were conflated in the course of Census activism, and this conflation emerged as the primary way to politicize multiracialism. To this degree, the multiracial movement sought to exist in the eyes of the state. As Kimberly DaCosta explains, "Gaining *state* recognition of social identities *requires* that activists make their claims on behalf of a putative group—to create a constituency. Activists' references to a 'multiracial community' were (in part) rhetorical devices self-consciously employed to bolster claims that they represented a constituency."[12]

This constituency was generally composed of multiracial organizations that began to crop up during the 1970s, in the decade after the Supreme Court deemed antimiscegenation laws unconstitutional in *Loving v. Virginia* (1967). The San Francisco–based Interracial/Inter-cultural Pride (I-Pride) was the first of these, established in 1978. Other groups developed throughout the 1980s. Two prominent multiracial organizations—the Association of Multiethnic Americans (AMEA) and Project Reclassify All Children Equally (RACE)—played key roles in the congressional debate over how to categorize multiracial identity on the 2000 Census.

They both continue to provide a range of advocacy and educational services for their constituency. AMEA, established in 1989, is a national umbrella organization for several of the regional organizations that emerged
in the 1970s and 1980s. AMEA represents the coalitional interests of these
groups, and many of them, including Getting Interracial Families Together
(GIFT) and Biracial Family Network (BFN), focus on creating communities among families defined by interracialism, multiracialism, and transracial adoption. Project RACE was established in 1991 and is most closely
identified with its cofounder and executive director, Susan Graham, a
white mother of biracial children. Her initial concerns for her own children's classification meshed with the overall concerns of the organization.
Both wanted to see "that children have an identity, a correct terminology
for who they are," and this terminology would be multiracial. The primary
objective of Project RACE is still to set up "multiracial classification on
all school, employment, state, federal, local, census and medical forms
requiring racial data."[13]

Between 1994 and 1997, AMEA president Ramona Douglass and Project RACE's Susan Graham partnered together in order to bolster the political influence of the multiracial community. Their differing backgrounds
were thought to benefit the diverse profile of the movement. As Douglass
explains in a brief account of the movement's development: "Graham, a
European Jewish American woman who was interracially married with
two African American/Caucasian children, and Douglass, a multiracial
adult of African, American Indian, and Italian descent, represented major
blocks of interest within the community."[14] This description Douglass
provides of both Graham and herself anticipates the break they and their
organizations made in 1997 over a disagreement on how the government
should tabulate multiracialism. Graham—a white Jewish woman who
is politicized by her affective relationships with a black husband and biracial children—was decidedly less interested than Douglass in forging
alliances with traditional civil rights organizations.[15] Graham wanted a
separate, catchall "multiracial" box added to the Census, which would not
account for the racial and ethnic disparities among multiracial individuals. Douglass—who self-describes as a multiracial adult of partially black
descent—wanted to address how the emergence of multiracialism could
potentially undermine the political clout of black, Asian, and Latino organizations. Douglass describes the end of the three-year partnership between AMEA and Project RACE in terms of Graham's alienation from

the general will of multiracial activists. The general sensibility within the movement was in line with Douglass's own. She writes:

> The participating organizations [of the Third Multiracial Leadership Conference in 1997] from across the country reached a consensus that a "check one or more box" format rather than a separate multiracial identifier would serve the highest community good. It would: a) allow for the celebration of diverse heritages; b) support the continued monitoring of existing civil rights legislation that impacted multiracial people directly; and c) it would also provide the most information for the accurate collection of racial/ethnic data for medical diagnosis and research. . . . Only Project RACE rescinded its initial endorsement of the Multiracial Summit Statement.[16]

The account given here represents an ideological rift between Douglass and Graham, between AMEA and Project RACE, and less obviously between some stakeholders with the movement. Graham held a prominent leadership position and testified during the congressional hearings on how to tabulate multiracialism, and her position was in line with a decidedly vocal fringe of the movement. For instance, Charles Byrd, founder of the Web-based *Interracial Voice,* also advocated for an autonomous stance for categorization from the multiracial community that was irrespective of the concerns of traditional civil rights organizations. Still, with regard to the Census debate, Douglass's perspective—that continuity between the past of race-based civil rights struggle and the potential of multiracial recognition supports the "highest community good"—won out. The enrichment of public life, in this way, depended on the recognition of diversity in traditional and emergent forms, the protection of rights, and medical responses that problematize biological differences between races and therefore lead to equitable care.

   This version of public welfare is capacious enough to include subjects who identify with a variety of communities, and in so doing choose a variety of lifeways. The victory over the Census notwithstanding, what Douglass's account reveals is a profound disparity between the means to achieving the highest communal good—the tabulation of multiracialism on the Census—and the potential outcome—the expansion of a social imagination and of a politically and intellectually fortified public sphere.

Checking boxes on a state form was the social practice prioritized by both ideological camps of the Census debate. Although the implicit difference between the two ideologies is temporal continuity with liberationist and rights-based movements of the 1960s and 1970s, and temporal rupture between the racial past and the multiracial future, neither version was ostensibly concerned with proliferating the array of social practices to counter social norms. So whereas the state implemented the prospectively more capacious version of policy, the multiracial movement's overall political goal of obtaining state recognition through official tabulation methods generally contributed to a temporal ending of concerted development of a broader understanding of social engagement, collaboration, and expression. What emerges in its place is the privatized temporality of family, or the time of reproduction, progenitors, and progeny.

To a large degree, the heteronormative family had organized the beginning and ending of the movement's goals years before the congressional debate on reforming the Census. Interracial (married) couples, on behalf of their multiracial children, and multiracial adults developed a putative multiracial constituency and mobilized around official categorization in order to prevent the social, cultural, and political eclipse of their experiences. The organizations under the AMEA umbrella were generally family organizations, and Project RACE prioritized identity issues for multiracial children. Aside from their work on legislative reform, many organizations offered support of families within relatively small, like-minded communities. However, if the rift between temporal continuity and rupture defined the conversation on the Census, the same rift marked the disagreement between members of these smaller communities. Confronted with this temporal fork in the road, the movement seemed uncertain of the direction it should travel. It was as if multiracial family organizations labored under the condition of being motionless within a racial timeline of progress. In a real sense, two objectives were simultaneously at play. One objective was to focus on the public organization of race and ethnicity for the sake of opening the field of identification recognizable to the state; the other was to foster inclusive communities that downplayed the politics of race and ethnicity in order to prevent the sense of alienation often felt by multiracial people and their families.

Heather Dalmage explains the complication that this balancing act produced. As she explains of GIFT and BFN in particular, a pressing struggle emerged:

Is it possible to create communities and spaces of comfort that do not exclude yet also challenge racism and social injustice? History has shown that multiracial family organizations can stay whole and strong by focusing on the shared experiences of border patrolling while avoiding larger racial politics. Indeed, this is the inherent flaw of multiracial family organizations: the very groups able to elucidate the dynamics of racism avoid these issues for fear of creating boundaries and exclusions and thus falling apart.[17]

The priorities that Douglass outlined emphasize the role that multiracialism ought to play in "elucidating dynamics of race" and "challenging racism and social injustice," yet the location of this activism within organizations that focus on the family reveals an impasse. This impasse might be described as the interface between the logic of public development—how would race be elucidated, and for whom?—and the logic of privatization, where it is the family that negotiates all racial meaning and action. The risks of fortifying the public as an intellectual and activist terrain are internal conflicts and the eventual dissolution of community. Dalmage explains that the fear of collaborating on social justice projects comes from the potential of alienating some members of the community. However, rather than reifying boundaries and ideological standpoints, one might imagine an alternative outcome of politicization: multiracial groups might have exploited this impasse between public and private in order to dabble in the realm of political and intellectual conjecture. Because no one was clear about how the multiracial family could have been instrumental for effectively dismantling racial and social injustice, this lack of clarity could have been the engine of invention. What version of racial time would be noncommittal, or even disloyal, to two available modes of inheritance—the first being that of previous liberationist movements, and the second being biological kinship? Simply put, by avoiding racial politics, and therefore the foundational analyses for this politicization, multiracial organizations seemed to be at a loss for how to account for its own place in history or for its own temporal movement.

Producing Family Time: Feminism as the Unspoken Precondition

The expression of the multiracial movement's flaw in this way—as a recognition that neither separatism nor virulent inclusion can sustain a movement—indicates the ostensible outcome of multiracial politics. Multi-racialism appears as a politics that no longer fortifies the public as a space for addressing the specifically racialized, gendered, and classed dimen-sions of inequity, but instead transforms public challenges to racism and social injustice into the neutralized space of the loving family or into com-fortably inclusive communities of families. What Dalmage pinpoints is the manner in which the discursive presence of familial love emerged at a time when the question of sustaining a neoliberal, antiracist movement was uncertain. Ramona Douglass, as a representative of family organizations and an ally of racially traditional civil rights groups, expressed interest in moving toward a future of meaningful social action. However, neither the Census controversy nor the impasse of multiracial politics in general leads to this outcome. Instead, when one considers the broader scope of multiracialist discourse, it appears that, eventually, the movement veered toward the universalization of personhood. Familial affect was a ready vehicle for travel in this direction.

However, the multiracial movement's self-account did not directly address its own temporal movement toward personhood, nor did it address familial affect as a means of achieving it. Cynthia Nakashima argues that multiracial discourse had three prominent voices, and although this claim does not overtly address the temporality of multiracialism, I submit that it reveals a key aspect of the process. She explains these voices as separate components of an integrated conversation, and so I list them here to con-sider what they mean in totality:

1. The struggle for inclusion and legitimacy in traditional racial/ethnic communities.
2. The shaping of a shared identity and common agenda among racially mixed people into a new multiracial community.
3. The struggle to dismantle dominant racial ideology and group boundaries and to create connections across communities into a community of humanity.[18]

Nakashima notes that "although there are important commonalities to being racially mixed in America, how individuals approach their multira-ciality can vary dramatically—from person to person, and within a single person over time and place."[19] What is of particular interest to me is how this three-part ideological structure presents a tacit chronology that begins with racial consciousness and ends with racial transcendence. Although it seems that all three elements of this structure unfold simultaneously, one can trace a tacit logic of development in its articulation of personal experience with community building. The chronology would look like this: first, multiracial individuals become conscious of their lack of inclusion and legitimacy in older racial and ethic communities. Second, these individuals form collectives to create a new, albeit still racial, community. Third, the racialization of mixedness is undone to create a community where both public and private experience and activity amount to achievement of universal humanity.

If such an implicit racial temporality is discernible within the context of multiracial discourse, then how does this version of racial time weaken the feminist outcomes of recognizing that "the personal is political"? In other words, why does the potential neutralization of race as a site of political action instrumentalize one of the most important revelations for politicizing gender? Multiracialism tacitly undermines a major feminist analytic while implementing it. Therefore, it is crucial to consider an afterlife of feminism: instead of a historiography that orders the emergence of an un-self-conscious, neutrally white feminist movement before the emergence of race-conscious black feminism, we can consider how racial entanglement marked the inception of feminist thought of the mid- to late twentieth century. The legacy of feminist thought and activism was treated with a profound ambivalence during the 1990s. This ambivalence was a product of tacit recognition that the public sphere, by this time, had been weakened as a site of social justice projects, even as the memory of a fortified public prompted multiracial politics.

At this point, I have claimed that the recognition that private and public lives are inextricable was the precondition for the emergence of the multiracial movement. This claim risks implying that one can construct a lineage that extends from the feminist movements of the 1960s and 1970s to the multiracial movement of the 1990s, as if the latter self-consciously replicated, expounded upon, or transformed the contributions of the former. Yet general participants of the multiracial movement did not overtly describe their political work as feminist. Instead of drawing such a reductive connection, overstating the family resemblances between the two movements or boldly claiming that the multiracial movement had over-arching feminist goals, I argue that the multiracial movement lacked self-consciousness regarding its relation to earlier projects that centralized the production, organization, and function of gender. This lack of self-consciousness or concerted theorization of gender is notable because 1990s-era discourses on multiracialism frequently evoke the concept. At times it is as if categorical delineations of gender underpinned the overt goal of theoretically and politically undoing racial categorizations. It is as if gender politics were foundational to the manner in which multiracialism was developed as a racial politics, even as multiracial activists and scholars seemed to be either unaware or unconcerned with this foundation. Rather than emerging as a self-aware progeny of an earlier feminist interven-tion, the multiracial movement emerged in an unwitting embrace with the phantom of this political past.

Even when activists and scholars of mixed-race studies openly addressed the category of gender in the context of theorizing mixed racialism, there was often a lack of thoroughgoing analysis of how gender and race are inextricable. One example comes from philosopher Naomi Zack's preface to Kwan and Speirs's collection. Zack is one of the architects of mixed-race studies, and her contributions to the area have established the study of multiracialism as a political knowledge project.[20] In the preface to *Mixing It Up,* Zack does three key things: she asserts that race is an onto-logical fiction; she affirms the personal nature of critical work on mixed racialism; and she claims that "there had to be middle-class multiracial Americans before such a thing as multiraciality could even have a voice on a printed page." She then offers this parting provocation:

> It is not an accident that most who write about mixed race are
> women and that most mixed-race symbols in the mass media are
> women. Women are the main players in the politics of the family.
> Women have traditionally enforced the racial identities and
> purities of American families, and women, now financially
> independent and politically and intellectually empowered, can
> revise such strictures. . . . The fact that women continue to be
> responsible for disproportionate amounts of compassion and
> communication in their roles as daughters, sisters, aunts, cousins,
> grandmothers, and friends, as well as wives and mothers, means
> that we are in many ways on the front lines of the negotiation
> of racial identities and perhaps, eventually, of all fictive racial
> taxonomies.[21]

Zack's primary goal here is to give a general overview of emergent themes in the collection, and a short preface is not the place for a lengthy exegesis. Still, Zack's remarks raise the question of how exactly multiracialism is political. What sort of multiracial politics focuses on personal experience, middle-class status, cultural representation, and womanhood? More to the point, how are these points of emphasis the outcome of a political reevaluation of normative standards, and what, exactly, was the mode of analysis that led to this reevaluation?

The passage above implicates a feminist politics because it empha-sizes the social relations of power that operate through various facets of experience, and because it specifies the perspectives and agency of women in particular. Furthermore, the passage refuses to neutralize the manner in which gender signals inequity. Joan Wallach Scott's definition of gender in the production of history is helpful here: "The core definition rests on an integral connection between two propositions: gender is a con-stitutive element of social relationships based on perceived differences be-tween the sexes, and gender is a primary way of signifying relationships of power."[22] However, what is interesting about Zack's passage above is that it exemplifies a tendency to evoke womanhood without exploring gender. I submit that this tendency to resist openly naming or explaining feminist theories of gender is a hallmark of multiracialist thought. Feminist theo-ries of gender are the unspoken prerequisites for multiracial politics. Zack mentions that it is "not an accident" that mixed-race studies has been pri-marily developed by women, and that representations of multiracialism are inextricable from womanhood. The refrain "it is not an accident" is a placeholder for a previous and deliberate analysis of how women are differentiated in relation to men and how this process of differentiation signals the operation of power. "It is not an accident" is shorthand for a previous development of feminist thought that, presumably, we now know very well. Because feminist paradigms are a given for how we now under-stand the status and agency of women in a decidedly reductive sense— women are now present and accounted for as subjects in history—the passage above suggests that there is no need to go on inquiring about the specific contexts and conditions for their status and agency.

The politics of multiracialism did more than ignore how feminist thought was foundational to its own development. Multiracialism also had the capacity to diminish the contributions of feminist thought when such thought could not be neglected. This could pinpoint a primary scheme: the political and intellectual interventions of feminism were foundational for multiracialism, and multiracialism undercut this foundation upon its recognition. According to the historical construction offered in Zack's preface, there is no socially determined difference between this particular phenomenon—"women have traditionally enforced the racial identities and purities of American families"—and this one—"women, now financially independent and politically and intellectually empowered, can revise such strictures." In this case, there is no way to discern whether one is the product of coercion and the other of liberationist action, or whether such discernment even matters. Rather, both conditions suggest that women have been the primary agents of racial discourse, still have such agency, and will continue to have it into the future, when "eventually, [women will negotiate] all fictive racial taxonomies." According to this passage, womanhood, unlike multiraciality, can be fixed and fully apprehended, to use Kwan and Speirs's words. Although the passage grants gender with specificity—womanhood—and thereby refuses to neutralize a history of power inequity that has been played out through gender, the striking result is another version of neutrality. This time, woman, and not simply gender, is the rubric under which analyses of inequity, antagonism to structural subjugation, or the politicization of private life is neutralized by a transhistorical universalization of experience.

By undercutting the feminist import of its concerns, multiracial discourse facilitates the replacement of one version of neutrality for another. More precisely, multiracial discourse utilizes a version of "the personal is political" and the evocation of specific identitarian categories to promote a politically neutralized ideal of personhood. This was possible because 1990s-era multiracialism benefited from the fact that the ideological rift between the personal and the public no longer required careful dismantlement. Further, the movement did not need to reinvent a thorough explanation of just how the personal is in fact political. Instead, a curious occurrence within some facets of the movement was a reversal of this scheme. The privatization of public discourses became an attempt to forge an alternative approach to the achievement of personhood. A 1990s-era multiracialism attempted to make particular racial, gender, and sexual relations political by neutralizing them through discourses of familial and maternal affect, and the ideal potential of childhood.

So far, I have given a general account of the multiracial movement, with the specific goal of explaining how feminist politicization of gender could be posited as the unspoken precondition of multiracialism. My purpose in emphasizing the contributions of 1960s- and 1970s-era feminist movements is to trouble the implicit timeline of multiracialism. In other words, I would like to consider alternatives to thinking about multiracialism as either a contributor to the end of social justice politics that were identity conscious, or to the beginning of another political project, underpinned by an ambivalent analysis of social justice. My intention is to reveal what has been operative, but seldom acknowledged, within 1990s-era multiracial discourse. Among the dimensions in operation was the exploitation and curious conversion of the analytic "the personal is political," which in turn rendered "the political as private." I turn now to discuss what this enervation of gender politics—and the knowledge it produced about motherhood and family life—meant for a multiracial discourse that was fixated on maternity and family. In general, white and black feminist communities of the 1970s could not resolve their divergent racial politics: black feminists roundly challenged white mainstream and radical feminisms for largely ignoring how gender politics are inflected by race. I argue that the trouble between white and black feminists did not completely disappear by the 1990s.[23] Rather, this political dissonance was muted by the emergent discourse of white women who loved their black husbands and had particular concern for their multiracial children.

On the surface, multiracial time was the time of family. This ordering of subjects within familial units adhered to a naturalized sequence of maturity, and by extension social participation: adults were the agents who developed a discourse of recognition for their own interracial intimacy and for their incipient multiracial children, who would not be granted full agency until the future. As Judith Halberstam explains in the epigraph above, the temporality of biological reproduction produces the recognizable, naturalized, and normal understanding of life progression: childhood or its outer limits (adolescence) is strictly delineated from the privileged time of adulthood. As Halberstam elaborates, "The time of reproduction is ruled by a biological clock for women and by strict bourgeois rules of respectability and scheduling for married couples.... Family time refers to the normative scheduling of daily life.... This timetable is governed by an imagined set of children's needs, and it relates to beliefs about children's

health and healthful environments for child rearing."[24] In a sense, the multiracial movement's focus on the family, and on multiracial children especially, was an attempt to conflate the timeline of multiracialism, which
begins with the legitimization of interracial marriage and ends with the
health and well-being of the multiracial child, and the ostensibly naturalized timeline of family and reproduction.

"White Women Took the Lead": Multiracial Motherhood

Within the general context of multiracial discourse—specifically in public
debates about Census categorization and in popular memoirs—one ostensible emergence of personhood was that of white motherhood. White
women described their development of an antiracist politics from within
black/white, interracial couples and families, and as the mothers of black-
appearing, multiracial children. As Peter Wallenstein and Erin Mooney
note: "In the 1990s . . . a collection of books came off the press, some of
them by women who described themselves as the mothers of mixed-race
children and others by children with multiracial identities."[25] To go further, the culture-producing mothers of mixed-race children seemed most
saliently white. Hershini Bhana Young explains the instrumentality of
whitening motherhood in multiracial discourse this way: "The mixed-race
movement's membership consists largely of monoracially identified parents, almost always white, who claim to act on their children's behalf. One
could argue, then, that the mixed-race movement attempts to extend the
hitherto denied privileges of whiteness to children who historically would
be black."[26] Another explanation of why white femininity and maternity
were so prominent is offered by Kim Williams: "The preponderance of
black–white couples in multiracial organizations, the race–gender breakdown of these couples, and a gendered division of labor combine to explain why relatively affluent suburban white women took the lead."[27] This
lead is ostensibly political in Williams's study, but it is also cultural. Further, it is driven by a sense of lost privilege or agency. In this way, the discourse of white maternity tied together three key approaches to framing
notions of identity: it captured a second-wave feminist sensibility in which
the personal lives of women are a starting place for political analysis; it
created wide recognition of multiracial identity; and it positioned white
subjects as challenging white supremacy by aligning themselves with the

racialized experiences of black, intimate partners and black-appearing children. As Williams notes, "Many white respondents seemed stunned by the treatment to which they found themselves subjected as members of interracial families. . . . Indeed, many white women . . . had been effectively disowned by someone in their family."[28]

Proponents of 1990s political multiracialism have attempted to move beyond the antiblack logic of the 1980s and to render a new logic of racialization that emphasized the kinship that white women share with black and multiracial subjects. Kimberly DaCosta cautions against the presumption that cross-racial kinship can globally eradicate ethnoracial boundaries, thereby tempering the general optimism of white women within the movement. DaCosta is careful to recognize ongoing ethnic/racial distinctions and hierarchies before acknowledging a liberatory potential of multiracial kinship. About this potential she writes: "The attempt to obtain some form of multiracial classification grew out of a desire to make visible those bonds that are easily elided—recognition of not only a varied racial heritage, but of *relationships*. The MOOM option ["mark one or more," for self-selecting racial and ethnic identity on the 2000 Census] institutionalizes and records in statistical form a trace of those relationships."[29] She goes on to reference Patricia Williams's often-cited provocation from *The Alchemy of Race and Rights* (1991): "Is there not something unseemly in our society about the spectacle of a white woman mothering a black child? A white woman giving totally to a black child; a black child totally and demandingly dependent for everything, sustenance itself, from a white woman."[30] Both moments fuel the claim that a focus on the family is most generative when it eschews biology and genealogy in order to expand the parameters of affection and care.

In this sense, the centralization of family and children is a proxy for the more radical potential of political multiracialism, which may grant various relationships beyond the heteronormative family a public importance and political relevance. "Those bonds that are easily elided" can appear in any number of varieties once they are made visible. They need not resemble the affection between husbands and wives, or parents and children. Indeed, those bonds, no longer elided, can be capacious enough to capture the affection between unrelated adults who enter multiracial family organizations—mothers whose relational experiences, shared sense of purpose, and vision cannot be relegated to any classification except multiracial politics in general.

The citation of the once unseemly prospect of a white woman who mothers a black child—and not, significantly, a white mother—already leads us toward a version of interracial affection that does not quite conform to the normativity of legal or biological bonds. As discussed above, children have often been the figure of relational cohesion between adults who do not share racial/ethnic identities or the same strategies for achieving social justice. In this way, they signal proxies for the not yet visible or emergent mediation between adults. What if the unseemly event of a white woman—who may or may not be a mother—caring for and perhaps fully submitting to the needs, desires, and demands of a black subject had more capacious implications? There is a trace of nuanced, elided, or not yet visible affect that the state now accounted for through official methods of racial tabulation. However, what if such a trace cuts across multiracial politics of the 1990s to make visible a residue of a prior political moment?

In her examination of the rift that occurred between black and white socialist and radical feminists during the 1960s and 1970s, Winifred Breines describes the poignant sense of nostalgia and mourning that white women purport they feel over the loss of interracial feminist collaboration as they experienced it during the early years of the civil rights movement. Regarding the collective memory of white subjects who were involved in social justice activism of the period, Breines describes this schema of love and loss. First:

> It is significant that many white civil rights movement activists remember the interracial connections of the early 1960s as the high point of their lives. For those who write about it, crossing the black/white racial divide in political work, interracial friendships, cooperation, hope, and devotion to racial justice transformed everything. Their lives became meaningful in an American culture rigid with repressive racial and gender rules; it moved them and moves them still.[31]

Breines—a white woman who was active within the movements she documents—goes on to describe the lack of sustainability of this interracial political collaboration and form of intimacy: "The image of community that I 'missed' could not have lasted precisely for the reasons that radical political activists understood by the late 1960s: the American political and

economic system does not foster equality, justice, freedom, or community. We often forgot to apply that insight to our own fledgling organizations and relationships, blaming each other and mourning instead."[32]
I cite these moments to highlight a notable resemblance between this
schema of idealist collaborative project building and subsequent disen-
chantment with that of the multiracial movement. Breines's description
above could easily describe many of the proponents of the multiracial
movement, and in particular the white mothers of multiracial children.
She describes the nostalgia above as a sense of the lost ideal of integration.
In Breines's description, and in the depiction of white maternal involvement in the multiracial movement presented here, there seems to be a
near simultaneity of beginnings and endings.

This is not to produce one historiography of the 1960s and 1990s in
which hope and loss are the conflated outcomes of feminist social action.
Rather, I would prefer to point out that both early second-wave feminists
and the 1990s-era multiracial activists were aware of their movements'
potential for creating social justice, even as, for very different reasons in
both cases, "equality, justice, freedom" could not be understood in racially
neutral terms by an activist community. To differentiate the two movements historically, perhaps the mourning of 1960s-era radical feminism is
for the limits of action waged in various public, political, and social contexts, and the mourning of 1990s-era multiracialism enunciates the loss of
a public terrain where social justice projects could be worked toward.

In a sense, the unresolved tension between feminists over racial politics emerges in the racial time of the multiracial movement. As I discussed
earlier, the rift between Ramona Douglass and Susan Graham presented
two ideologically opposed directions for the movement of multiracialism.
Douglass—a self-identified multiracial adult who allied with traditional
communities of color—took a perspective on history and social engagement that encompassed, but was not limited to, the production of heteronormative family units. Her attempt to maintain discursive and political
continuity between the past of social justice projects and the emergence
of multiracialism tacitly indicates grief over the ending of such social engagement. Yet the movement itself seemed to go no further than to rele-
gate the meaning of social justice and action to the private terrains of the
family, and the personal practices of self-identifying racially for state tabulation. Although Douglass's account of the movement explicitly specifies
that the ideological differences between her and Graham were a matter of

racial politics, the subtext is that the two simultaneously diverged over a gendered analysis that underpinned their respective strategies. When Douglass specifies that Graham is a "European American Jewish *woman* who was interracially married" and that she is a "multiracial *adult*," I do not believe that an attempt to naturalize what is in fact historically contingent is at play. Rather, I believe that both designations undercut the primacy of both the heteronormative family and maternity as requisites for granting multiracialism with social and political relevance. Douglass implies that Graham's womanhood need not be relegated to the neutralized, tacitly white, gendered position within the family. Douglass wages this critique by choosing a designation for herself that is ostensibly gender neutral, but also strikingly detached from a clear connection to the heteronormative family. The risk of using a racial discourse to eclipse any thoroughgoing analysis of gender is the relegation of public action through the bolstering of domestic life. Once again, Douglass was on the winning side of the Census debate. However, Graham seemed to have won the culture war.

Public and Private Affairs: Politicizing the Multiracial Family

Graham strenuously argued for a single "multiracial" category on the Census around the same time as that the anti–affirmative action Proposition 209 was voted into law. Graham, out of step with other prominent multiracial activists, found an eager ally in Newt Gingrich, then the Speaker of the House of Representatives. Despite Graham's previous coalitional work with leaders of other multiracial organizations, she and Gingrich met privately in June 1997. During this period, Gingrich pronounced that "adding a multiracial category to the census" and "doing away with affirmative action" were two parts of "building a better America."[33] Fundamentally, both Graham and Gingrich were voices of racial transcendence, the third voice of Nakashima's ideological structure. Kerry Ann Rockquemore and David Brunsma summarize the primary reason why this alliance produced such a sense of foreboding for the traditional left: "The spectacle of Susan Graham (a white mother of biracial children . . .) and Newt Gingrich (the personification of the conservative right) joining forces . . . confirmed the worst fears of civil rights leaders, who saw the multiracial movement being used as a tool to dismantle civil rights gains by stripping the government of the capacity to enforce that legislation."[34] As both examples demonstrate, it becomes difficult to disaggregate the goals of one ideological facet of multiracial politics from the state's desire to relinquish its obligation to redress inequality—an obligation that stemmed from civil rights legislation of the 1960s and the inception of affirmative action policies in the 1970s. This one anecdote of multiracialism in 1997 captures Graham and Gingrich engaged in a personal and political embrace. However, it is important to emphasize just how crucial the racial dimension of motherhood was. White motherhood might have facilitated multiracialism's neutralization of racial and gender political discourse, but this process required a slightly reworked (although deeply historical) discourse on black motherhood. Indeed, the multiracial anecdote I just recounted wrote blackness out of the family.

By the 1990s, it was widely accepted that the personal was inseparable from the political, but saying so became part of a value system that privileged individualism outside of social context. Rainier Spencer noted that "Project RACE's embrace of Gingrich is [an] example of the degree to which at least some multiracial activists are willing to sacrifice civil rights enforcement for the sake of self-esteem. Gingrich's record on civil rights issues leaves no doubt as to precisely why he would support a multiracial category. Asserting otherwise goes far beyond even naïveté or wishful thinking."[35] If we narrate the end of civil rights advancement and affirmative action with the alliance between a naive, white mother turned activist and a savvy neoconservative statesman, then what emerges is an ironic cautionary tale. What emerges is the end of public expansion that begins during the liberation movements of 1960s and the return to the (white) family. This return, it might be reasoned, is the proper outcome of liberationist teleology: once the state identifies with maternity, recognizes the vicissitudes of racial belonging, and grants racialized subjects a sense of fulfilled personhood, then what further need is there to antagonize the state? What analysis would motivate further antagonism? The caution is that a maternal multiracialism that neutralizes identity politics—or strips them of specific, historical relevance—through the pursuit of self-esteem will inevitably lead to the total privatization of what were once public and state-regulated issues. Civil rights enforcement is somehow reconfigured, through maternity, as antithetical to state recognition of personal liberty, which exceeds the discourse of rights and governmental regulation. This is all figurative for the reunification of the white American family after the enervation of the public as the terrain on which individuals and collectives can antagonize hegemonic forms. It is the story of white women coming home after the reinstatement of white patriarchy. It is a postracial and postfeminist story. White maternal womanhood and the state speak with the same ideological voice, and since both confer in private, ideally there would be no telling where one set of interests ended and the other began.

During the Census categorization debates, Gingrich proclaimed, "I believe that we can begin to address the country's racial divide by adding a multiracial category to federal forms and the United States Census while simultaneously phasing out the outdated, divisive and rigid classification of Americans."[36] Although color-blind on the surface, this rhetoric was not out of line with the racially divisive policy that congressional Republicans had proposed just a couple of years earlier, in 1995. Republicans of the House offered the Personal Responsibility Act, which was part of the Contract with America. As Dorothy Roberts describes, the Personal Responsibility Act rationalized welfare reform by asserting that the reproductive practices of black Americans produced a disproportionate dependency on the welfare system:

> The act referred to the rising illegitimacy rate for Black Americans and stated that "the likelihood that a young black man will engage in criminal activities doubles if he is raised without a father and triples if he lives in a neighborhood with a high concentration of single parent families." In promoting his Contract with America, House Speaker Newt Gingrich attributed Black people's poverty to their laziness.[37]

The Republican rhetoric about black familial irresponsibility laid the groundwork for the color-blind rhetoric Gingrich espoused later on because, in both cases, racial politics are inextricable from the state's attempt to relinquish its obligation to provide financial support for families and children. The deeply entrenched myth of the pathologically dysfunctional black family spins out this way: black reproduction occurs irrespective of constructing two-parent, heteronormative family units. Black single mothers bear the brunt of the state's judgment for birthing and raising children without black fathers or marriage agreements. When black fathers are absent, the state is obligated to take on a blurrily public/private role of patriarchal substitute. The welfare state financially supports the black children that black men leave behind, and the carceral state disciplines the black men that those children become. By 1997, the country's racial divide had been cast as a divide between responsible privatization and irresponsible dependence on the public. Perhaps this is why the neoconservative Gingrich reached a conclusion similar to that reached by the liberal Daniel Patrick Moynihan thirty years earlier: there should be a return to a liberal theory of the state in which the public and private are separate terrains. In part, the racial divide was solvable through the private, self-sustaining unit of the family.

When Graham argued that racial classification reform would ameliorate the indignity of being racialized in this country, one might safely presume that she was not thinking about black women or black mothers. When Gingrich and Graham forged their own informal contract, one might imagine that their shared version of political multiracialism did not have an analysis of the distribution of public resources or of how the intersections of race, gender, and class undercut the individual freedom of choosing one's family. Black people in general, and black women especially, are far less likely to belong to multiracial families when these families are defined by interracial marriage and the production of biracial offspring. According to Moran, black women marry partners of other races—that is, they outmarry—far less often than black men do, despite a long history of (illicit) interracial intimacy between black women and white men, and despite the higher degrees of education and employment black women have in comparison to black men. Moran explains this inconsistency: "When black men achieve educational and economic success, they become suitable marriage partners for white women. Their accomplishments 'lighten' and 'masculinize' them. Success does not have the same impact on the appeal of black women. Black 'superwomen'—who are resourceful, self-sufficient, and employed outside the home—are labeled 'sub-feminine' and 'castrating.'"[38] When it comes to black women and family, black welfare mothers are single and therefore irresponsibly dependent on the public, whereas black middle-class women are heteronormatively undesirable and therefore unsuited for marriage. Because the multiracial movement located itself within discourses about the family, the movement was rife with opportunities to become self-reflective about its own investment in racializing and gendering heteronormative desire, and in characterizing economic success in volitional terms.

However, the movement's lack of self-reflexivity signals an impoverished context for social engagement as the backdrop of multiracialism's emergence. Furthermore, the creation of a putative multiracial community—comprising subjects with diverging interests and disparate personal histories—seemingly led to the suppression of social contestation through substantive dialogue. To a degree, this suppression fostered an inequitable dimension to how white women (who took the lead) and black women were positioned within the movement. In this condition, one might recognize the vestiges of divergent racial politics among an earlier generation of feminists. As Kimberlé Crenshaw has explained, while white women were able to develop a feminist sensibility without attending to intergender privileges of whiteness, black feminists were compelled to complicate the singular focus on racism held within black communities.[39] This is all to suggest that the antiracism of political multiracialism could not attend to the historical conditions of (black female) marginalization because it foreclosed the public sphere as a terrain where the contestations of social engagement take place and where the politics of identitarian belonging and difference are complicated. As mentioned above, political multiracialism relegates social life to the private realm, thereby obscuring critical outcomes that are generated through public contestations and identitarian complications. Because the public sphere only supports a private sphere that does not attend to the historical scope of political meaning, political multiracialism approaches antiracism through a refusal of historical vicissitudes of gender/racial subordination. What is left is a universalization of difference, which arises through the organization of the interracial family and is transcended through discourses of intimacy and reproduction.

Liberal Personhood and Modes of Affect

The salience of racial time as the time of the heteronormative, reproductive family denies critical perspectives from which to see—or, more precisely, to know—what occurs within the intersections between subjective and social effects, private and public domains. With regard to the ideal potential of childhood, Tavia Nyong'o makes this point: "The mixed-race child as a harbinger of a transracial future is emplotted within the straight time of heterosexuality, wedded to progress. And yet in our everyday performances of intimacy and obligation, we continuously and unself-consciously deviate from that plot, enmeshing ourselves in other, queerer temporalities."[40] Nyong'o makes use of paradigms made available through performance studies in order to work toward alternative versions of the not-yet, and therefore toward alternative temporalities.[41] The implication here of how queer family formations are deemed invisible by the desire for multiracial transcendence also signals the problem of making the intimate and every-day, nonheteronormative possibilities of personhood and its practices pub-lic. The teleological straight time Nyong'o identifies and the conflation of time that I suggest is the result of privatizing politics both reveal tautological stasis: the present always already signals progress (and therefore the present accounts for itself as the future), and the beginning of social life is also the end of it. Avery Gordon, like Nyong'o, makes use of temporality as a struc-ture for perception through the metaphor of haunting. To Gordon, haunt-ing is "a process that links an institution and an individual, a social structure and a subject, and history and a biography."[42] Haunting is a process that mediates queerer temporalities such as the ghostly remainders of history, and what seems easily present as history, sociology, and social knowledge. In her reading of Toni Morrison's novel *Beloved,* Gordon explains: "Reck-oning with ghosts is not like deciding to read a book: you cannot simply choose the ghosts with which you are willing to engage. To be haunted is to make choices within those spiraling determinations that make the pres-ent waver. To be haunted is to be tied to historical and social effects."[43]

Affect was the process through which one reckoned with ghosts in the era of political multiracialism. Political multiracialism reconfigured the terms of racial affect. For both Nyong'o and Gordon, affect is not the engine of tautology, which would then mean that "the personal is politi-cal" because politics are personal.[44] Instead, affect invites conjecture, which becomes a process that cuts into the readily present plotting of the histor-ical and sociological. According to Jared Sexton, affect's ability to make the present moment uncertain is denied across the wide swath of multi-racialism's self-account. With regard to interracial sexuality—the unavoid-able foundation for multiracial subjects and the futurity of the multiracial child—Sexton makes this important point: "Multiracialism claims not to be about interracial sexuality where its sexual acts are associated with the depths. It is, rather, about love, romance, family, and trust where these ideals are associated with the heights of racial harmony—it is the eleva-tion of the interracial relationship up and away from the low areas of the body, the putative site of racism's pernicious effects."[45]

The depths of sexuality—which conjure the down and dirty effects of violence, coercion, or prohibition of miscegenation at various junctures from slavery onward, including racial fetishism and the dehumanization of flesh—must be denied to keep the ghosts that threaten to disorganize multiracial kinship elsewhere. If affect is, in this case, the rhetorical prevention of sexuality's involuntary, spiraling engagement with its spectral other, then one might recognize how this moral appeal to love, romance, family, and racial harmony in general strongly ascribe to the promise of human agency and the apparatuses that render such agency effective. The guarantees of affective elevation are ostensibly derived from the contractual arrangements of marriage, from the liberal forms of personhood granted from the legal legitimization of interracial intimacy, of propriety over multiracial children. In other words, attention to the elevation and depths of interracial sexuality leads to a question of which version of interracial sexuality promises the purchase of liberal personhood. Elevation seems to offer such a promise; the depths do not. The fall into the depths would signify the manner in which subjects of interracial intimacy could be enacting "racism's pernicious effects," but also how the body in the raw signifies a problem for the promises of liberal personhood.

Robyn Wiegman offers another version of this temporal distinction and another viewpoint on the rawness of bodily material. While Sexton makes this distinction by referring to the depths of personhood denied and the heights of personhood achieved—the before and after shots of liberalism's teleology—Wiegman directs our attention toward another significant discourse of the 1990s, which is that of reproductive technologies. Sexton argues that interracial sexual relations threaten the moral underpinning of the multiracial movement's rhetoric; the health and well-being of multiracial subjects and interracial families is naturalized within social consciousness through a process of avoiding the historicity of violence and coercion. Wiegman makes a similar claim by analyzing a legal case in which the technological possibility that a white woman can claim nongenetic maternity of a black child through gestation led to the mistake a fertility clinic made with genetic material turned property. Wiegman's analysis indicates the manner in which race is naturalized through familial affect. Wiegman explains, "Through the mistake, multiracial kinship, *for the white subject*, was disarticulated from the maternal lineage of coercion and cultural disavowal that has governed, quite literally, interracial sex and reproduction in the United States."[46] A white woman who was mistakenly inseminated with the genetic material of a black couple "could embrace the idea of her own maternity, in short, without encountering the specter of her own participation in sexual miscegenation."[47]

   This horrific, ghostly dimension that is held at bay by liberal legitimacy
of cross-racial affect has a more obvious presence when the woman inseminated with the genetic material of an ostensibly white couple is black. In
the case of *Anna J. v. Mark C.* (1991), Anna Johnson was denied maternity
of the child she gestated and gave birth to because of the contractual
agreement she had entered with Mark and Crispina Calvert, an interracial
couple who had been largely represented through the press as white.
While Johnson's position as a black woman who is denied the child of
her gestational labor does evoke, as Wiegman confirms, "the theft of the
body that slavery enacted," Johnson cannot be strictly understood as
sharing the same racialized status as a slave because "the contract serves
to secure the ideology of liberal personhood as that which, precisely,
differentiates the past from the future."[48] In this way, the contract—and
legal decisions that reinforce it—does not prevent the specters of U.S.
racialization from being evoked into present-day consciousness. Yet the
obtainment of liberal personhood is predicated on a denial of history's
horrors, which leads to different roads for the white subject and for the
black subject. For the white subject, one road leads to a version of multiracial affect that bolsters late twentieth-century white privilege. For the
black subject, another road leads to the ambivalent condition of living
within the historical juncture of liberalism's past and future. Legacies of
bodily theft and coercion always have a ghostly presence, even as the ideology of liberalism persuades subjects to behave as if ghosts are not to be
grappled with.
   To think of ghosts, or to imagine that political multiracialism emerged
at the end of the twentieth century as the specter of earlier iterations of
identity politics that countered cultural and statist forms, is to be confronted with a particular absence. In other words, what emerged was not
the newness of multiracial identity, disarticulated from the past, but the
ghostly matter upon which the appearance of newness depends. If multiracialism seemed to emerge as a new social identity, then this suggests that
multiracial subjects—those whose identities are comprised of multiple
racial and ethnic heritages—make up a coherent categorical group. Yet
the moment when political multiracialism enters this system, at the end
of the twentieth century, is also a time when the instrumentality of social
categories had already begun to erode. This has particular consequences
for black identity. With the rise of multiracial identification, does blackness—the historically but implicitly mixed category that has heretofore

incited racial politics—disappear? Is the dawn of multiracialism the dusk of blackness?

Considering an inclusionary politics that interfaces with a seemingly exclusionary one is yet another approach to charting the temporality of racial formation. The temporal fork in the road that multiracialism and blackness index is the emergence of one formation and the waning of the other, respectively. Kathleen Odell Korgen explains that "prior to the existence of multiracialism, there was little debate on how biracial persons should identify themselves. Black nationalists opposed interracial marriages. . . . Biracial Americans were racially defined by both blacks and whites as simply black. . . . Today, however, racial identity is neither so quickly nor so easily defined."[49] If, as Wiegman put it, the "cultural disavowal that has governed, quite literally, interracial sex and reproduction in the United States" was the imperative of both white and black nationalists, then biracial subjectivity disarticulates the present from past regulatory practices. However, because the condition of being "simply black" is no longer "so quickly or easily defined," blackness, unlike whiteness, is under particular pressure to account for itself "today." What contributes to this pressure of a self-account is that blackness is stuck on the road of a liberal teleology: it must move toward the horizon of neutral personhood even as it understands itself to be a historical product of American negation, and therefore a sign of nonpersonhood.

Black nationalism of the 1960s and 1970s discursively established that black identity is composed of shared experiences, heritages, histories, and cultural practices. Black self-determination, opposition to Eurocentrism, and an embrace of pan-Africanist epistemologies together make up the economic, political, and cultural outcome of black nationalist sensibilities. However, black nationalism lacked a general attentiveness to the politics of gender and sexual difference.[50] As Wahneema Lubiano notes, "Within the terms of black nationalism, blackness and the black dreamed-of, autonomous subject is inevitably male, heterosexual, and in training to be a powerful patriarch—only in and on 'black' terms, terms that are both separate from and continuous with those of the hegemonic culture."[51] This form of nationalism had produced its own antagonisms toward itself from within. Black nationalism of the 1960s may have sought the achievement of personhood by means other than those facilitated by state power, such as legal reform, contractual arrangements, and institutional integration. In its more radical articulation, black nationalist thought exceeded the logic and limits of statehood to develop an intellectual project that provided an internal analysis of nationalism's limitations. Just as political multiracialism alluded to statism (again, think of the Census) in order to claim that the time of state-sanctioned legitimization had its ultimate conclusion in the autonomy of private life, so versions of black nationalist thought also antagonized the state in order to build a universalized paradigm for activism.

What if we consider that the imperative to have black racial coherence, or to "unite in a universal black liberation movement to strike the universal slavemaster at *one time, one blow, one war*," as the spectral presence that tangles with the newness of multiracialism?[52] What if we imagine that late multiracialism could not simply choose which ghosts it would reckon with? What if the question is not whether the objectives of multiracialism are simplistically plotted in the same sequence as modern black nationalism, but whether the present of multiracialism is rendered irresolute as a result of historical entanglement with a black nationalist legacy? Ostensibly, multiracialism did not account for itself as a form of nationalism, nor did it want to proscribe nonblack heritages, histories, and so forth. Ostensibly, a radical organization such as the Revolutionary Action Movement (RAM) sought not just the universalization of blackness but the flattening of racial time. Structures of dominance—imperialism, colonialism, slavery, capitalism—do not simply index the various moments in which race gains its logic in particular ways. To strike the transnational, transhistorical slavemaster, at one time, in one war, suggests that liberation occurs as the universal and generic horizon, so that what one gets through the paradigm of revolution is a discourse in which blackness is always already recognizable to itself, and in opposition to the signpost of slavemaster. Multiracialism sees the horizon differently: as mentioned above, political multiracialism configures the private sphere as the universalized horizon of meaning and action. However, what if we imagine that both discourses present a temporal conflation of sociality that forecloses perspectives from which to view not only subjective and social effects, but also the self-production of their own antagonisms?

Nation Time(s): Black and Multiracial Heteropatriarchy

I have asserted that familial and especially maternal affect were central preoccupations within the personal narratives of multiracialism's activists, proponents, and culture producers. The recognition that many of those producing such narratives were women suggests a particularly maternal, or womancentric, dimension to multiracial discourse. However, there were two prominent modes of affect at cross-play, with each attaching itself to gender differently. Another discourse produced a racial entanglement between blackness and multiracialism that was most vociferous when it is accompanied by an imagined nationalist unity. This other, non-maternal, version of entanglement—another version of affect—reveals how the summons to "unify for nation time" makes an uneven appeal across gender.[53]

The central question that emerges is this: why is it that both political multiracialism and black nationalism, having been developed at markedly differing moments under markedly differing auspices, both move toward universalized horizons with similar certainty, and without grappling with self-produced antagonisms? In his discussion of these movements, Sexton does not address this similar mode of transit. Rather, he emphasizes their ostensible point of departure:

> In essence, the multiracial intervention argues not only that its concerns are an extension of, and therefore equivalent to, those of historic black freedom struggle and that if the terms *black* and *multiracial* work at cross-purposes today, it is the former term that is in the wrong, but also—its most insecure and hence most vociferous point—that multiracialism is not, in itself, a discourse and a politics of antiblackness. This is the point of transit between the debate regarding the history of interracial sexuality under slavery and the dispute around contemporary interracial relationships and multiracial identity politics.[54]

Sexton pinpoints two dichotomous arrangements for blackness and multiracialism. The first is a version of Korgen's explanation, which in this instance points to multiracialism's supposedly correct relation to freedom struggle, and to blackness as the wrong approach to reference such struggle. The second, which is paradoxical to the first and of which Sexton is skeptical, is an aspect of a multiracial self-account that rejects antiblackness. This self-account gathers its logic from indexing blackness as outdated. Blackness is wrong as an indicator of the present. As a politics that indexes what once was and what currently is, multiracialism cannot be antiblack because it simply distinguishes one historical juncture from another.

This provokes another moment of conjecture: what if the point of transit that marks the distinction between the one temporal moment and another allows for movement in both directions? Mike Hill points out that the emergence of multiracial politics presents the delineation of time into the before and after of liberal statism, or the utility of identity for jurisprudence. While citing work that heralds the onset of the multiracial nation by Werner Sollors, Ross Posnock, and David Hollinger, Hill makes this suggestion: "They are . . . temporal provocations that bespeak a curious disjunction between the past and future significance of racial self-description."[55] He raises this not to reiterate a now-familiar observation, but to make a less expected claim, which is that as relations between categories "change over time, racial categories tend to turn against themselves and redivide, leaving only traces of whatever previous political significance they may formerly have had."[56] Both Sexton and Hill are pointing out that multiracialism emerges as that which outlives the category of blackness. As that which seemingly breathes new life into the historically political efficacy of racial categorization, multiracialism can appear to continue its liberation struggle even as it evacuates the political significance of racial categories. This evacuation—an emptying of a category of its political content—provides the space from which to see a possible divergence between Sexton and Hill. While Sexton's metaphorical point of transit illustrates that multiracialism transforms itself from being an antiblack discourse to an antiracist discourse by relegating blackness to the past, Hill's metaphorical traces effectively do away with the temporal disjuncture of past and future, or before and after. Those traces of political redress through either jurisprudence or counterstatist liberation struggle once facilitated by race, and which are no longer viable in a neoliberal era where race is empty, still remain. Those remainders are precisely the particles melted into air that make the outlines of multiracialism, which seems to rise from the horizon, visible.

It is for this reason that I would like to return to Sexton's metaphor, and then to the unwitting similarity between black nationalism and multiracialism. If blackness is not only obsolete but emptied of its political efficacy, and therefore present but ghostly, then multiracialism also loses its solidity through its entanglement with blackness. To be sure, this is what Sexton is driving at. That the very point of transit between ideologies is visible at all indicates how the past continues to leave its mark on the present. Rather than moving from antiblack to antiracist, the only transformation that takes place is between the efficacy of racial categorization to bear political content for redressing historic inequities and the loss of this efficacy. However, in addition to this, what interests me about points of transit is the possibility this metaphor has to reveal traces or incomplete transformations other than those specifically pertaining to racial categorical vicissitudes. I have mentioned that multiracialism did not account for itself as a nationalist discourse.[57] I also suggested, however, that multiracialism was akin to a version of black nationalism because of its universalization of racialism's outcome—in the politically evacuated private sphere—and its temporal conflation of sociality. In this way, the only temporal disjuncture that matters is that which separates blackness—which, in versions of black nationalism, is always already recognizable to itself—and multiracialism—which arises out of blackness's rubble. This false, or incomplete, disjuncture is a point of transit between the universalization and historical flattening of nationalist collectivity on the one side, and the theorization of identity politics as that which challenges the universalization or flattening of temporality on the other. *Troubling the Family* situates the transit point—or perhaps more precisely, the passageway—in the interventions of feminist thought. This bears repetition, albeit in a slightly changed way: if one sees blackness and multiracialism as locked in dubious battle, with each referencing the other as its negation in order to gain self-recognition, then one can begin to focus on this heavily emphasized schematic of negation more broadly. If, when all is said and done, blackness and multiracialism are present and accounted for, then what is really missing? What I will refer to as an affect of denial or revulsion between blackness and multiracialism appeared in its most salient forms when facilitated through the channels of masculine normativity.

One might think of a 1990s-era nationalist paradigm of marching: in 1995, the Million Man March, organized by Louis Farrakhan, drew hundreds of thousands of black men to the Washington Mall for a day of atonement. The separate but equal event scheduled on the day of the Million Man March was referred to as the Day of Absence, during which black women were encouraged to stay at home, attend to their children, and privately support black male collectivity. In the following year, multiracial activist Charles Byrd spearheaded the much smaller 1996 Multiracial Solidarity March. If Byrd could not garner the level of attention and participation that defined the Million Man March, he made sure to place black leadership at the heart of his remarks that day. It was as if a subli- mated desire to have his gaze returned could only be expressed as a vehe- ment renunciation of black separatism. He asserted that "black leadership today" was "more separatist-inspired and too often exhibit[ed] the same racist mentality of the long-standing white power structure. . . . *Afrocentric nationalism* polarized and hurt the civil rights movement, replacing effec- tive strategy with empty shouting and posturing of the sort that allowed America the opportunity to avoid both identification with black people and the job of bettering this nation."[58] Byrd egregiously blames the black community for "allowing America" (which is composed of nonblack denizens? Or is it of local and federal government officials?) to abandon its work toward social justice. He yokes separatism to racism, and while it is difficult not to think of "black leadership today" as referring precisely those involved with of the highly publicized march that took place only the year before (Louis Farrakhan, Jessie Jackson, Martin Luther King III), he explicitly indicts members of "the black political intelligentsia"—Jon Michael Spencer, Henry Louis Gates Jr., and Gregory Howard Williams— for their supposed endorsement of the "one-drop rule."[59] Byrd's unre- quited yearning for "identification with black people" and with black men in particular becomes the *ressentiment* that appears as an unwanted unity with blackness through the rule of hypodescent, and an overarching frus- tration with a racial politics that either coerces multiracials to identify as black or simply leaves them out in the cold.

This rechanneling of masculine intimacy into racial antagonism misses a connection with the remarks on nationalist separatism by black feminist Jewell Jackson McCabe, founder of the National Coalition of 100 Black Women in 1981. To the Million Man March/Day of Absence, her re- sponse was, "How dare anyone ask us to show unity by silence?"[60] This indignation over the sexist structure of the Million Man March seems to echo Byrd's indignation over the implied demand to be silent about one's multiracial identity. However, this unwitting similarity most poignantly highlights the lack of open connection between these two perspectives. With nearly a full year between the two marches, Byrd could have waged a critique of Afrocentric nationalism through an observation of gender separatism. However, from a masculinist ideology, it is easy not to see this gender divide, which is why Byrd inadvertently, though profoundly, repli- cates the absence of his adversaries. Although Farrakhan's Million Man

March ostensibly sought to organize gender roles horizontally, the organization of public masculine and private feminine work is ultimately hierarchical. This careful (re)constitution of gender was a troubling reminder
of how racial unifying projects have historically marginalized or undercut
the labor of women, and therefore invited the political and intellectual
challenges of black feminists. In contrast, Byrd's affect toward black masculinity that is rechanneled into a repudiation of black neonationalism
seems always already to take for granted that blackness is normatively
male. The empty shouting is not the historical silence that black nationalist or social justice projects have coerced its subordinated participants to
be. While attempting to play the role of a race leader, Byrd seemed to wage
his biggest complaint at being denied a mode of masculinity that is somehow inextricable from blackness.

Political Ends and the Rise of Multiracial Sons

Byrd's complaint demonstrates how a particular vision that places blackness and multiracialism within each other's sight lines relegates womanhood as a requisite blind spot. Perhaps this is the particular mode of vision
that had a nation focused on the racial battle for Tiger Woods in 1997.
This battle not only symbolized the latest vicissitude of racial categorical
possibilities, but also illustrated that the horizon for entangled varieties of
blackness and multiracialism was ultimately the emergence of a native son.
    I have argued here that multiracial family organizations labor under the
condition of being motionless within a racial timeline of progress. This
motionlessness is akin to the appearance of black female personhood in
the neoliberal teleology outlined by Robyn Wiegman. Wiegman's analysis
of black gestating womanhood bound in a (patriarchal) contractual agreement highlights the fraught nature of neoliberal teleology: the reproductive
black female is stuck somewhere between the past of slavery and sexist–
racist coercion, and the future of personal volition and the equal recognition of personhood, which is mediated through the neutral channels of
contractual agreements. While this example implies that movement on the
road forward requires that one disregard the manner in which the specters
of history reemerge and require their acknowledgment, multiracial family
organizations grapple with historical aporia by adamantly investing in a
future. As Dalmage explains, "As organizational boundaries become defined by racial politics rather than social experiences, individuals may feel

alienated and less inclined to maintain membership. Such a concern led one former BFN president to conclude that 'the organization needs to focus on the children, or it will fall apart.'"[61] In this way, children may function as mediation between racial politics and the social experiences and personhood of adults.

Considering this function of childhood—and more generally, the privatization of public action—immediately evokes Lauren Berlant's discussion of citizenship during and after the Reagan era of the 1980s. She describes yet another version of nationalism or "a nationalist politics of intimacy" that invest heavily in "the family":

> The intimate public sphere of the U.S. present tense renders citizenship as a condition of social membership produced by personal acts and values, especially acts originating in or directed toward the family sphere. No longer valuing personhood as something directed toward public life, contemporary nationalist ideology recognizes a public good only in a particularly constricted nation of simultaneously lived private worlds.[62]

This "intimate public sphere" not only reduces the meaning of citizenship to preoccupations with private activity, but also magnifies the infantile icon of ideal citizenship in lieu of adult civic participation. Again, here's Berlant: "the nation's value is figured not on behalf of an actually existing and laboring adult, but of a future American, both incipient and prehistorical: especially invested with this hope are the American fetus and the American child." The significance of this observation for my argument here is that "the fetal/infantile person is a *stand-in* for a complicated and contradictory set of anxieties and desires about national identity. . . . these anxieties and desires are about whose citizenship—whose subjectivity, whose forms of intimacy and interest, whose bodies and identifications, whose heroic narratives—will direct America's future."[63]

The resemblance between Berlant's assertion and the rhetorical and activist agendas of multiracial family organizations is striking. Dissent over "the dynamics of racism" and racial alienation is directed toward an enervated version of public life, and specifically toward the family. Alienation is consistently explicated through personal, individuated experiences. Alienation becomes the conduit through which challenges to racism and social injustice go from being public activism to private concerns about self-esteem and care for intimate relationships. Further, a focus on the children acts as a deferral mechanism: it keeps at bay adult grappling with the complications of political subjectivity. It staves off the open acknowledgment of how very limiting a project that prioritizes unification at the expense of political thought, action, and negotiation can be. A focus on the children seems to conclude with a national retreat from the fortification of the public as a sphere for political activity. The literal child becomes the iconic child, and the icon stands in for an open acknowledgment that politics leads to the falling apart and the dispersion of collectives. In this way, the only public life that can sustain itself is one that fortifies the meaningfulness of private lives.

This account seems to explain what multiracialism promised its proponents during the 1990s: it promised a public existence in which social organization leads to the value and recognition of personhood. Political focus on racial inequity is converted into social organizations focused on families, and more precisely, children. The problem of openly posing and debating the national question—whose subjectivity, whose forms of intimacy and interest will identify us?—was the multiracial movement's problem writ small. However, what interests me is a mode of subjectivity whose importance is substantively diminished by this account: the existing and laboring adult stakeholders of multiracialism. This is not to recast the versions of black and multiracial ideologies that respond to the national question—whose subjectivity, whose forms of intimacy and interest, whose bodies and identifications, whose heroic narratives—with a reductive reinforcement of heterosexual masculine citizenship. Further, this is not to recast the version of multiracial rhetoric that figures the (feminized) private sphere as the neutral horizon of racial conciliation as an alternatively more generative formulation of citizenship. Instead, I want to pinpoint the often-neglected gender divide within multiracial discourse, and how this divide attends to the anxieties over disparate adult interests that threaten to break collectives apart.

The affect of denial and revulsion play these anxieties out openly: heteromasculine entanglements between blackness and multiracialism are demonstrative of how national leadership requires the delineation of whose subjective positions and which bodies ought to represent a national identity. The implied masculine lineage of race leadership, stemming from civil rights–era activism of the 1960s, is the starting point for this mode of entanglement. Alternatively, affect that is directed toward the family and toward the interfamilial experiences of parenthood, and motherhood especially, is magnified in order to avoid the antagonisms that racial politics produce between adults in public. Both versions are decidedly ambivalent forms of affect: the first is repressed desire for cross-racial masculine unity that expresses itself as revulsion, and the second is a desire for cross-racial kinship that renounces the careful development of racial analysis. Neither of these gendered versions, which operated within the larger scope of multiracial discourse, offers the promise of a vitalized public in which minoritized or subjugated subjects can express their pleasures, needs, and challenges to dominant and normative forms of identity and behavior. Neither gendered version offers the potential of an expanded social scene in which to develop alternative analyses to identify us.

The movement's overall neglect of its theoretical foundations, and a careful assessment of theories of gender in particular, has restricted the mechanisms through which multiracialism promises the fulfillment of personhood. Just as the ~~black~~ multiracial Frederick Douglass has given us an idiom for a cycle of conversion that has one gendered referent—"You have seen how a man becomes a slave. You will now see how a slave becomes a man"—the supposed fulfillment of multiracial personhood became discursively inextricable from masculinity. If blackness in general offered a fraught version of liberalism's teleology—which is the insistence that black subjects accept a horizon of neutrality, and move toward it while under the shadow of racial history—then black womanhood in particular offers a yet more fraught version. She signals in the most pronounced ways how what seems like a teleology produces its own logical other, which is immobility. This approach is especially necessary for exploring the vicissitudes that political multiracialism simultaneously expresses and obscures in relation to black racial politics. In the chapter that follows, I demonstrate how black feminism, like multiracialism itself, can act as a heuristic for exploring alternative strategies for attending to U.S. racial histories while speculating about potential ways of becoming political.

CHAPTER 2

Legitimizing the Deviant Family

Loving v. Virginia and the Moynihan Report

Loving suggests, in a fleeting and inadequate way, the possibility of a corollary principle that when state power is being used to determine who "the People" will be . . . strict scrutiny is necessary to disrupt the establishment of caste.

—Angela P. Harris, "*Loving* Before and After the Law"

The years in Washington were not happy ones for the couple. Richard [Loving] struggled to maintain permanent employment while Mildred busied herself tending to the needs of their three children. During this time, they remained oblivious to the civil rights movement that was unfolding in their midst. "I just missed being at home," [Mildred] told me years later. . . . I wanted my children to grow up in the country, where they could run and play, and where I wouldn't worry about them so much. I never liked much about the city."

—Robert A. Pratt, "Crossing the Color Line"

Origins

This chapter explores how two significant state documents of the 1960s—Daniel Patrick Moynihan's "The Negro Family: The Case for National Action," or, as it is more widely known, the Moynihan Report (1965), and the U.S. Supreme Court decision of *Loving v. Virginia* (1967)—together mark the historical basis for the multiracial movement's preoccupation with the family. When read together, these two documents reveal a seemingly contradictory national stance on the American family. On the one hand, the state wanted to tighten its regulation of black, supposedly unstable families. On the other hand, the state wanted to loosen regulation by abandoning racial restrictions on marriage. Although seemingly contra-dictory, the Moynihan Report and the *Loving* decision were concomitant. Both were state initiatives to reinforce heterosexual marriage, and by exten-sion the heteronormative family, as private units that fortify national well-being. The ideological concomitance of these two documents marks the enduring significance of the family as a unit of both private and national interest. Although this ideology pervaded the treatment of the family in 1990s-era multiracial politics, there has yet to be a genealogy of the move-ment that addresses it. The combined legacy of the Moynihan Report and *Loving* figured so largely within discourses on the multiracial family that one could trace it through the major components of movement: the legit-imization of multiracial families, the primacy of (white) maternal love for multiracial children, and suburbanization as the racially normalized con-dition of family development. This chapter explains the manner in which this profile of 1990s-era multiracialism owes an unacknowledged debt to the governmental policy and legal decision of the mid- to late 1960s.

Building American Families: Reading Loving before the Moynihan Report

Why did the family become the central arena for transforming public matters of inequity—such as the unequal distribution of rights and racial stratification—into private matters? In the first epigraph above, Angela Harris notes that family, in terms of marriage law in particular, has a deep history of state regulation. In fact, the state, to some degree, produces itself by constituting legitimated families. The *Loving* decision reveals the inextricable ideologies of race and gender—or racialized gender—as the "prepolitical reality on which government . . . must build."[1] Marriage as a state institution tacitly requires the distinction of castes. Our close analy-sis of the establishment of castes is necessary because marriage is so closely tied to our understanding of the natural foundations of citizenship. Harris writes that a "productive approach to *Loving*'s legacy is the argument that in both antimiscegenation laws and prohibitions against same-sex mar-riage, governments have incorporated caste distinctions into their mar-riage law, which should be considered a violation of the Reconstruction Amendments of the Constitution."[2] In this way, the sort of scrutiny that Harris is advocating has the potential to make the law instrumental in pro-ducing a more egalitarian vision for the affective dimension of citizenship.

The potential is to recognize other viable forms of how the people can feel their connectedness. An ideological dimension of citizenship—an affective dimension, or the manner in which people emotionally belong to nation—is based on racial and gendered orders of inequity that are understood as natural. Chief Justice Warren's language in the *Loving* decision draws attention to this ideological component, explicitly mentioning white supremacy as a rationale for antimiscegenation. Differences between the races do not emerge prior to the politics of the state; rather, the people are understood to emerge through state mechanisms that determine differentiated and unequal castes. Harris explains that citizenship has been the mode through which we understand our affective connections with others as natural in addition to legal.

Harris's comments on how the state operates through affective connections have further use for exploring how the state defines the stability of families. In a sense, stable families relieve the state of its decidedly patriarchal responsibility as welfare provider. At the same time, however, the state still takes on regulatory responsibility by promoting marriage as a requisite for familial health. If 1960s-era discourse singled out the black family for being pathological and simultaneously for bleeding the state of public resources, then the black family figured those subjects who are structurally, culturally, and historically disconnected from the affective dimensions of citizenship. In this way, an additional imperative to Harris's claim that we attend to the caste inequities built into marriage law is that we attend to the manner in which families do not emerge prior to public policy. Rather, what makes the functionality of some families recognizable and acceptable is the inequity of caste embedded in legal and policy-driven constructions of family.

The production of families is controlled by the built-in caste differentials of marriage law, and then the status of families is determined by public policy analysis. Both aspects were significant to the *Loving* case, in which a white man was prohibited from marrying and building a family with a black woman. However, the *Loving* case demonstrates another dimension of state control: in order to keep their legally illegitimate family intact, the Lovings were forced to move geographically, from one state to another, from the country to the city. In the second epigraph, Robert Pratt refers to the period between the 1959 forced exile of Richard and Mildred Loving and their children, and the enactment of *Loving v. Virginia* in 1967, after the Supreme Court's decision. The white Richard Loving and black Mildred Jeter were legally married in Washington, D.C., in 1958, and afterward, they immediately resumed residence in their home state of Virginia, even though their marriage was in violation of Virginia's Racial Integrity Act of 1924.[3] Soon after their marriage in D.C., the Lovings were arrested for living in Virginia as a married couple. They were subsequently indicted; forgoing their right to a trial by taking a plea, the Lovings were sentenced to a year in jail, or given a suspended sentence on the condition that they live in exile (that is, not in the state of Virginia) for twenty-five years.[4] Judge Leon M. Bazile defended the course of action this way: "Almighty God created the races white, black, yellow, malay and red, and he placed them on separate continents. . . . The fact that he separated the races shows that he did not intend for the races to mix."[5] Of course, this ruling did not account for the actual intimacy between the races as it existed in Central Point, the region in Caroline County that had a long history of interracial sexuality when Richard and Mildred met. The ruling before the Supreme Court heard *Loving v. Virginia* goes to great lengths to police the affective dimension of citizenship by interpreting its caste distinctions as natural and therefore legal. At this time, the difference of caste prohibits marriage rather than becoming embedded in it. In 1959, the Lovings chose to leave their Virginia home to live in the District of Columbia. The time of exile was difficult: in Pratt's account, Richard Loving "struggled to maintain permanent employment while Mildred busied herself tending to the needs of their three children."[6] Mildred Loving was troubled by having to raise her children in the city, as opposed to the preferable country. In this way, the state-imposed exile of the Lovings impinged on the family's capacity to function well and autonomously.

Because the state recognizes legal marriage as a precondition for legitimate, autonomous family life, and because *Loving v. Virginia* is the eventual outcome of a 1959 court decision, I read *Loving* before the Moynihan Report. In 1959, the state had a mandate to deny the legitimacy of some nuclear families on the basis of interracial intimacy, rather than support them. From thereafter, however, the state began to revise its position on family, and this included the transformation of marriage law. *Loving* overturned the 1924 Racial Integrity Act in Virginia—legislation that intensified existing antimiscegenation policy by limiting the definition of whiteness. The 1924 legislation prohibited a purely white person, now defined as someone having no "blood other than Caucasian," from marrying a non-white person.[7] This legislation, part of a continuum of antimiscegenation policy in Virginia extending back to the colonial era, was understood in the *Loving* decision as a breach of the Fourteenth Amendment and equal protection under the law. As Chief Justice Earl Warren's decision notes, "The fact that Virginia prohibits only interracial marriages involving white persons demonstrates that the racial classifications must stand on their own justification, as measures designed to maintain White Supremacy. We have consistently denied the constitutionality of measures which restrict the rights of citizens on account of race."[8] The *Loving* decision falls within an era of civil rights legislation that can arguably be bookended by *Brown v. Board of Education* in 1954 and the Fair Housing Act in 1968. By 1967, the dismantlement of antimiscegenation legislation was in line with the times. As Randall Kennedy notes, "The decision was practically a foregone conclusion, especially since, in *McLaughlin v. Florida* (1964), the Court had already invalidated a Florida statute that criminalized interracial fornication."[9] Carlos Ball notes that "by the late 1960s, this remaining vestige of white supremacy could no longer be made consistent with our constitutional values."[10] The *Loving* decision redresses the unconstitutional denial of legal protection on the basis of race, and it prohibits government interference from the personal, discretionary process of choosing a marriage partner across racial and ethnic lines. By the end of the 1960s, the problem of interracial marriage had been diminished legislatively and culturally. However, the issues that motivated such regulation were actually still on the forefront of national concern: the disadvantageous difference of black Americans, and the geographic proximity between blacks and whites.

What this implies is that marriage—as the legal site from which to redress racial inequity—had the potential to obscure the varying arrangements surrounding intimacy and affect that nonetheless continued to be shaped by white supremacy and state-sanctioned civic policy. One interpretation of the legalization of interracial marriage in *Loving* is that the state wishes to endow fathers with the responsibility of taking care of the family. As it happened, the Lovings were a family: Mildred and Richard had the first of their three children in 1958 and their second in 1959. This is where the court-order exile of the Lovings that began in 1959 overlaps with the outcomes of the Moynihan Report: by 1965, it was decidedly inconvenient for the state when fathers "struggle to maintain permanent employment" and perhaps abandon their families as a result. However, this concern over the fulfillment of fatherhood was racially uneven, as absent fathers were perceived to be black. The *Loving* decision coincided with the perceived crisis of the growing number of black children receiving public assistance. In this way, the Lovings' period of exile, between 1959 and 1967, offers not a snapshot of official discourses on the family but a negative of that snapshot. If Richard Loving struggled as a provider during this period, then this certainly did not signal a cultural phenomenon among white men or for white families. Conversely, if Mildred Loving "tended to the needs of her three children," then this certainly did not install black motherhood as a symbol of family functionality or responsible citizenry. By the mid- to late 1960s, the positive impression was that the state supported the production of American families irrespective of caste or color. But what happened to the negative?

From 1963 to 1965, Daniel Patrick Moynihan served as assistant secretary of labor and policy. During that time, in March 1965, he drafted the policy paper "The Negro Family: The Case for National Action." The report begins by acknowledging the achievements of the "Negro revolution" of the 1950s and 1960s, then claims that "the major events of the onset of the Negro revolution are now behind us." He lists these seminal events as the organization of the mass movement; "the Kennedy–Johnson Administration['s]" commitment to "the cause of Negro equality"; and the public support of this unprecedented federal commitment, as demonstrated during the 1964 presidential election.[11] Moynihan explains how the Johnson administration had been strongly responsive to redressing the economic disadvantages of black Americans. These measures of redress included the Manpower Development and Training Act of 1962, which responds to racial inequities in the labor market, and the Economic Opportunity Act of 1964, which "began a major national effort to abolish poverty, a condition in which almost half of Negro families are living."[12] A third measure was the Civil Rights Act of 1964, which "marked the end of the era of legal and formal discrimination and unequal treatment." To follow this account of federal activism, Moynihan quickly notes that the era of legislative redress that began with *Brown v. Board of Education* had produced a judiciary climate in which inequality for black Americans would be struck down "wherever it appears." Moynihan's bottom line is that the state had completed the task of responding to the demands of the civil rights movement and creating legal conditions for racial equality. The state could guarantee that expanding public accommodations led to greater equality, but other measures, like job training, "only make opportunities

available. They cannot insure the outcome." State-sponsored opportunities for economic advancement marked only the beginning of racial equality. Responsibility for "insuring the outcome" lay elsewhere. The subtitle
of the first section, "The End of the Beginning," is how the report represents the timeline of state responsibility for inequitable conditions for
black Americans.

The end of governmental responsibility marked the beginning of family responsibility and hence personal responsibility. While Virginia had
issued a mandate that made the state's force on family life explicit, the
federal government simultaneously attempted to mask its interference
with the quality of families. Before *Loving*, fifteen state governments were
out of sync with an emergently national antiracism. They were also out of
sync with an emergent national historiography. Virginia's antimiscegenation law eclipsed a long history of interracial intimacy such as that in the
Lovings' native Caroline County. Pratt says of Central Point that it has "an
interesting history of black–white sexual relationships [developed] over
the years, which over time had produced a community in which a considerable number of the blacks were light-skinned."[13] At the same time, the
federal government began to historicize the production of families as if the
interference of state power in this process has come to an end. The federal
mandate to establish antiracist public policies and to promote equal rights
as a rule of law allowed Moynihan as a state official, and allowed the state
more generally, to produce a discursive index between the past and present. There was no denying that historically, state power had produced a
caste system in the manner Harris describes, which thereby produced
an inequitable politics of citizenship. However, the state's antiracist mandate meant that the historical vestiges of inequity were going to be neutrally examined rather than forcefully reproduced. The outcome of *Loving*
signals that the federal judiciary attempted to align the mandate of state
governments along this version of racial time.

The Moynihan Report claims that "the heart of deterioration of the
fabric of Negro society is the deterioration of the Negro family," a schema
that makes the private realm the cause of a social outcome. At its core,
the report takes as its primary concern the underemployment and absence
of fathers in households run by single mothers. After a lengthy historical explanation of how black men have been subjugated by slavery, post-
Reconstruction segregation, the "abrupt" migration from rural space to
urban space, and finally unemployment and low-wage earnings, the report

notes in its conclusion: "Since the widespread family disorganization among Negroes has resulted from the failure of the father to play the role in family life required by American society, the mitigation of this problem must await those changes in the Negro and American society which will enable the Negro father to play the role required of him."[14] This is not to say that patriarchy was not operative in black families; ostensibly, the state compensated for the inability of black men. Actually at issue was the increasing dependence of mothers on federal aid to support the needs of their children. In part, the legacy of the Moynihan Report was the figure of the deviant black mother who, absconding from the functional dimensions of family like marriage and patriarchal domesticity, created a national crisis that consisted of an increasing drain on federal resources. As the report states in its opening section, the dysfunction of the black family "will give unity of purpose to the many activities of the Federal government in this area [of addressing the relational disadvantage of the black community], directed to a new kind of national goal: the establishment of a stable Negro family structure."[15] According to the report, "Among ever-married nonwhite women in the nation, the proportion with husbands present declined in every age group over the decade. . . . Although similar declines occurred among white females, the proportion of white husbands present never dropped below 90 percent except for the first and last age group."[16]

If part of the crisis was the absence of husbands, and if white husbands signaled the endurance of a functional family, perhaps the publicity of the *Loving* case—including photos publicizing the victorious Lovings after the Supreme Court decision—indicated not only a newly vindicated form of intimacy, but also the state's solution to the decline of blackness and its increasing dependence on the state. Never mind that a black woman and her white husband were parents of (light-skinned) multiracial children, because what Harris refers to as "race pollution" and miscegenation are problems of the past. The current concern was whether such children were likely to become wards of federal programs that were increasingly compensating for the lack of fathers. Again, here's the Moynihan Report:

> The majority of Negro children receive public assistance under the AFDC [Aid to Families with Dependent Children] program at one point or another in their childhood. . . . The AFDC program,

deriving from the long established Mothers' Aid programs, was established in 1935 principally to care for widows and orphans, although the legislation covered all children in homes deprived of parental support because one or both of their parents are absent or incapacitated. In the beginning, the number of AFDC families in which the father was absent because of desertion was less than a third of the total. Today it is two thirds.

Although it appears that the years that produced the Moynihan Report and the years after were directed toward the preservation of the black family as an institution that could facilitate the privatized care of black children through the presence of fathers, Dorothy Roberts argues that this period actually heralded the intensification of state intervention with regard to the care and custody of black children. As the Moynihan Report points out, AFDC was derived from the New Deal–era Aid to Dependent Children (ADC), which not only provided federal support for mothers, but, as Roberts explains, "was created primarily for white mothers, who were not expected to work."[17] This expectation was contingent on an ideological assumption about the responsibility of mothers to their children. Roberts continues, "[ADC] also included the racist exclusion of Black mothers based on discretionary standards. Southern states notoriously expelled thousands of Black children from their welfare rolls in the 1950s because mothers weren't married."[18]

 The protocols for federal aid were increasingly linked to ideological assumptions about gender roles within families, unevenly rationalized with regard to race—black mothers were presumably unmarried without the moral justification of widowhood, for instance—and suggested that the onus be on fathers to act as financial providers unless this was otherwise not viable. Not coincidentally, these protocols provided a rationale for punishing needy black mothers at a time when the political climate finally permitted them more federal support. "A new kind of national goal," in this way, was to shift the direction of governmental resource distribution away from needy black mothers, which ironically had been an old kind of national goal. Yet even as the state subtly reverted back to racially inequitable distribution practices, the *Loving* decision seemed to emerge as an event that was tangential to this fiscal goal. Just as *Loving* struck down the last vestiges of antimiscegenation in judicial review, the black family was highlighted as antithetical to the values of the state. Just as the nuclear family became the site where the races can now intermingle and amalgamate according to personalized discretion, the black family was rhetorically singled out for its unique inability to integrate the values of American society and achieve the recognizably healthy qualities that families should demonstrate.

The missing negative of a snapshot in which the state became anti-racist, or either benignly or neutrally concerned with "family disorganization among Negroes," is the exile of the Lovings rather than the decision in *Loving*. The exile conjures a few key aspects that are eclipsed by the subsequent law: state interference in the economic self-determination of family life, and the explicit importance of geography. The Moynihan Report notes that "in every index of family pathology—divorce, separation, and desertion, female family head, children in broken homes, and illegitimacy—the contrast between the urban and rural environment for Negro families is unmistakable," with urban environments comparing unfavorably.[19] "A new kind of national goal" implicitly pivoted around the blackness of the ghetto by focusing on the excesses of black cultural history. There are two tendencies of the era worth tracing in tandem: first, the state's new goal accounted for the way in which the interracial work of the civil rights movement was rendering the city inoperable as a site for disposable labor and racial sequestering. Alternatively, the national goal could have targeted the increasing lack of opportunity for labor in cities, rather than on the increasing lack of responsibility of black men in black families. Second, the city had to gain its character of deviance from a naturalized affinity with black people, who are not coincidentally determined by black families. If the ghetto was a place for sequestering, criminalizing, and regulating blackness, the new national goal tautologically suggested that blackness transformed the city into a dangerous, dysfunctional ghetto, and blackness was dysfunctional, which then justifies the growth of the carceral apparatus.

States of Migration: Making Color-blind Families

The state's interest in the nuclear family during the 1960s is taken up in Siobhan Somerville's assessment of *Loving* as the case through which 1990s and 2000s analogies between equal protection of interracial relationships and same-sex relations are often made in debates on judicial review.[20] Somerville usefully calls for a movement away from a focus on the identitarian particulars of race and sexuality to consider how the *Loving* decision can become a critical tool for assessing how varying intersectional politics reveal a cold war–era interest in codifying heterosexual, monogamous marriage as part and parcel of American nationality. She refers to how the 1952 amendments to immigration policy, the Immigration and Nationality Act (INA), conflate the privileging of national origin—rather than race—with the uniting of family, and the production of deviant homosexuality for U.S. national belonging. Significantly, Somerville points out that in 1967, just before the *Loving* decision, the Supreme Court decided in *Boutilier v. Immigration Service* that Clive Michael Boutilier was in violation of the federal provision "that excluded homosexuals from eligibility for immigration and naturalization."[21] Having disclosed that he had engaged in sexual activity with men during the process, he was classified as a "psychopathic personality" and "sexual deviate," which prohibited migration to the United States at the time, and prompted his deportation.[22] Somerville argues that although the INA had removed the explicit language of race, this indicated a shifting, albeit continually prohibitive, discourse on the conditions of legitimate U.S. citizenship. She writes, "The INA suggests a larger shift in federal discourses of marriage, family, and citizenship that would become visible in the coincidence between *Loving* and *Boutilier* in the Supreme Court docket of 1967.... These provisions suggest that lawmakers brought closer scrutiny—and the power of the state—to bear on sexual acts and identities that seemed to threaten the normative status of monogamous heterosexual marriage."[23]

Indeed, Somerville goes further by pointing out that the later twentieth-century and early twenty-first-century tendency to render interracial and same-sex marriage analogous through the judicial decision of *Loving* overlooks the way in which downplaying race has been a mechanism for excluding nonheterosexual modes of sexuality. As Somerville explains:

> *Loving* . . . effectively consolidated heterosexuality as a privileged prerequisite for recognition by the state as a national subject and citizen. . . . By establishing a fundamental right to marriage regardless of race, the federal state in effect shored up the privileges of heterosexuality through a logic that was on the surface antiracist and anti-white supremacist. *Loving* was decided, after all, at a moment when marriage as an institution was being widely questioned in the in United States.[24]

I raise Somerville's argument here to extend her overall concern for the ways in which policy discourses mark shifts in the state's approach to designating proper modes of national belonging. Somerville illuminates the unexpected concomitance of immigration policy and antimiscegenation law, particularly as both begin to deploy color-blind rhetoric to produce and codify the prevalence of heterosexual family formations that are being challenged and disavowed by the 1960s. This inextricability between race and sexuality—and I would add gender—residually emerge in the discourses of the multiracial movement decades later.

Before I elaborate on this point, I would like to consider how the matter of intranational migration—from the country to the city—is also a crucial part of how marriage is normalized as a tacitly white, heterosexual enterprise. When immigration policy was reformed in 1965, a highly featured rationale was the unification of family members from abroad with those in the United States, or the aim "to principally reunite nuclear families."[25] Somerville points out how this seemingly neutral rationale is racially and ethnically coded, given the exclusions of previous immigration and naturalization policies. Similarly, I suggest that the problem of racialized intranational settlement from Southern rural spaces to urban centers in the United States also demonstrates a heightened concern for the state's interest in properly ideal families during the 1960s. To evoke Harris here, racial, ethnic, and sexual differences emerge through the state mechanisms of marriage law, and as Somerville points out, immigration policy. The mid-1960s marked a period in which neutral, color-blind rhetoric begins to disguise how caste distinctions have been built into marriage law, and how racial, ethnic, and sexual caste inequities have been built into immigration laws. Both marriage law and immigration policy, as attempts at rendering the state's stake in family as neutral—or a forgone conclusion, given the climate of the times—do not explain how knowledge was generated about black family formations at the time. This rift between the appearance of state neutrality and overt statist interest in the black family entail two regulatory approaches. On the one hand, it entails the color-blindness of marriage and the antiracism of heterosexuality. On the other hand, it entails the heightening of black visibility, which is arguably demonstrated through the Moynihan Report. The appearance of neutrality is required to produce particular forms of racial visibility. Ultimately, I understand this rift as an originating strategy employed by the contemporary multiracial movement: blackness, black sexuality, and its naturalized location in the city, is underattended to in generating a politics about the multiracial family.

Black citizens have been migrating from the rural South to Northern urban centers since the end of Reconstruction and throughout the early decades of the twentieth century, but the promise of the city began to wane from the 1960s into the 1970s. Madhu Dubey points out that while the legislative advancement of the civil rights movement had extended the rights of black Americans, the limits of such advancement were becoming apparent due to the increasing discontent within cities. Here's Dubey: "Outbreaks of violence in numerous cities prompted the 1968 Kerner Commission Report on Civil Disorders, which drew attention to the prevalence of de facto racial segregation in northern cities, officially certifying that the racial problem had moved from the rural South into the cities, and in fact become nationalized."[26] I want to follow Somerville's lead by deliberating on whether the concomitance of state regulation of black families and the urbanization of the racial problem reveals another mode of critical intersectionality. Somerville addresses efforts to elide the specific categorical qualities of race and sexuality through color-blind rhetoric when it comes to interracial intimacy and immigration. I suggest that this ostensibly color-blind acceptance is accompanied by an opposite tendency in which intimacy and migration are exactly the terms targeted as problematically black and antithetical to color-blindness as a policy ideal in cities. In this paradoxical way, the city is rhetorically configured as the locus for open policy initiatives that separate blackness from the dominant citizenry in terms of public interaction and interracial sexuality. Even as the protocol of color-blindness was becoming a useful mechanism for constructing the conditions of proper citizenship while simultaneously allowing the state to target and penalize nonnormative racial and sexual identities, the city was an increasingly potent symbol of a particularly black form of difference.

Somerville points out that a heightened concern for families through marriage became an indicator of a benevolently antiracist, antiwhite supremacist state, yet the other side of the coin is that race openly and undeniably appeared in the form of race riots in Rochester and Philadelphia in 1964, the same year as the passing of the Civil Rights Act, and in Watts in 1965, shortly after the Voting Rights Act was passed.[27] This appearance of race as a sign of ongoing conflict and disparity unmitigated by legislative reform might be connected to the perception that the integrity of marriage and family had become tenuous. The *Loving* case performs a paradox that is an effect of the moment's shift in policy: while it produces an approach to codifying marriage and family as heterosexual and color-blind through a liberal discourse, it also indicates that the conditions of marriage are contingent on the profound racialization of geography. In the report, Moynihan writes that "the mass media and the development of suburbia have created an image of the American family as a highly standardized phenomenon." Suburbia, while not explicitly mentioned as such, is a space where the white middle class have produced functional family structures apart from black community. According to the Associated Press, "The black population [in Washington, D.C.] peaked at 71 percent in 1970 as tens of thousands of white residents left Washington for the suburbs."[28] By comparison, as the report notes of the early 1960s, "Negroes are now more urbanized than whites."[29]

This urbanization is not only clearly incongruous with a color-blind ethos. It also implies that there is a thoroughgoing rift between blacks and whites that is as much geographical as it is affective. The urban space that black people were now staunchly identified with was associated with violence, the race problem, and a deterioration of the fabric of family and community. As Peter Wallenstein mentions with regard to the status of Mildred and Richard Loving during the nine years between their marriage in 1958 and the Supreme Court decision of their case, "they lived as defendants, felons, exiles, fugitives, litigants, and even as prisoners—all for the crime of interracial marriage."[30] These various modes of delinquency are clearly the result of antimiscegenation as the state law of Virginia, but I would assert that each also indicates fluctuation in and relegation to either urban or nonurban spaces: the very defiance of a plea agreement specifying the terms of geography, or the rejection of having to live in the District of Columbia as opposed to the rural community of their home state, created a set of criminalized positions within the law. The opposition to the city as even a concessional space for racially marginalized families to live implies that the city is a deviant and undesirable designation. While marriage is the condition contested in this case, one of the modes of contestation is mobility—the manner in which the Lovings secretly and illicitly returned to Caroline County, for instance, or the very desire for a home outside of black-designated ghetto—that reveals the material consequences of the choice of a marriage partner. Such consequences include (unwilling) relegation to a space rife with socially constructed, racialized meaning.

In a recent explanation of how the findings of the Moynihan Report were received by the public with disdain upon its initial circulation, William Julius Wilson writes that the development of a Black Power sensibility influenced how African Americans interpreted the report as a racist assessment of black cultural life in black communities. According to Wilson, this sensibility, "proclaimed as the 'black perspective,' signaled an ideological shift from interracialism to black solidarity."[31] The interracialism that marked civil rights activism was overridden by a tendency toward black self-determination, which sought to affirm black racial pride. Wilson argues that the "black-perspective explanation" of the report "does not even acknowledge self-destructive behavior in the ghetto. . . . This approach side-steps the issue altogether by denying that social dislocations in the inner city represent any special problem. Researchers who emphasized these dislocations—such as persistent unemployment, crime, and drug use—were denounced, even when their work . . . focused . . . on the structural roots of these problems" rather than on individual responsibility.[32] In a sense, what is useful about Wilson's not uncommon historicizing of 1960s politics as a teleology that moves from interracial collaboration to Black Power self-determination is that the Moynihan Report tacitly marks the shift from one sensibility to the other. The 1950s and early 1960s was a time when the United States, its exceptions notwithstanding, drew a liberal consensus around the task of reforming racial inequities. By 1965, however, the interracial consensus around redressing black subordination had given way to a distinctly noninterracial perspective of racial politics. This is an interesting assessment if one considers that the breakdown of interracial consensus around racial equality also coincides with the rise of color-blindness. Although policy that would codify heterosexual marriage as legal and color-blind was a forgone conclusion in this era, a narrative that, according to Wilson, highlights the structural conditions of racial division as insurmountable begs the question of how the future of color-blind families were to be constructed. Is color-blindness a possible public imperative when it is politically and geographically unlikely, vis-à-vis black determinism and the black ghetto?

This reiteration of racial divisiveness seemed to lack a structural analysis that considers the economic disadvantages that the inner city presents, along with an analysis of how the state itself had continued to structure racial division according to geography. In this way, the Moynihan Report marks the delineation between legislative redress of racial inequity and a new narrative that connects black self-determination with a naturalized affinity between blackness and ghettos. While Wilson wants to emphasize that the renouncement of the Moynihan Report was contingent on a racial sensibility that was self-defeating insofar as it ignored the "structural roots" of disempowerment for black families within cities, this observation still suggests an extricable link between the casting of blackness as unemployable, drug using, and criminal, and the vicissitudes of the shifting economic conditions within urban spaces. Such a structural analysis refrains from a problematic tendency to blame the victim—to villainize the individuals who suffered from the conditions of ghettoization, or to infer an intrinsic insufficiency of black subjectivity.

However, it does not seem to account for the manner in which urbanization—which becomes the loaded problem of the ghetto—is disarticulated from interracialism. For instance, consider again Wallenstein's description of various markers the Lovings were subjected to: "defendants, felons, exiles, fugitives, litigants, and even as prisoners." The proximity to imprisonment and criminality that the Lovings were so close to, should they leave the city, is akin to how the city at the time was structured as a holding place for deviance, not unlike prisons. As Loïc Wacquant points out, the de facto segregation of race is akin to earlier regimes of racialized structures of capitalism—slavery and the later Jim Crow forms of agrarian labor—as it deploys black labor while keeping black Americans separated from dominant society.[33] He writes, "For the ghetto in full-fledged form is, by its very makeup, a *double-edged sociospatial formation:* it operates as an instrument of *exclusion* from the standpoint of the dominant group; yet it also offers the subordinate group partial *protection* and a platform for succor and solidarity in the very moment whereby it sequesters it."[34]

This was not untrue for the Lovings, perhaps. While in the District of Columbia, they lived with family, Mildred's cousin and his wife, in the northeast quadrant of the city. Historically, the vicinity was a mixture of immigrants and African Americans, but it was becoming increasingly inhabited by blacks.[35] The dominant group from which the Lovings were separated was not exclusively white. Rather, the clear appearance of miscegenation—the sort of appearance that being sequestered in a ghetto structurally prevents—resulted in their exclusion from (racially mixed) Caroline County. And protection in the full-fledged ghetto potentially means making an alliance with others who are also not fit for dominant society ("defendants, felons, exiles," and the like). In this way, the Lovings' most transgressive gesture was to challenge the way in which geography—the ghetto itself—was a prominent form of regulation. Wacquant also writes that "when the ghetto was rendered inoperative in the sixties by economic restructuring that made African-American labor expendable and mass protest that finally won blacks the vote, the carceral institution offered itself as a substitute apparatus for enforcing the shifting color line and containing segments of African-American community devoid of economic utility and political pull."[36] In a sense, if the *Loving* decision is a forgone conclusion in 1967, this may have as much to do with the state's shifting stance on sequestering deviant sectors of the population in cities.

The plea agreement that gave the Lovings the (false) option of either spending time in prison or moving out of Virginia, with the District of Columbia emerging as a convenient site—because it borders the Loving's home state and granted their interracial marriage—seems like a conflation between antimiscegenation and a state-sanctioned structuring of the city as a dumping ground for expendable labor.[37] Perhaps in 1959, when the plea agreement was reached and after the Lovings had their first child, the expectation was that they would migrate permanently to a place unlike the Southern and rural space of racial segregation, such as a city where industrial labor was still viable. Embedded in this assumption was the understanding that Richard Loving would obviously lose the privileges of whiteness, and the Loving children would not be granted the privileges of his caste. One might go on to speculate that by the end of the 1960s, when the *Loving* decision was reached, the state's approach to structuring the city as a dumping ground for expendable labor no longer made sense. What seemed like an overturning of racist regulation was concomitant with a shift in the means through which racialized regulation would continue to take place.

Indeed, in a *New York Times* profile of Patrick Moynihan published in 1966, it is mentioned that the policy maker interested in "the entire spectrum of urban problems" and "one of the country's most prominent authorities on the family" lived with his own family on "a 100-acre farm near Cooperstown, N.Y.," when not in Cambridge, Massachusetts, out of "a desire to lead a rather less hectic life."[38] The comparison between this desire and that of the Lovings is an easy one to make. Before the staging of the ubiquitous photos taken after the Supreme Court decision—with Richard's arm triumphantly draped around a smiling Mildred's neck, the many laws books visible behind them in their lawyers' office—this is what we know: "From their farm home in Bowling Green, east of Fredericksburg, Mr. and Mrs. Loving drove north to Alexandria for a news conference. . . . The new house, in which the Lovings' three children grew up, symbolized the family's freedom to have a permanent dwelling where they could live in peace in their home state."[39] In the end, the triumph of having the vestiges of antimiscegenation legally dismantled was translated into the restoration of a time prior to the necessity of the modern ghetto, where "Mr. Loving" (who literally built the "farm home") is granted the status of familial patriarch through the stability of a permanent country home. Furthermore, the family symbolically thrives when it is couched in a tacitly emergent discourse of color-blindness or nonblackness, and this deracialization somehow appears once the institution of family is separated from the site of the ghetto.

In part, the legacy of the *Loving* case is a naturalization of family that undermines a fuller range of racial and sexual possibilities for this institution. However, I want to make the additional suggestion that *Loving*, by legitimating the interracial family and therefore inoculating the state from the appearance of racism and antimiscegenation, prevented a focus on how the political discourse of urban blackness was as much a manufactured narrative as an effect of objective policy. As Dubey notes, "The War on Poverty and community development programs of the 1960s . . . could no longer garner public support by the end of the decade, when the short-lived national consensus on black civil rights dissolved into moral panic about African-Americans as the prime threat to urban security and national community."[40] However, this moral panic extends to the "psychopathic personality" and "sexual deviate" migrating into the United States, the African American who has troubled the urban North by migrating from the South, and among this group especially, the black matriarch who has displaced the healthy function of black masculinity from families. The interracial family was a formation that challenged white supremacy, as the decision goes, but not the manner in which the state punished an array of deviate subjectivities through public policy narratives aimed at policing highly politicized geographic boundaries and borders. Closer attentiveness to the white urban man who cannot find work in the city and who cannot return to Virginia accompanied by his own family, or to the black mother who shares Moynihan's sensibilities about family and geography might have the potential to illuminate a wide-scale critique on how the state refers to geography, race, and the family to expand its control of security and national community more generally.

As Pratt mentions in his commentary, the Lovings were not ostensibly interested in the civil rights activism that had gained momentum during their exile. However, one might speculate that by the later stage of the era, the complication of what exactly comprised the outcomes of civil rights— liberal color-blindness, the contrary hyperattentiveness to the racialized city, the paradoxical rift between the races after legislative reform—determined the Lovings' seeming ambivalence. Pratt mentions that the Lovings were oblivious to the civil rights movement, but this is not the same as the lack of an activist consciousness in terms of resistance to state prohibition. Indeed, it was Mildred who wrote a letter of complaint to then–attorney general Robert Kennedy, which provoked responses from the Justice Department and the American Civil Liberties Union (ACLU), who took on the case. Perhaps the privacy of Mildred's activist gesture opens questions about how to attend to the multivalent forms that comprise political action, including those forms that are not clearly public or completely oblivion. Mildred's simple, seemingly apolitical refrain, recounted by Pratt—"I just missed being at home"—is private sentiment with public, political, and historic implications.

Legacies

From the 1960s to the 1980s: The Crisis of Black Motherhood

While Mildred continually underplayed how her right to marriage, and more pertinently her decision-making process of mothering, were political, she was participating in a narrative that leads back to slavery. Indeed, black women were denied the volition to be at home, to raise their children—when given the opportunity—where and how they saw fit. A long historical condition of black motherhood has been the denial of the right to decide where and how one rears one's own children. The historical moment I have accounted for here, which spans from the late 1950s to the late 1960s, is a part of this longer historical trajectory. Back in 1958, Mildred Loving had no claim to her family in Virginia. As a black woman, she was in a sense prohibited from having a volitional family. However, by 1965, the Moynihan Report posited black women as completely volitional. They were the matriarchs that displaced the patriarchal function of normative family life. Each of these moments, connected together, suggests a consistent inability to understand black motherhood as either integral to or normatively functional within families. This perceived inability, I argue, is ironically achieved by focusing on the family: the structures that determine how families are positioned within particular geographic locations are not only regulatory. They also produce discourses about the family. The question of legitimacy—whether it is temporally possible to recognize a black woman as the mother of interracial children before the legal legitimacy of *Loving*—coincides with the way in which black motherhood decades after 1958 is delegitimized through social pathology or criminality. The black mother—ostensibly an urban figure—becomes a symbolic marker of how the inextricable link between blackness and urbanization translates into the potential death of children and the nuclear family in general, which is the very institution the state wants to preserve as a heteronormative, nonurban, and tacitly white sign of social health.

Mildred Loving's marriage and motherhood coincided with the state's belated attentiveness to providing support to black mothers as a result of the civil rights movement.[41] As the Moynihan Report suggests, the numbers of black children who were being supported by federal aid during the 1960s were reaching troubling heights. The unprecedented expansion of federal aid to black families was a response to historically inequitable practices of distribution. However, the new goal of the state was to relinquish its newly acquired obligation to redress racial inequality by distributing public resources to needy black families. The result was a state-sanctioned shift from a politics of public resource distribution to a politics of personal responsibility. As Roberts explains: "With the growing numbers of Blacks in the welfare caseloads came the stigma of 'welfare dependency,' work requirements, and reduced effective benefit levels. The welfare mother transmuted from the worthy white widow to the immoral Black 'welfare queen.'"[42] The state developed a rationale for abandoning equitable aid distribution practices even as it became a highly intrusive force on needy black families. Roberts is ultimately arguing that there is a strong correlation between the long, shifting history of welfare policy and the vastly disproportionate tendency to remove black children from unfit homes— impoverished households and biological families—into state custody, which includes "foster care as well as . . . juvenile detention, prisons, and other state institutions."[43] If a long-standing public mandate has been to protect the family as a central institution for producing and sustaining subjects who have a normalized, affective connection to nationhood, then this shift in welfare policy suggests that impoverished black families are distinctively expendable. The further outcome is that black motherhood itself is inoperable.

Kimberlé Crenshaw notes that as of the late 1980s, "The latest versions of a Moynihanesque analysis can be found in the [Bill] Moyers televised special, *The Vanishing Black Family* [1986], and, to a lesser extent, in William Julius Wilson's *The Truly Disadvantaged* [1987]."[44] Each suggests, according to Crenshaw, that black men feel no obligation to take care of their children because "someone will take care of their families," and that the welfare system has allowed black women to leave the fathers of their children. In each case, the site of familial dysfunction is centered on an underanalyzed condition of patriarchy (one that excludes single white mothers), and of course an implied abuse of welfare programs. If black motherhood abuses the provisions the state has in place, provisions that stem from ideological assumptions about proper motherhood, then the extension of this—and the rationale for policy that again excludes black mothers from federal support—is the illegitimate abuse of street drugs. Once black women are untethered from the formations of patriarchy, the result is unbridled illegitimacy: children have no fathers; mothers implicitly use federal funding for uses other than the state-intended one, which is the care of children; and once a mother can potentially not feel the affective pull toward her own children, then the most impoverished black women are susceptible to the lures of street crime. The illicitness of sexuality—the sort that is part and parcel of reproductive practices that neglect adequate parental care—rhetorically leads to the illicitness of drug abuse. Both suggest the indulgence of adult gratification at the expense of childhood well-being. Street drug consumption was never sanctioned by federal policy, and therefore the severity of state intervention is supposedly justified.

For this reason, it is appropriate to point out how the salience of sexuality or immorality, widely construed, has been used to activate a set of representational assumptions about poor and working-class black mothers. Patricia Hill Collins describes the prevalence of 1980s-era criminality concerning financially underprivileged black women:

Crack cocaine was primarily confined to Black inner-city neighborhoods, and women constituted approximately half of its users. In the 1980s, news stories began to cover the huge increase

in the number of newborns testing positive for drugs. . . . Fictional
treatments followed soon after. For example, in the feature film
Losing Isaiah, Academy Award–winning actress Halle Berry plays a
woman on crack cocaine who is so high that she abandons her
baby. A kindly White family takes Isaiah in, and they patiently deal
with the host of problems he has due to his biological mother's
failures.[45]

The policy logic that was developing over twenty years earlier contributes
to what the popular film *Losing Isaiah* means.

Losing Isaiah (1995) tells the story of a black crack-addicted mother
who abandons her infant son in a trash heap in order to get high. The child
is subsequently rescued by sanitation workers and brought to a hospital,
where Margaret Lewin (Jessica Lange), a white social worker, encounters
the crack-addicted baby and immediately develops an affective attachment to him. We learn that Margaret is happily married, has a healthy
teenage daughter, and lives in a large, attractive home in what appears to
be a middle-class neighborhood. She and her husband successfully adopt
Isaiah, and although his presence causes occasional disruptions—attrib-
utable to drug abuse while in the womb of a black woman—the more
prevalent outcome is that this white family is raising a black subject who
is developing into a happy, loving child. In the meantime, Isaiah's biological mother, Khaila Richards (Halle Berry), serves prison time for her
drug offenses, lives provisionally with a black woman who is clearly strug-
gling with her own drug addition and inability to parent adequately, and
develops general conscientiousness during her visits to a rehab center. It
is here where she learns that her son, who she had thought was dead, is
still alive and living with a white adoptive family. The wife-mother of the
family has become particularly attached to her adopted black child. With
the help of a tenacious lawyer (Samuel L. Jackson), Khaila challenges the
legality of the adoption on the grounds that she had never officially for-
feited her rights as the mother to her son.

Two points are clear here: this is a narrative about deviant black motherhood—she does not know who her child's father is—and a story that
demonstrates the affective attachment white mothers can so easily develop
for black children. Ultimately the judge decides that Isaiah should be raised
by his rehabilitated biological mother. However, the movie ends when
Khaila, now able to act as a responsible mother, is unable to persuade

Isaiah that she is in fact his mother, or to feel comfortable in black community. At this point, she asks Margaret to temporarily resume caring for Isaiah, and the final shot is of the two women—not a husband and wife—attending to the newly comforted child. There is, on one hand, an elision of the black mother who, in the end, is actually capable and willing to care for her own child, without the patriarchy of fatherhood or state funding. After all, the ultimate rejection of Khaila's motherhood comes from the innocent impulses of a prepoliticized black toddler, not from the court. On the other hand, we have the familial scene that curiously ends this movie: the future well-being of Isaiah is demonstrated through the interracial coupling of two women. Perhaps the black mother cannot appear in multiracial discourses about maternal responsibility because she presents the possibility of a functional, matriarchal black family formation. This raises the question of why multiracial discourse and the (matriarchal) black family cannot mutually support one another. Yet another question is whether the black mother potentially disrupts the affective bond white mothers have for children or husbands by being present as the illegitimate love object.

While the movie represents a crisis between biological black motherhood and white affective motherhood, it opens a critical space to ask what motherhood itself wants. It is not simply the reciprocal love of a child, the reproduction of normative family, or judicial legitimization. The matter of affect—the way in which one becomes interpellated into normative national investments, as Harris explains in the beginning of this chapter—requires the repetition of state regulation, surveillance, and criminalization because otherwise it creates the potential for intimacies and allegiances that cross normative boundaries of kinship.

Perhaps the post-*Loving* interracial family is a domain where intimacy between differently raced subjects is legitimated, but where sexuality and affect cause subjects to experience the precariousness of belonging. Or perhaps the multiracial subject appears politically—makes a public point about multiracial recognition—only when that subject occupies the politically aporic space of childhood, the space that adults affectively move toward, presumably in healthy, normative ways. It would seem that he appears for others: the mixed racial subject reproduces a politics that revolves around a child in need of parental and societal self-esteem, or alternatively, the mixed racial subject provides impetus for transforming white motherhood. For all multiracial discourses reveal about the challenges of having multiple races within singular families, they have little to say about the manner in which mixedness itself transforms the functioning and construction of patriarchal families and communities. Or, more to the point, they have little to say about how a politics of multiracialism itself might be transformed by a critique of what we mean by family. It seems clear that some subjects are parents and some are children, but what remains unclear is what, exactly, about the politics of multiracialism necessitates and perpetuates this particular structure of kinship.

This leads to two points of speculation. First, if multiracial politics must always take family as its central domain, then the outcome is a reproduction of normative regimes of recognition. Indeed, the family in multiracial organizations is overwhelmingly posited as heterosexual, and family often labels a condition in which mothers are responsible for the well-being of mixed racial children. If the institution of the family is where the production of race is located, and if family is what makes particular antiracist practices possible, then does an antiracist approach to family have the capacity to unmake this formation, to tear it apart, to wound it into a new grammar of kinship? This would be an effect that is ostensibly antithetical to the project of mothers who would very much like to keep the family intact and act as spokespersons for its legitimated coherence.

Thus, while much of multiracial rhetoric has been developed by white women and therefore centralizes white motherhood, multiracial discourse has not adequately theorized motherhood or family.[46] As Ruth Feldstein has argued, motherhood, from the liberal era spanning the 1930s to the 1960s, has been a vehicle through which to mobilize varying ideological claims. [47] In this way, motherhood provides a key domain through which to rationalize the normality of white patriarchy. The Moynihan Report is evidence of how motherhood encapsulates ideological assumptions about black women, men, and the civic functionality of black communities.[48] After the feminist movement of the 1960s and 1970s, and throughout the 1980s, there is theoretical deconstruction of the categorical integrity of womanhood and gender, and there are renewed considerations about maternity and reproduction. Yet it seems that motherhood, in the context of the interracial family's legal legitimacy gained after 1967, becomes an instrument that white women can use to revitalize the ethics of a feminist perspective without disrupting the value, integrity, or meaning of family.

What Motherhood Wants and Focusing on Children

I have argued in this chapter that reassessing the social policy initiatives of the 1960s can displace the primacy of *Loving* and its impact on legitimizing the multiracial family by considering the legislation through the lens of the Moynihan Report. While *Loving* has been taken for granted as a civil rights measure in line with its time, and while the ruling itself openly challenges white supremacy as a rationale for the state's regulation of marriage and kinship, the decision—and the personal narrative of Richard and Mildred's desire to create a heteronormative family and home away from the racially coded city—is actually concomitant with the a rising discourse on the dysfunction of black family formations, the futility of the state's continuing obligation to civil rights reform, and the social blight caused by black motherhood and the absence of (black) patriarchy. To read the celebrated *Loving* decision through the antiblack, narrow conditions for building families allows for the possibility to critique the manner in which multiracial discourse of the 1990s has done two things at once: ostensibly recognize *Loving* as the originating moment of the multiracial family's legal legitimacy, and carry the vestiges of a discourse that undercuts the legitimacy of various other family formations. The very issue of legal legitimacy is exactly what proponents of multiracial politics simultaneously cling to and understand as the ground that has crumbled underfoot.

I now turn to this question of legitimizing the family and the role that multiracial children play in late twentieth-century approaches to acknowledging the void that civil rights activism has left behind, particularly for white mothers. Jumping ahead to the multiracial movement of the 1990s, the legacy of *Loving* allows interracial couples to declare that interracial families require national recognition. This declaration leads to the politicization of multiracialism, particularly as a form of racialization that ought to be accounted for on the 2000 Census and other state forms. In her study on the political influences that lead to the overhaul of racial and ethnic categorization policy for the 2000 Census, Kim Williams points out that white mothers of mixed racial children consistently played a leading role in multiracial politics. Part of a general rationale for such activism, and for the movement overall, was the obligation of parents to bolster the self-esteem of their mixed racial children; as Williams writes, "self-esteem" was "the fall-back position of the multiracial movement in the 1990s."[49] This movement, understanding itself as an extension of civil rights activism, was overwhelmingly organized by the white mothers of interracial children, and the well-being of children became the primary impetus for multiracialism's claim to state-sponsored recognition vis-à-vis the Census. White mothers who were at the forefront of the 1990s-era multiracial movement take up family, particularly when it involves children, as an affective space connected to citizenship. However, there is a glaring absence of black motherhood. The epigraphs at the start of this chapter highlight the legacy of the *Loving* decision as an occasion to interpret the role of white antiracist mothering in the burgeoning multiracial movement of the 1990s. At this point, I want to consider how the contemporary multiracial movement opened the door for ongoing racial analysis but continued a tendency to render black motherhood as the illegitimate ghost of interracial affect.

In a sense, the discourse of the 1990s suggests that interracial legitimacy after *Loving* actually produces the unstable status of interracial children. As Rachel Moran notes, "Racial separation leaves little room for multiracial persons to define themselves on their own terms." This produces a kind of illegitimacy that allows for a politics of affect, the way (white) mothers move toward their differently raced children emotionally. It is also likely that Mildred Loving's children were given little room to define themselves as something other than black or mulatto. However, if the Loving children are often left out of *Loving* legal commentary, perhaps this is because the children themselves represent an impasse: they are subjects who have yet to come into being through a discourse that attends to their in-between status as, on the one hand, legitimated by a patriarchal law, and on the other, always already illegitimated by virtue of being simultaneously interracial and black. A black mother before *Loving*, in other words, has black children who are illegitimate—denied the protections of law and state recognition—but these children do not yet signal new interracial subjectivity. Although these children challenge the taxonomies of race, their legal illegitimacy and their black maternal parent stabilize the status of interracialism within blackness. Once legalized, interracial marriage deems "black" children the proper progenies of whiteness and the inheritors of white masculine property. However, this does not necessarily generate the problem of how distinctly interracial subjects can signal an impasse between legitimated and illegitimated forms of racial politics.

Although the *Loving* case is ostensibly about the legality of antimiscegenation, the circumstances of the case itself are perhaps a tacit statement

about why motherhood becomes the natural modality for initiating questions of legitimacy. As Hortense Spillers writes, "The African-American
woman . . . becomes historically the powerful and shadowy evocation of
a cultural synthesis long evaporated—the law of the Mother—only and
precisely because legal enslavement removed the African-American male
not so much from sight as from *mimetic* view as a partner in prevailing
social fiction of the Father's name, the Father's law."[50] I do not mean to
suggest at this point that Mildred Loving's white husband stands in for the
inability of black men to perform mimetically the law of patriarchy. I wonder, however, whether the white mothers who implicitly refer to Mildred's
condition decades later—annual Loving Day celebrations are a case in
point—without substantially accounting for black motherhood are demonstrating another claim that Spillers makes as a result of this inability. I
wonder whether their implicit reference to Mildred Loving demonstrates
an overarching disappearance of the law of the Mother, which made possible the coherence of American kinship and reproductive relations. Spillers
goes on to write, "The female, in the order of things, breaks in upon the
imagination with a forcefulness that marks both a denial and an 'illegitimacy.'"[51] Does the appearance of black motherhood during the late twentieth century, when interracial family has been granted legitimacy and
yet when white mothers are searching for a way to make the concept of
illegitimacy meaningful after civil rights legalism, threaten the political
foundations of the multiracial movement? The multiracial family, as a late
twentieth-century political formation, relies on a normatively patriarchal
logic for its legibility.

The impetus for prohibiting interracial sexual relations was the emergence of interracial children. This is why Ball argues for a stronger emphasis of the fact that Richard and Mildred Loving had children that were
born in 1958 and 1959.[52] Although this may not figure directly in the circumstances of their case, it illuminates a historical rationale for the law
in Virginia and similar laws in other states. A focus on interracial children
also clarifies the challenge of the *Loving* decision: "Interracial children
showed that racial categories, seemingly distinct and immutable, were
instead highly malleable. Therefore, from a white supremacy perspective, it was important to try to deter the creation of interracial children as
much as possible, and the ban on interracial marriage was a crucial means
to attaining that goal."[53] There is a long history in which children have
been deprived of legitimate recognition and legal protection, but this

deprivation is part and parcel of the potentially destructive effects interracial children have on white supremacy.

The focus on children demonstrates a condition in which the constitutional challenge to white supremacy has nothing to do with problematizing the child from within the category of family. The interracial child is now endowed with full protection of the law precisely because the law recognizes interracial marriage as a legitimate contractual agreement. In this way, children develop a paradoxical status: children are at once endowed with the potential to irrevocably disrupt the logic of a racial order—to blur the lines, as Ball would have it—while remaining dependent on the legal status of their adult parents for protection and recognition. As Ball points out, the legal legitimacy that children of different-sex partners are granted is accompanied by courts "deny[ing] *other* children (i.e., those raised by same-sex couples) the protections and stability that would be afforded to them through the legal recognition of the relationships between the care-giving adults" in same-sex relationships.[54] Also consider Claudia Card's assertion that "children [who] are raised by grandparents, single parents . . . are all in the midst of patriarchies. But these have been regarded as deviant parenting, with nothing like the prestige or social and legal support available to patriarchal mothers."[55] There is still much to be claimed about the legal manner in which children currently are denied protections, but these conditions for denial—the homosexuality of guardians, or the nonnormative placement within patriarchies—have decidedly been separated from the historical conditions of interracialism and families.

In a sense, multiracialism, as it has been narrated and made rhetorical, has not been connected to the broader range of circumstances in which children are made legally vulnerable, which would draw a focus on same-sex discrimination, the legitimacy of the extended family, or, as Roberts has argued, the manner in which mothers who are victims of patriarchal abuse are not always able to protect their children.[56] I argue that this paradoxical condition—the influence children have to disrupt the status quo while at the same time remaining terminally dependent on the existence and status of other categories—is what allows the multiracial child to become so forceful in post-*Loving* rhetoric. It allows adults who are concerned with multiracial politics to identify the historical illegitimacy of the multiracial child, always situated in the pre-*Loving* past, although now relevant for the psychological health of the child, as a foundation for current moral claims to a variety of investments. However, these claims do not—cannot, in order to retain their rhetorical force—acknowledge the ways in which the multiracial child, who is either protected or illegitimated by the status of adult relations to patriarchy and the law, is affected by sociopolitical and cultural norms like other children. According to multiracial discourses, not only does the black/multiracial child necessarily retain a degree of exceptionalism through a residual illegitimacy, but this exceptionalism also must foreclose a thoroughgoing attentiveness to other illegitimated subjects: multiracial proponents seem not all concerned with whether children who are raised within same-sex relationships, by single parents or nonparental guardians, and yes, by mothers subjected to varying forms of abuse, suffer from low self-esteem.

Given this foreclosure, when I refer to the rhetoric of children, or when I refer to the political positioning of the child, I am referencing the foreclosure that the multiracial movement has produced to consider the various ways in which non–mixed racial children are implicated by legal or social protections. The multiracial child justifies the movement's political claims. The difficulty I am describing here is not about particular individuals who wish to participate in multiracial politics, but about the multiracial movement itself. During a previous era, civil rights legislation can be understood to make constitutionally based ethical claims, which is to say that ethics is grounded in the stipulation the law makes for equal protection and due process, irrespective of racial differences. However, once the law is no longer deemed to be the primary domain for discerning the guiding principles on how to enact an ethical racialism, multiracial children reference this new void because they are at once a sociocultural extension of adulthood—and adult aspirations for the future—while they lack a self-determination that requires authoritative intervention. One can think of children as those who always already lack a kind of autonomy or legitimacy, and who therefore are in need of the social and legal protection of legally legitimated adults, such as heterosexual parents and patriarchal mothers. This is to say that children are in fact still implicated and impacted by ethical claims that can refer to the law as an instrument for enforcing protections, but there is a sector of multiracial rhetoric that wants to posit legalism as an instrument that signals a prior moment in mid-twentieth-century civil rights history. Children can be referenced because such a lack of self-legitimacy is akin to an earlier, pre–civil rights–era moment of egregiously racist nonapplication of constitutional law. In a sense, children signal the loss of the civil rights era's foremost ethical strategy, as well as the loss of the law as a central guideline for devising a set of antiracist principles or arguments.

In the face of this loss, children become construed as those who have the power to ground us to civic responsibility. Yet at the same time, children cannot produce a moment of postillegitimacy—a moment after the goal of achieving constitutional rights is reached—because they are not legally autonomous. As long as children are nonautonomous—which they must be—they can signal an ongoing claim to illegitimacy, which automatically implicates adults. But to be clear, there is an ethics that can recognize that children ought not to be completely self-governing for their own protection, that they not be freed from the authority of governing institutions. For instance, while Mary Lyndon Shanley considers the problem of recognizing the legal status of lesbian comothers and genetic donors, with theories that take up either the contractual rights of adults or the functional actions of parents, she argues for a primary focus on the needs of the child: "Child-centered theories look at the best interests of the child or needs of the child to decide who should exercise parental rights. . . . they emphasize the fact that the primary purpose of establishing legal parenthood is not to gratify adults but to provide the necessary condition for protection and nurture of children."[57] Shanley's perspective, with its overt concern for the children and its recognition that adult legalism should be most attentive to the well-being of children (at the expense of adult gratification) for its ethical foundation is in line with the tenets of multiracial motherhood. However, it needs to be underscored that the context for her concern—same-sex unions, the legal and social disputes among adults concerned with queer family formations—appear out of line with the way in which multiracial proponents have framed their concern for children. For one thing, questions about the legal claims that same-sex partners or sperm donors have cannot be relegated to a past historical moment that has already legitimized those claims. One key element of aporia this disjuncture highlights is the reluctance of multiracial discourse to rigorously suture a racial analysis with one on sexuality. Race and sexuality as objects of analysis produce an impasse for the multiracial movement's figuration of the family as the center of its political concerns. The law, as an instrument that might produce a comparative analysis with regard to family, seems inadequate: the law has been (and still is) the domain through which family formations are contemplated, while race and sexuality, for some proponents within multiracial discourse, have been inadequate or unacknowledged concepts to developing theories of the family.

Overwhelmingly, the tacit recognition that childhood's lack of autonomy is important leads to the revitalization of ethical claims about race. This revitalization occurs just when interracial couples—adults granted full protection of the law—arrive at the fulfillment of legal protection. The inexpressible condition that this legal achievement produces is the need for a new way of referencing a domain, other than the law, for reforming racial inequity. Therefore, children are at once legitimated by parents or legal guardians, and at the same time they are beyond the legitimizing effects of the law as autonomous subjects. In this way, for adult multiracial activists, the multiracial child can delay the sort of crisis that comes from an impassable confrontation with racial politics beyond the legalism of civil rights. If there is gratification in this process, perhaps it is the postponement of this crisis. The guiding principles toward race need not account for the undertheorization of maternity—or who can determine what makes a mother—and what this means for the agency of particular female subjects.

The Potential of Kinship beyond Family and Citizenship

The centrality of family, and in particular the recently legitimized multiracial family that still considers itself to be quasi-illegitimate or alienated, has been heavily attended to by multiracial activists and policy makers. Kimberly DaCosta asks why the multiracial movement has been as much about family and as it has been about race. Of participants in multiracial family organizations, DaCosta mentions that "these parents were relatively uninvolved in the issue of federal racial categorization and are more focused on local projects that provide support for themselves and their families."[58] This might be thought of along with Williams's similar claims about the involvement of white mothers and their families in multiracial organizations. She writes, "When [affluent, well-educated, suburban white women were] asked, 'Why did you join this group?' one-third of all respondents answered, 'To socialize with other multiracial couples.' . . . Friendship and support for both parents and children emerge as the central factors explaining parental involvement."[59] She also notes that "these women were looking for community—not for a census designation."[60] While family, as a legal category, entails privatized contractual agreements

and reproductive rights, I want to emphasize here that both DaCosta and
Williams reveal a desire to develop relations that supplement those simply legitimated by normatively patriarchal, nuclear families. This is a
desire that becomes buried by the more overtly ethical claims about
maternal care of interracial children. Yet this submerged desire presents a
potential for multiracial kinship politics that moves away from the rubrics
of legitimacy that construct the investments of multiracial family as a
political entity. Uncovering this desire allows us to consider it along with
the bygone and unmourned viability of post–civil rights legalism, and to
consider whether family might possibly be a substitute for another mode
of relation.

In "Friendship as a Way of Life," an interview that first appeared in the
French magazine *Le Gai Pied* in 1981, philosopher Michel Foucault insists
that the goal of uncovering the truth of homosexual desire is less useful
than working toward homosexuality as a way of life. This is to say that
exploring the relational practices of homosexuality, aside from sexual con-
summation, potentially illuminates the uneasiness of care: "Everything
that can be troubling in affection, tenderness, friendship, fidelity, cama-
raderie, and companionship, things that our rather sanitized society can't
allow a place for without fearing the formation of new alliances and the
tying together of unforeseen lines of force."[61] On the surface, it would
seem that the endgame for the aforementioned white mothers of black–
biracial children was to foreclose these sorts of contingencies, this precariousness and these new coalitional effects that Foucault fleetingly suggests
as the potential for friendship—or kinship—as a way of life. An ethics that
would codify maternal desire as that which is the impetus for recognizing the always already illegitimacy of black/multiracial childhood and, further, produce a mode of activism that is based on this codified, naturalized
desire does not account for the possibilities of alternative relational practices between those members who are considered family. This is not an
easy project to imagine when relational practices between adult parents
and children are already circumscribed by a set of legal and cultural ethics
that are meant to protect children from potential abuses. What if this very
set of ethics—the shared interest between mothers and children—was
investigated in a manner that encompassed the discourse of multiracialism but wasn't completely undercut by it? What if investigation, rather
than conviction, of what it means to be politicized by available possibilities of multiracial kinship was taken seriously during a moment when white

mothers found themselves on the troubled terrain of what an ethical, antiracist approach to family is?

In "Is Kinship Always Already Heterosexual?" there is a moment when Judith Butler asks about the disjuncture between legitimacy and illegitimacy, particularly with regard to gay marriage and sexuality, but more generally in terms of the political potential between these already recognizable concepts. Butler suggests that the risk of investigating the space that can trouble the legitimated and illegitimated ways we recognize sexuality—and perhaps affection, friendship, and kinship—is being apolitical. This is because investigation is a mode of criticality, a mode of asking about particular formations without asserting a stance in one way or another. The idea is not simply to question "taken-for-granted conditions" as an end, but rather, to go "through suffering the dehiscence, the breakup, of the ground itself."[62] When Butler asserts that the "hybrid regions of legitimacy and illegitimacy" are "not precisely places where one can choose to hang out, subject positions might occupy," she is discussing a set of critical acts and practices of becoming that refer to Foucault's earlier assertion.[63] These hybrid regions are not yet expressible or occupiable, unlike the conviction that racial hybridity is a space from which subjects can rally and know themselves. Butler continues, "There are middle regions—hybrid regions of legitimacy and illegitimacy that have no clear names and where nomination itself falls into a crisis produced by variable, sometimes violent boundaries of legitimating practices that come into uneasy and sometimes conflictual contact with one another."[64]

While it seems that the mothers of interracial children were in fact looking for something that was not the legitimization of state recognition, nor the illegitimization of anomalously interracial families, I want to suggest that these women were approaching something like a development of the not yet expressible, not quite political space of a hybrid criticality. If "a politics which incorporates a critical understanding is the only one that can maintain a claim to being self-reflective and nondogmatic," then I want to suggest that the ultimate lack of a critical perspective points to the missed opportunity of these women who did not necessarily want or need to take a particular stand on the nature of multiracial kinship.[65] One might go further to suggest that this lack of criticality reproduces historical and subjective absences that contribute to normalizing forces, making recognizable particular kinds of and conditions for affection, friendship, and parental care, while deeming other kinds invisible.

I want to speculate that the intersection of legal legitimacy for the post *Loving* interracial family, and the discursive illegitimacy produced by the lack of an overarching national recognition, had lead to vehement foreclosures of political ruptures of "unforeseen lines of force" because the possibility of such unpredicted ways of being kin or companions was so near. The violence of insistence that particular patriarchal family formations and particular kinship figures signal multiracialism could well have clashed with the desire to be multiracial in ways that recognized various sexual practices, maternal forms of resistance within normatively patriarchal formations, or engagement with the troubling aspects of tenderness and affection. This would require an experience that prevents the actors within the multiracial movement (the primarily white women looking for support or community) from understanding the terms of communalism as based only on maternal desire, and a tacit sense of white femininity. For the experiential knowledge that the ground itself has broken, such mothers must experience the manner of this breaking, including the way black womanhood is the condition that disappears in the memory of what multiracial kinship means as a political formation. To break into *that* void, which is not the one left in the wake of civil rights legal ethics to be filled by the care of children, or to experience the absence of Mildred Loving as a mother of multiracial children, or the illegitimacy of black womanhood that Spillers alludes to that breaks into the legitimated logic of national recognition and reproduction, might allow for a disorienting critique of multiracialism.

Roberts's argument is useful here. She argues that criminal law is more likely to punish women for parental negligence if they are perceived to actively resist domestic violence, without taking into account the full political context of familial violence. She suggests that the myth of "idealized motherhood"[66] is in part responsible for the disparities the law displays with regard to punishment that often reveals racial and class-based inequities. Roberts makes two assertions. The first is:

> Although feminists have demolished false conflicts between
> mothers and children, the truth is that mother's interests and
> children's interests often conflict. And mothers sometimes choose
> against their children in order to be safe, to pursue their own
> ambitions, to hold on to a man.[67]

The second assertion is:

> The ideal of mother's exclusive responsibility for children also
> justifies punishing Black mothers in particular. Black women's
> style of mothering is often misinterpreted as child neglect
> precisely because it violates this standard. Black mothers have a
> long-standing cultural tradition of sharing childraising with other
> women in the community. These cooperative networks include
> members of the extended family . . . as well as nonblood kin and
> neighbors. . . . Social workers and judges often believe that Black
> children raised in these arrangements are neglected. . . . This is yet
> another way in which the law punishes women's resistance to an
> oppressive maternal role, thwarting the potential of alternative
> visions of motherhood.[68]

The first of these provides an auxiliary legalist trajectory to the one that
suggests interracial families are centralized around the legitimacy of *Loving*. Mothers who were the most active proponents of the multiracial
movement argued that the self-esteem of their children was the primary
impetus for making multiracialism political. Shanley, like Roberts, points
out that there can be disparities between the desires of (same-sex) parents
that do not always take the well-being of children into account. In a sense,
both Roberts and Shanley demonstrate the manner in which two different
contexts—a woman's heterosexual desire for her man, a lesbian partner's
desire for parental rights—could potentially complicate the multiracial
narrative of mother work as racial advocacy and a shared interest with
her children. Each context makes clear that adult sexuality is complicit
with one's impact on childhood caretaking. More pertinently, each context breaks opens a space through which a critique can occur about the
nature of political and legal assumptions that are taken as granted.

In contrast, as I have asserted, the inability of making claims about
multiracialism that are based on civil rights–era legalism has presented
an ethical crisis that required an intensified concern by mothers for their
interracial children. This concern need not be motivated by currently
viable questions of law, such as physical child abuse or neglect, the lack of
legal entitlements granted to children because of the illegitimacy of their
guardians, or the way in which the needs of children are subordinated to

those of adults. These last concerns are all viable legalist matters around which collective mobilization can be directed. I raise Roberts's first assertion to provide a generative tension between the ostensible narrative of the interracial family—that its primary concern is make sure that interracial children develop a self-confidence that is not prevented by the violence of the family itself—and the possibility that mothers may not always have their children's interests in the forefront of their minds. While Roberts is addressing women who need to choose between the abusive men in their lives and the welfare of their children, the salient discourse about multiracialism not only does not address the possibility that a masculine presence (or maternal presence, for that matter) in families might be potentially dangerous, but it does not address openly that white, affluent mothers might be motivated by interests that are not shared by their children. Indeed, the domains that typify the multiracial family often seem to be represented as healthy, functional, nonviolent spaces for children, who are at risk of experiencing the violence of misrecognition from outside the home. The partners of white motherhood are primarily subordinated presences, but they appear when negotiations around the well-being of children or the production of mixed racial analysis are required.

However, the observation made by both DaCosta and Williams about the initial motivation of these mothers can be thought of as a fissure that tacitly reveals an ideological failure of the always coherent, always functional multiracial family. Again, when DaCosta asserts that these maternal subjects "are more focused on local projects that provide support for themselves and their families," and when Williams emphasizes that these same women were looking for "support and friendship" rather than national recognition that the interracial family form is coherent, healthy, and outside of the multitude of violence that might be an effect of family, it seems that there is an opening for thinking about coalitional politics that extends beyond the ostensible project of multiracialism. "Local projects that provide support" can clearly be understood as the sort of gatherings among multiracial families that indeed replicate the centrality of how proponents of multiracial politics understood the stakes of recognition, visibility, and so forth. "Support and friendship" can easily imply that interracial families continue to understand themselves as having a marginal relation to the normativity of monoracial families. However, both suggest the potential of deliberation on relational forms, with their varying and contingent lines of force that can be contextualized in a number of ways politically, among

white mothers who have been the ostensible architects of the public perception of coherent, legitimate multiracial family. There is an extension of
what I'll refer to here as kinship, an extension beyond the institutional
mechanism of family. While multiracial families share the condition of
mixedness and resulting minoritization, the conditions that woman experience are not, as DaCosta and Williams phrase it, relegated to the conflated identities of mothers and children, or of the support gained from
patriarchs who might organize the experience of safety or legitimacy, or,
finally, a set of intimacies that might privilege the needs of mothers over
their children. In this way, the fissure that I argue is raised by DaCosta and
Williams allows for a consideration of varying and multiple practices of
multiracialism that are in a state of emergence when the motivations of
communal support, friendship, and project building are brought to the fore.

    This brings me to Roberts's second assertion, which addresses the
communal nature through which family has been practiced—and officially undermined—within black communities. The ideological myth of
motherhood insists that mothers are the primary caregivers of their children, and that in this capacity, mothers are obligated to protect the best
interests of their children. To some degree, this is precisely the ideology
perpetuated by maternal proponents of multiracialism. Their work prioritizes the significance of a mother's responsibility to her children, which is
implicitly made exclusive by the generic nature of memoir and by the particularized situation of being white in a black–biracial family. However, it
seems that these proponents also wish to construct an alternative vision
of white mother work that comprises this as an antiracist practice. The
implication is that unlike normative whiteness, which is produced in monoracial white families, the interracial family, and in particular the white
mother who gives birth to black/multiracial children, has a responsibility
to develop an analysis that puts pressure on the assumed privileges of
whiteness. The impetus is to recognize that a practice that disperses the
responsibility of mothering, just like a practice that overemphasizes the
mother's primary responsibility, both belong to a racialized, state-driven
narrative. The ways in which multiracial activists emphasize their roles
as attentive mothers that are self-identified with their children to some
degree undercuts an antiracist agenda.

    However, this is a key reason for my speculative consideration of what
DaCosta and Williams state when it comes to what white maternal proponents of multiracialism potentially could have worked toward. What

DaCosta and Williams refer to as the potential of multiracial collectivity—the force through which multiple ideologies might clash through the denaturalized, unsanctioned relations between friends, mothers, kindred—suggests that the enduring perceptions of black motherhood could potentially trouble the conceptualization of what an antiracist practice means for white mothers and for multiracialism generally. The memoirs I address in the next chapter decidedly do not openly render problematic the conditions of patriarchal motherhood or family. I attempt to draw out the tacit desires for support networks and friendships in relation to what is understood institutionally—and legally—as family. The always already illegitimacy of the black/multiracial child within the legally legitimized space of the post-*Loving* interracial family and the overly attentive white maternal parent arguably are the most salient rhetorical nodes of the 1990s politics of multiracialism. However, in the following chapter, I would like to consider whether memoirs reveal an acknowledgment that even within what seems like a newly coherent way of formulating the multiracial family, there are a set of impasses, disjunctures, and spaces of contestation that would lead to a multiracialism that cannot be ethically stabilized, but rather produced and reproduced through a process of becoming multiracial.

CHAPTER 3

The Whiteness of Maternal Memoirs

Politicizing the Multiracial Child

Crossing the Color Line *is not* about *black people, although it is about race: it is about whiteness, about trying to cross the color line at many places, about meeting points of whiteness and blackness, about the politics of feminism and antiracism, about mothering black children in a society that does not value children, and particularly does not value black children.*

—Maureen T. Reddy, *Crossing the Color Line*

What is this whiteness that threatens to separate me from my own child?

—Jane Lazarre, *Beyond the Whiteness of Whiteness*

THE PREVIOUS CHAPTER focused on how *Loving v. Virginia*, the 1967 Supreme Court decision that marks the beginning of legitimacy for interracial marriage, is the originating moment for 1990s-era discourses on multiracialism. While the legacy of *Loving* allows for ongoing consideration of the legitimization of deviant family formations, which not only include multiracial families but also same-sex marriage and parenthood, the 1967 legislation actually shared the same political logic of the Moynihan Report, published in 1965. By comprehending the nine-year period of exile imposed on Richard and Mildred Loving by the state, and by keeping the subsequent *Loving* decision and the Moynihan Report in mind, we can begin to reveal how both of these legal and policy decisions normalize family by rhetorically naturalizing several of its components: patriarchy, color-blindness or racial neutrality, heteronormativity, and distance from urban location. This revelation indicates that an emphasis on legitimizing the family is couched in the civil rights–era, antiracist dismantlement of antimiscegenation laws throughout the country; in addition, the forgone conclusion of racial equity was concomitant with a decidedly insidious and paradoxical attempt by the state to alleviate its obligation toward racial, sexualized, and economic redress by privatizing these responsibilities through a new national focus on the family.

In this chapter, I turn to two multiracial memoirs: Maureen Reddy's treatise on interracial family, *Crossing the Line: Race Parenting and Culture* (1994), and at briefer length, Jane Lazarre's treatment of similar subject matter in *Beyond the Whiteness of Whiteness* (1997). I argue that efforts to politicize multiracial children reveal a problematic condition: while the multiracial family has gained legal, rational legitimatization, romantic preferences and marital ties are still overwhelmingly monoracial. I argue that these memoirs pinpoint political business left unfinished by *Loving*, which is an attendance to how, precisely, one makes the crossover from the legal unfettering of affective (heterosexual) relations irrespective of racial differences to actually producing a trend of interracial intimacy. Although heterosexual adults are free to choose marriage partners across the color line, this legal liberty has made the practice of romantic love itself seem neutral and individualistic.[1] As Rachel Moran argues, *Loving* was able to legitimate interracial intimacy, but the ruling provided no method for enforcing it. Because the post-*Loving* era recognizes the legal rights of the interracial family, children emerge in this era as a highly important focus for proponents of multiracialism because they are at the forefront of the gaps in *Loving*'s logic: how do parents of differently raced children politicize intimacy and affect? How are children granted or denied agency within a conventional familial structure that is nonetheless interracial? How do mothers themselves understand their relation to the legacy of *Loving*, the paradigm of family, and kinship relations more expansively to include friendships with other mothers and women?

Those invested in multiracial politics have tended to avoid fully grappling with questions about adult intimacies in order to concentrate on the decidedly uncertain space of the multiracial child. By uncertain, I mean to suggest that adults and children negotiate questions of intimacy and common interests on uneven ground. Adults, primarily parents and guardians, focus on an ethics of caregiving for children. This focus required the development of an analysis of why parental caregiving of the multiracial child was political. While Reddy or Lazarre do not—indeed, cannot in a post-*Loving* era—have a sustained concern for the particular matter of legal illegitimacy when it comes to interracial children, both develop affect as a theme that allows them each to politicize multiracial identity through families that were already properly recognized by the state. This chapter explores the context in which producers of multiracial discourse attempted to work out a new ethics about race by pointing to two historical changes associated with the late 1980s and early 1990s: first, the law seems to vanish as a privileged site for claims on behalf of an ethics of racial equity after *Loving*. The question for proponents of multiracial politics, particularly white mothers of multiracial children, is how to find a new site through which to claim such an ethics. In this way, the uncertainty I mentioned earlier can be more aptly described as a moment in which the white women who took the lead were forced to reckon with what might have seemed like the vanishing of historical touchstones. If the multiracial movement generally lacked an awareness of how to position itself in a larger temporal context, then the sense of a vanishing past is one effect of this. Perhaps children were the most appropriate icons of an antiracist future that could somehow be temporally separated from a history that seemed to vanish, and from a subsequent present that seemed uncertain.

However, what vanishes does not completely disappear. Forgotten history reemerged as altered (and alternative) versions of what had been normalized about maternal agency. For example, if motherhood had been naturalized as a race-neutral category, then the version of motherhood that reemerged in the late 1980s was a category that was most legible through race. Thus, in the second change associated with the 1980s and 1990s, black motherhood—at once deviant and ideal—seemed to signal a return of what had historically vanished. The radical negation of black women's claim to their own children during slavery, and the silence that shrouded a collective will to remember the subjugation of slaves, was brought into national consciousness slightly before the publication of Reddy and Lazarre's memoirs. Toni Morrison's Pulitzer Prize–winning novel *Beloved* (1987) is particularly significant here because Reddy turns to this novel to explicate cross-racial relationships between women. Morrison's novel troubles the naturalized, temporal distinction between one moment of subjectivity and another. Children are transformed from prepolitical and prehistorical symbols to a forceful presence that troubles the inequitable bond between childhood and adulthood. In these ways, *Beloved* is a significant pre-text for the general concerns of white maternal affect for the multiracial child because of the novel's central plot: the uneasy return of a child. Beloved is spirit and flesh, child and ancestor. Her return from the dead troubles the ideological position of motherhood.

This sort of return is manifest in the memoirs of Reddy and Lazarre. Even as these memoirs imply the existence of a void to be filled with the politics of motherly affect, within this void emerge vestiges of a racial history that undercuts the authority of motherhood, ultimately revealing a major impasse on the way to developing an antiracist politics that leaves the ethics of love unquestioned. Beloved explores how black women's right to claim children was broken by slavery, and how children return to reveal an alternative version of ethical relations. In contrast, or perhaps obliquely through this context, white women's memoirs seek to make a positive claim to loving their multiracial children to secure the presence of interracial sexuality and affect as real family.

The Vanishing Law: Building Bridges for Cross-racial Intimacies

Proponents of multiracial politics such as Reddy and Lazarre are quite interested in the uncertainty of racial ethics when it comes to the interracial family. However, their approach to exploring this uncertainty is to occupy the era after Loving as if its only legacy is a hands-off government. They forego the new potential that deliberating on the effects of Loving in both society and law might yield, which would allow them to see how vestiges of law continue to produce inequitable outcomes for marginalized subjects, multiracial identity notwithstanding. In particular, alternative readings of Loving would reveal how the exclusion of nonheteronormative and nondomesticated intimacies has been central to the legitimation of interracialism. Instead, they see the law as no longer intruding in kinship arrangements because they no longer restrict the formation of heteronormative, nuclear families, as Wallenstein points out: "After the Supreme Court ruled in the Loving's case, couples no longer had to worry about the law of interracial marriage. That law had vanished, vanished so completely that people growing up a generation later typically had no understanding that such laws ... had ever been in place."[2] Wallenstein is obviously referring to a generation of children who did not experience the force of Jim Crow firsthand, but I would suggest that this condition—the vanishing law—is also if not more applicable to white adult subjects who are politicized for the first time as a result of having multiracial children. In this case, it is of course not true that these adults had no understanding that antimiscegenation law ever existed; they remember this history of racial restriction. However, their own reported politicization as subjects of interracial relationships coincides with what seems to them as the vanishing of the law (as either obstacle to or instrument of racial equity).

This is a key paradox of the vanishing role of law in multiracial ethics: one must remember a law in order to see it vanish. Within this logic, antimiscegenation law is more politically forceful for those who remember Jim Crow, rather than for those younger subjects growing up a generation after *Loving*, because it is this sense of disappearance that presents a logical gap to be filled with a new strategy toward racial progress. Reddy and Lazarre treat the law as if it were a gaping absence that requires them to invent new strategies for legitimating the affective ties and cultural value of their already legally legitimate families. This is why the multiracial child emerges as an important figure for devising an antiracism to which a politics of the interracial family can be tethered: the child indexes uncertainty about the privatization of relationships that implies the absence of state interest in the realm of intimacy. In so doing, it also enables maternity to emerge as the new ground from which racial, particularly interracial, politics can be reconstructed.

Indeed, the overwhelming concern for the self-esteem of multiracial children was the engine behind much multiracial activism. This politics of self-esteem signaled a tacit assumption that legalism had vanished as an effective recourse for addressing how race still functions in both the romantic creation of families and the ongoing state regulation of families. Legal scholars R. A. Lenhardt et al. suggest that "one might contemplate the reverberating effects of *Loving* for other kinds of intimate associations [besides marriage] and their place in American society and law. What of the relationship between a parent and child? Or the relationship between extended family members or even friends? Does *Loving* offer a way of thinking about handling matters of identity that might arise within them?"[3] In general, the multiracial memoir does contemplate cross-racial intimacy through the central domain of mother/child relationships, thereby downplaying husband/wife relations. However, the genre's general reluctance to speculate about a fuller range of intimacies, along with their social and legal statuses, signals a mourning of *Loving*'s passing, the vanishing of clear legal recourse, or a racial divide that is no less palpable after the civil rights era. If the rallying focus on childhood self-esteem is the new approach to developing an ethical position on race, then this new approach adopted the goal of filling the void left by the legal redress of the civil rights era. As a new national goal, childhood self-esteem eclipsed other approaches to thinking about racial intimacy. The vanishing law has the effect of producing a gap to be filled by a new racial logic that centers on nuclear familial affect as well as on the self-esteem and well-being of children.

I want to lay out how this analysis relates multiracialism, and multiracial children in particular as symbols of an incipient condition, to the wider terms and assumptions of motherhood. As I asserted above, those invested in multiracial politics generally avoided questions about adult intimacies in order to focus on the decidedly uncertain historical space of the multiracial child. Reddy and Lazarre raise the question of how to bridge the gap between the reality of racial separatism—even within singular families—with the ideal of transcending racial differences through mother love or by being particularly race conscious because of motherly affect. Developing the work of legal historian Robert Cover, Rachel Moran describes this condition, albeit through the overt matter of race-conscious adoption procedures and the degree to which the law should handle racial constructions of family this way:

> In weighing the bonds of love in the racially divided world that we know against bonds that might have been in a world free of discrimination, the law of custody and adoption becomes "a system of tension or a bridge linking a concept of reality to an imagined alternative." The bridge is a shaky one, subject to shifting understandings of both race and intimacy. As a result, legal standards remain highly contingent and contested.[4]

Reddy and Lazarre use their memoirs to describe the shaky ground of negotiating between sharing identities with their biological children and recognizing the differences between their own white subjectivities and those of their differently raced children. However, Reddy and Lazarre do not—cannot—allude to the law to stabilize the uncertain space between an ideal of racially transcendent love and the reality of enduring racial separatism. Indeed, the domain of law can neither provide a clear-cut approach to regulating how race should figure into matters of custody and adoption—whether a child should be placed in a differently raced family—nor produce feelings of affect or intimacy across the color line. Therefore, the shaky bridge that Reddy and Lazarre both describe is akin to the shifts and contingencies of the law, yet it marks the absence of legal logic with an uncertain space. Where legalism cannot be relied on to do the work of stabilizing a racial ethics of affect, mothers such as Reddy and Lazarre understand the uncertainty left in the wake of absent legal logic as a space for deliberating on how the mother/child relationship can be a conduit for explaining the complications of the color line.

Yet the child, while ostensibly an index of racial ethics outside of the regulating space of law, only becomes a site for encounters with the shakiness of traversing the realm of racial ethics once, ironically, one takes for granted the naturalized conditions of motherhood. M. M Slaughter points out, "Women are not 'given' as Mothers. Rather, mothering is constructed as a woman's role."[5] While Slaughter is concerned with how the Mother is constructed in relation to the differently gendered and labor role of the Ideal Worker, I would argue that the contrivance of the Mother is dependent on a number of assumptions: (1) particular gendered assignments of labor domesticate women as Mothers on the one hand and externalize the labor market for the (male) Ideal Worker on the other; (2) this contrived relation between gender and labor roles is naturalized, so that women are presupposed to be Mothers; and (3) Mothers, as those who nurture and raise children, have a responsibility to make this sort of labor their foremost priority, at the expense of their own adult desires and gratifications. Ruthann Robson makes this last point most explicit in her discussion of lesbian motherhood: "Exclusion of a lesbian's lover from her home is asking a lesbian to choose between her lover and her child. This is not the type of choice that any lesbian legal theory would seek to promote. . . . It is difficult to disagree with the legal standard of 'best interests of the child,' but a lesbian legal theory has a different focus. Its central focus is lesbian."[6] Together, both Slaughter and Robson claim that motherhood need not naturalize the self-sacrifice of sex, adult intimacy with other adults, and other forms of gratification for women in order to attend to the best interests of children, including self-esteem.

At this point I want to provide an example of how this condition of affect between white mothers of biological children is undercut not only by the devaluation of adult desires, but also by the devaluation of blackness in a manner not often recognized in the memoirs to be discussed. During the early 1980s, Linda Sidoti, a white mother of a three-year-old daughter, divorced her white husband and gained custody of their child. Her former husband filed for custody after she began to live with a black man as an intimate partner. It was at this point that Linda Sidoti had to present a legal challenge to retain custody: "The trial court [. . . stated], 'It is of some significance . . . that the mother did see fit to bring a man into her home and carry on a sexual relationship with him without being married to him. Such action tended to place gratification of her own desires ahead of her concern for the child's future welfare."[7] Like *Loving*, *Palmore v. Sidoti* (1984) eventually was decided in the Supreme Court, which determined that government has no concern with intervening when it comes to race and family.[8]

Still, *Palmore* demonstrates that interracial intimacy as it is directly related to mother/child relationships—the presumption that the self-esteem of the multiracial child is in need of fostering—has a ghostly opposite. While the rationale of attending to a child's self-esteem has been part of a larger concern for responsible antiracist mother work that to a large degree has been naturalized by the legitimization of the family and non-black, biological motherhood, this fairly recent case suggests that self-esteem—like motherhood and family—are not neutral terms that have an integral tether to an ethos of affect. In a lower court at the late date of 1981, the myth of unbridled black male sexuality emerged, revealing the perception that some subjects—black men—cannot foster the self-esteem of children within an interracial, familial context. More to the point at hand, however, the criminality of black motherhood that was so prevalent in the 1980s and 1990s is part and parcel of the conditions that have socially and legally constructed what we mean by motherhood: the desires and gratification of women, even when they do not appear as criminal breaches of welfare policy or drug abuse, are antithetical to the contrivance of motherhood.

If motherhood and parenthood more generally are not racially neutral contrivances, then the multiracial, parental concern for childhood self-esteem is not innocent as antiracist practice. In the *Palmore* case, the primary contention waged by the former husband in a lower court was that Linda Sidoti was not fit for motherhood because her self-gratification—not coincidentally, her sexual partnership with a black man—was incompatible with her obligation to place her child's best interests first. Relegating mother work to women seemingly suggests that this relegation naturally requires the denial of female adult gratification, even as its legal theorization disavows the needs of homosexual women, figuring the child's best interests as being commensurate with racist white patriarchy, the

restriction of women within a segregated labor market, and homopho-
bia—all for the sake of children. This sort of racialized marginalization
could have become fodder for a progressive multiracial critique. An alternative version of multiracial politics would take into serious consideration
the manner in which one of the foundational aims of 1990s-era multiracial politics—protecting the self-esteem of multiracial children—has an
antiliberatory connotation. If there is potential in focusing on how mothers are responsible for the best interests of their children, I argue that
it involves a critique that considers multiracialism as inextricably linked
to the pitfalls of mandatory domesticity, the racism of patriarchy, and
antiqueer politics as determinants of the "proper" family.

The way in which the white mothers of multiracial children rely on the
morality of maternal love or affect exploits, to a large degree, the manner
in which black mothers have little purchase to this emotional connection
when it comes to their own children. This is not to say that the white
mothers who wish to describe or construct a politics around the meaning
of multiracial maternity are actively invested in devaluing black motherhood. However, the very project of creating either a moral framework or
a politics through maternal affect requires a paradoxically unsettling critique of the (shaky) ground that makes this seem viable. In the epigraph
at the start of this chapter, Reddy points out that her politics as a white
feminist is "about mothering black children in a society that does not value
children, and particularly does not value black children." Here Reddy
references without explicating a historical condition in which the value
that black mothers did indeed grant their black children has been consistently ignored, disrupted, undercut, and torn apart by the demands that
national and transatlantic labor structures have made on black families.
Because Reddy's perspective on white, antiracist mothering of black children focuses on children and not patriarchy, her epigraph does not suggest how her politics of mother work neglects the racialized dimensions of
patriarchy. Consider Moran's comments on the relative lack of value black
women have been attributed in the dominant cultural imagination:

Black women marry out at a substantially lower rate than black
men. This paradoxical outcome reflects in part the impact of
ongoing racialized sexual imagery. Both black men and women
have been stereotyped as hypersexual and promiscuous. Unlike
the image of the "black macho," however, the myth of the "black

Jezebel" is countered by another view of black women. Because they often played the role of caretaker in white homes, black women have been portrayed as asexual and motherly.[9]

What this indicates is that the condition Reddy and Lazarre write about—being white mothers to black/multiracial children—is a condition that is less common for black women who are deemed as less desirable than their white counterparts on the ostensibly open, post-*Loving* marriage market, but nonetheless are understood as properly domesticated, insofar as they have traditionally cared for white homes.

This paradoxical mythology about black motherhood, which on the one hand is pathologically unfit for motherhood and on the other hand is overly motherly and domestic (without the privileges that patriarchy grants normative domestication) suggests that the bridge of negotiation reveals more about the social status of white motherhood than black motherhood in the memoirs to be discussed here. In this paradox, black motherhood itself is a space of uncertainty: it is a space where legal intervention deems black women as criminal, who abuse a prereformed welfare system and are prone to drug addiction. However, they are embedded in the cultural imaginary as either unfit to be mothers or lacking the self-consciousness of being mothers. In this imaginary space, one might infer that black motherhood cannot perform the critical act of reconceptualizing multiracial politics in the same way with the same agency and with the same self-consciousness that white motherhood can, even as the white mothers of these memoirs are invested in conventional forms of heteronormativity and domestication.

The memoirs of Reddy and Lazarre construct the role of the white mother as that which completely identifies her self-interest with that of her black/multiracial children. Both memoirists express deep concern that their parenting styles should attend exclusively to the needs of their children, producing a narrative that does not challenge the legal rationales for how black mothers are punished for resisting the expected protocols of motherhood. In so doing, they neglect the varying contexts in which (racial) patriarchy impacts the health and safety of women and children within families and in the definition of family. I propose that the memoir form—as opposed to the legal truth, the sanctity of *Loving*—reveals a space of unwitting critical uncertainty (shakiness) over the multiracial movement's ethical purchase on family. More specifically, I explore whether the particular memoirs discussed here—Reddy's *Crossing the Color Line* and to a lesser extent Lazarre's *Beyond the Whiteness of Whiteness*—can be read to produce a generative contestation between the antiblack discourses over functional mothering and the conditions of white, antiracist maternal practice. This would entail a careful attentiveness to the privileges and depravities accorded to race within the cultural dimension of motherhood. The paradoxical status that both Reddy and Lazarre demonstrate as self-identified feminists who nonetheless are not actively or ostensibly critical of conventional structures of family is a condition that does not insidiously "become part of the unconscious psyche" like "the assumed meaning of Blackness," as Roberts puts it. It also is not a moment for self-reflexivity, much in the same way that Reddy and Lazarre tread a shaky bridge that centers their politics on their own biological children, rather than on the fuller implications of how their emergent racial politics implicates both the personal, private space of intimacy and the enduring societal questions of law and government. These memoirs want to focus on the processes of producing and challenging racial orthodoxy when the color line is blurred in the most intimate spaces, or when the process of racial production leads to ambiguous outcomes within single families. Even as these memoirs do not traverse the space between privacy and vestiges of legalism and public policy that may have led us to where the family is today, Reddy and Lazarre do evoke the spatial metaphors of bridges and barriers to work through the difficult dimensions of history.

History under the Bridge: Crossing the Color Line

Maureen Reddy, a white woman who is married to a black man and raising black–biracial children, posits the family as the primary site for engaging matters of racial formation. In *Crossing the Color Line,* Reddy narrates "family" as the central domain from which to devise a racial politics, precisely because of its capacity to both create consensus and enable deconstruction: the interracial family is a legal unit that confirms the intimate integration of multiple racial identities, while at the same time it produces a condition of racial alienation within the domain of intimacy, as opposed to in public. This dual capacity—interracial unity and racial distance—makes sense from Reddy's own perspective: while she diligently attempts to account for the experiences of her black husband and her black/multiracial son, and while she recounts conversations with various extended family and friends, *Crossing the Color Line* overwhelmingly documents Reddy's own subjectivity as a white woman who is constantly negotiating her relation to racial difference, the political potential of motherhood, and the exceptional conditions of belonging to an interracial family. In other words, her memoir is a text that wants to explore what "politics" means when it is experienced most profoundly outside of the domain of legalism, social collectivity, and historically rooted racial injury, and inside the realm of lawful kinship structures, and motherhood in particular.

As a genre, the memoir publicizes such an individuated experience as an index for particular historical moments; in this case, Reddy is aware of how varying historical narratives of race circumscribe but do not exactly inscribe her singular condition of interracial familial belonging as a white woman. Reddy's memoir accepts the normality of family and motherhood as statuses that, for interracial couples, have already been hard won by civil rights activism. In the aftermath of such civil rights victories, she wants to construct motherhood as a form of political subjectivity that results from this earlier moment. Reddy's *Crossing the Line,* like Lazarres's *Beyond the Whiteness of Whiteness,* pivots around the unique challenges white mothers face while raising their biological, black/multiracial children that presumably "society does not value," and how such mother work leads to an antiracist perspective that becomes antiracist practice. For Reddy, this means, in part, that mothering entails an active redressing of a pervasive lack of value accorded to black children, and blackness in general, in dominant society. A politics that centralizes motherhood as the modality for developing antiracist practice has the capacity to denaturalize the terms for how family is produced, and therefore to destabilize the way in which mothers and children understand their relationship to each other, and their responsibilities as kin.

Although the family can cohere—from her self-conscious perspective, it can bring a white, Irish American feminist in the fold of black kinship— it can just as easily break down into multiple misidentifications. It is this dual capacity for coherence and deconstruction that provides Reddy with her most forceful metaphor: on several occasions throughout the memoir, Reddy describes herself as a bridge. Being a white mother of black/multiracial children "is about living as a racial 'insider' who stands outside prescribed racial arrangements, a position that affords unique insight into those arrangements. It is about being a bridge."[10] Reddy begins the memoir by describing a panic attack she had in 1985, while she was driving her

two-year-old son across the Tappan Zee Bridge in New York. She describes an enduring "bridge phobia," which seemed to have emerged
unexpectedly and was inexplicable. The first chapter, entitled "On Lines
and Bridges," recounts this episode:

> I am seized by a paralyzing terror as I involuntarily and vividly
> imagine the bridge splintering to pieces, sending cars tumbling
> into the Hudson. . . .
>   My two-year-old son, strapped into his car seat in the back,
> must sense something amiss, as he stops singing to ask, "Is this
> Grandma's? We there?" "No, Sean, but we're almost there," I reply
> in a high-pitched, strangled-sounding voice. Speaking seems to
> lessen my terror, and so I continue.[11]

The bridge, which is both metaphorical and actual, is a ground above
water that provides a safe passageway, bypassing fluid that does not easily
sustain bodies. What is underneath the bridge is potentially dangerous.
The imagined potential of the bridge "splintering to pieces" is particularly
terrorizing if the metaphor includes a sense of temporal disruption: the
road that once offered a guaranteed ground for progressive movement—
civil rights reform, for example—can be violently destroyed and can therefore destroy all those who would depend on it to live their lives. The terror
that comes from a realization that there is nothing yet available to substitute the previously supposed continuity between an antimiscegenationist
past from that one travels safely into an antiracist moment where a mother
may guide her differently raced child home. In this new temporality, an
older, monoracial generation awaits its multiracial progeny.
    In a sense, the two-year-old child who sits in the backseat—both the
literal son and an icon of futurity—implicitly demonstrates a hopeful outcome for the breaking ground of temporal continuity: to him, Grandma,
an originating maternal presence, or an antecedent to both Reddy and
her son, is never cut off from where they are. Reddy imagines that they are
not only moving away from the familiar, the safe, or any viable relation
to history, but also, and more devastatingly, she imagines that movement
itself may cease to be possible. Sean could be detecting that this movement itself is a problem—the something amiss that he senses—although
his version of this crisis is not the inevitability of social or literal death.
Instead, the manner in which he signals the crisis of temporal movement

suggests an emergent analytic that time is not most viable on a linear plane. Indeed, the trip across the Tappan Zee suggests a movement toward the past in terms of antecedents, generations: *Grandma* is the goal, not the symbol of future subjectivity. Sean disrupts the linear logic of time—through generational progression, movement forward—with the infantile inquiry, "We there?" "There" could easily be where they are, in addition to where they are going. It could be a generative confusion of what it means to be in Grandma's space, on a bridge between temporal moments and spatial designations.

Further, it could be an incipiently made challenge to Reddy's own commitment to linearity. The breaking of ground in her account means certain death. The provisional nature of the road for the infant Sean means that the vicissitudes of movement is necessarily conjectural. Ultimately, "We there?" does not so much require an affirmation of what "there" is, or a distinction of how it is particularly distinctive from "here." However, the moment of conjecture is mitigated through Reddy's reinforcement of maternal authority over her child: speaking, or providing an explanation that stabilizes a normalized reality—"we're almost there," we are moving ahead as mother and child—is less of a comfort to her son than a comfort to herself. She talks to Sean to convey that they are moving toward safety in an attempt to undercut her own tendency toward self-destruction: Reddy recounts that she was "mumbling quietly to [herself], 'You're not going to die, you're going to drive across this bridge.'"[12]

When Reddy writes, "For years, bridge phobia rides along with me whenever I drive, lessening across time but never really gone, always ready to spring, like some malevolent ghost in the back seat,"[13] we might wonder about just what—or who—this "malevolent ghost" signifies, the reason for its malevolence, the reason for its literal positioning behind Reddy—a position of belatedness that is the condition of ghosts, those absent presences signify the problem of the past. A provocative aspect of Reddy's description is that her infant son, who is the only other passenger in the car when she describes her first panic attack while crossing the Tappan Zee, is likely to be traveling in the back of the car, fastened in a child's car seat. This provokes the possibility that she is implicating her own son as a ghostly presence, suggesting that her son exists alongside this "malevolent ghost," or conflating the two. I would contend that this unwitting confusion when it comes to the role of motherhood and the haunting history of race evokes the uncertainty of motherhood as an ethical tether to a new

racial politics. Why is there a confluence of Reddy's anxiety about the spa-
tial/temporal crossing of a bridge, the problem of responsible mothering
that accompanies this anxiety, and the implication that her son is not only
unknown to her, but also a malevolent remnant of an inescapable past?

Perhaps Reddy experiences the past as a specter that denies reconciliation or understands it as a set of circumstances that cannot include her
own subject position as a white woman of a black/multiracial child, and
that also carries residually dangerous spitefulness toward her position. In
other words, the rupture with a past that is signaled with palpable mali-
ciousness by what one might guess is a black collective presence coincides
with the sense that there is no integrity to the ground on which one treads.
If the legalism of the civil rights movement is moot in the 1990s, if blackness is an identity that has historically prevented subjects from legitimizing their kinship relations, if multiracialism is a formation that cannot
come into nationalized recognition through blackness, then all of these
aspects of uncertainty haunt Reddy's own ethical authority as the driver
of interracial politics. In this case, it seems that this haunting signifies
the absence of recognition, but not of white mothers of black/multiracial
children per se. Instead, it signifies the absent recognition of how motherhood is racialized, nationalized, or historicized politically. The malevolence is itself an implicitly racialized refusal to have the ground so neatly,
safely experienced for white feminists without the subordinating engagement of a multitude of contexts that encompass those subjects who are
apparently ghostly, like so much water under a bridge.

Although this memoir "is not *about* black people," I would submit that
it is about the specter of blackness, which can trouble the manner in which
one inhabits her own historical moment. Reddy's most ostensible concern
is about the (white) mother work of raising a black/multiracial child, but
at this point I want to describe how, ultimately, the memoir is concerned
with interracial relationships between women. Reddy builds the potential of motherhood (as an imaginatively shaky bridge) to make way for the
memoir's conclusion, which imagines a revitalized, interracial feminist
movement based on a shared interest in raising children. In a sense, one
might speculate whether Reddy's appropriation of already legitimated
terms, such as interracial family and (white) motherhood, is itself a bridging strategy that stretches across the legitimacy of post-*Loving* patriarchy
to the unrealized potentials of a second-wave feminism that can unify black
and white women around racial politics.[14] This is to suggest that although

Reddy is openly anxious about mothering a black/multiracial child from the very beginning—as her bridge phobia illustrates—she is implicitly anxious about her relationships with black women. In the beginning, this is not manifested in the overt description of her fear of crossing bridges but rather immediately afterward, in the representation of her (black) female friend as a figure who easily defers to Reddy and her experience of assimilation or a metaphorically successful bridge crossing.

Crossing the Color Line begins with Reddy describing the overwhelming anxiety that came with crossing bridges. She implicates her multiracial son, Sean, as part of the significance of crossing the Tappan Zee described above. However, Reddy's epiphany about her anxiety occurs during a conversation in which a female friend—whose race she does not specify—makes these remarks: "I don't think I would ever marry a white man; there'd be too much trouble with his family, I assume. But if I did, he'd know from the start he'd have to assimilate into the black community, like you have."[15] This validation from her (presumably black) friend leads Reddy to refute the assumption that a white person can assimilate and to offer an alternative positionality: "I don't think a white person can really *assimilate*. . . . I think I stand on the color line itself, not on one side of it. Or maybe I'm like a bridge, stretching across the line, touching both sides, but mostly in the middle somewhere."[16] This is where the epiphany occurs. She suddenly realizes that her panic regarding actual bridges is an effect of this condition: "The panic is . . . about metaphor and race."[17] This is to say that the panic was produced by the challenges of mothering a son that she identifies as black. Significantly, just as her child started to ask "searching first questions about race," Reddy comes to understand her particular capacity to act as a channel through which racial arrangements are uniquely interpreted.

I want to make more of the fact that her son's participation in this scene is an important critical intervention that exceeds Reddy's mode of analysis further on. According to Reddy's interpretation, to be a bridge is to remain unassimilated, to develop a subjectivity that makes interpretive connections between racial differences but does not absorb them or remains distinct from them. Yet the habit her infant son has of formulating "searching first questions" is precisely a starting point for actual critique: the deliberation about race that refuses to rely on a pregiven moral ground. This is significant in terms of the two figures represented at the start of this memoir: Reddy's multiracial infant son, and her (black) adult female friend. Whereas the first is unwittingly responsible for generating a new analysis for black/white racial relations after civil rights and after integration, the second seems unwittingly to reproduce an outworn strategy toward racial equality, which is referred to as assimilation. Why does the memoir begin this way? Or, more specifically, why are we offered what I understand to be an inversion of who may be responsible for an analysis on the conditions of cross-racial intimacy in the postintegration era? An infant is implicitly responsible for (malevolently) signaling to Reddy that her construction of motherhood is inextricable from the complications of race, while an adult (black) woman misses the connection between the marriage market and racial hierarchy. In a sense, it is not only that motherhood becomes the new center of racial ethical work, but because (black) women are less likely to belong to multiracial families, black feminist thought has little to contribute to the explication of intimacy across the color line.

There are a few notable details to track in this moment: first, Reddy refutes the possibility of assimilation while at the same time referencing the intimacy of interracial friendship and interracial family. She wants to mark a kind of racial adaptation that is recognized and acceptable to her presumably black friend, but then she is paradoxically compelled to insist on the persistence of racial separation, and implicitly, inequity. While Reddy's friend begins by raising strong doubts about familial or romantic interracialism as an instrument for uplifting the status of blackness, her friend ends by suggesting that, under some conditions, particular white individuals can volitionally renounce white supremacy in order to merge socially and culturally with blackness. I want to emphasize the point that Reddy's friend does not suggest the possibility or potential of having a white family or community accept her as one of their own. In other words, Reddy's presumably black friend is stating that interracial intimacy is possible when white subjects decide to be taken into the fold of black family and community, but such a decision, at the late date of the 1980s, is one-sided, insofar as black subjects cannot seem to be a part of whiteness. The condition of white assimilation, particularly when raised by a (presumably) black subject, is ostensibly a gesture toward the promise of a post-*Loving* society, where white supremacy is dismantled in part because of a new willingness on the part of white subjects to embrace black people, culture, and community. In this era, there is no "trouble with [a white] family" when the terms of integration do not involve a white man choosing a black woman for marriage. Again, black women outmarry at lower rates than other groups. In this way, Reddy's friend is signifying on the legacy of *Loving:* in the context of a (presumably) interracial female friendship, she is pointing out how black womanhood continues to inhabit a shadowy space in relation to whiteness. Yet her speculative assessment of race reads as simply the opportunity for Reddy to describe her decidedly more significant epiphany.

Because Reddy does not perceive her friend's act of signifying or the manner in which her own expression of subjectivity evokes its shadowy, but nonetheless real, other, this stands out as a teachable moment for Reddy. On the surface, her friend imagines that interracial marriage is possible because a sort of nullifying of racial difference can take place in this arrangement, a nullification that presumably would include white supremacy. Therefore, it is up to Reddy to explain to her (black) friend that the nullifying promise of racial intimacy and integration has not been achieved in fact. Indeed, within the context of the brief conversation between Reddy and the person that she identifies as her friend, Reddy is more aptly positioned to explain the failures of the family as that site where racial assimilation is viable, or more generally the failures of post-*Loving* culture to produce a de facto end to racial separatism. What Reddy's whiteness allows her to understand—with some narrative authority—are the legalistic limits to familial, and by extension national, belonging that her (black) friend is a bit belated in acknowledging. If her friend still understands that interracial unions can potentially undercut white supremacy—which is in part the premise of the *Loving* decision—then Reddy is corrective and articulately skeptical about the instrumentality of legalism to transform the attitudes of white individuals.

Loving raises the question of whether whiteness, presumably having its supremacy legally nullified, could be assimilated or integrated into a black and brown social sphere. Yet Reddy's friendship with a presumably black person, and her interracial family, positions her as a sort of informant that allows her to describe an ethical stance on race—one that recognizes the ongoing disparities between black and white social distribution—while simultaneously performing a similarly ethical practice of participating in an interracial form of intimacy with her friend. Her friend, on the other hand, becomes in this conversation the straw man who somehow misses the pragmatic circumstances of racialization, even as this (black) subject, like Reddy, is permitted the opportunity to narrate a kind of alienation and subordination that destabilizes the ground of interracialism.

It is more pertinent that Reddy's (black) friend is a catalyst for Reddy's own self-awareness and serves therefore as the sort of void that Toni Morrison theorized as the condition for constructing and distinguishing white subjectivities.[18] This is not entirely unlike the acknowledgment that it has been "through [her] experiences with Doug [her black husband]" that she "learned about the other side of racism, white skin privilege, which within a few years appeared to me like a vast underground network, whose surface I initially had mistaken for the whole."[19] Indeed, to return to Reddy's epigraph, this is not a memoir "*about* black people," although blackness is the taken-for-granted politicized subject position from which the whiteness of black/multiracial motherhood discovers its ethical stance on race. That the field of whiteness is represented here as an "underground network"— perhaps a metaphoric inversion of a historically black underground railroad—that does not appear on the surface of social or cultural experience as a whole suggests that "white skin privilege" is the ghostly other to a more obvious "side of racism" attached to blackness. This is perhaps an ironic perspective, because Reddy is unable to detect the way in which her friend is signifying on the obviousness of black political progress and integration. Also, with some degree of self-consciousness, white privilege can be inverted with (if not nullified by) the black holes that blackness has historically been for American nationality. The question is whether the encounter with these holes—these absences of critique, in a sense, because they, as black holes, are not visible or legible—actually makes room for the production of a differently racialized subjectivity, or a sort of whiteness that does not depend on the always already status of blackness.

In the brief moment in which Reddy converses with her friend, there is a significant distinction between her relationship to this (black) woman and to her son, (malevolently) situated in the backseat. Both relationships make telling statements about Reddy's two political allegiances, feminism and the racialism of motherhood. However, unlike motherhood, feminism is not problematized as a category that requires racial analysis. It is for this reason that Reddy takes her friend's statements at face value. In the contemporary moment, Reddy and her friend discuss the unevenness of racial stratification, but Reddy's (black) friend does not evoke the disorientating effects of critique precisely by being poised to affirm the viability of how the politics of interracialism are being constructed currently. In a sense, Reddy's friend is a catalyst for the epiphany that she has about her bridge phobia, which is to say that she provides affirmation that blackness stabilizes the ground for doing ethical work on race rather than haunting it. The friend also alleviates the problem of confronting an oceanic, treacherous waterway—evocative of the Middle Passage—that signifies the way in which the past haunts the present. The fear that Reddy describes is ostensibly about the bridges, the fear that they have no real integrity. However, I would suggest that the actual alleviation—the epiphany—is that there are no ghosts to haunt the back of Reddy's project, or that a bridge is rethought of as a sturdy foundation because it need not connect the contemporary moment of Reddy's subjectivity to a past that might destabilize it. Reddy herself is bridgelike because the troubling implications of her (black) friend's claim that she "would never marry a white man"— something that Mildred Loving, the ghost of a past Jim Crow era, in fact did—is construed as ameliorating after *Loving*, even as it opens the possibility of how a presumably black woman is still somehow tangential or belatedly irrelevant to the legacy of *Loving*.

Reddy spends much of the memoir describing her son as a figure that evokes interventionist questions. For example, in the chapter entitled "Why Do White People Have Vaginas?" Reddy focuses on Sean's consistent ability to challenge conventional, identity-based taxonomies, particularly in a context where cultural and social standards in advertising, literature, and playground etiquette rigidly reinforce them. This ability is partially represented as a result of politicized parenting—as Reddy wonders, "How powerful would our parental influence be? We waited, and hoped"[20]—it seems to emerge predominantly from Sean's childlike innocence, or a lack of investment in ossified constructions of race, sex, and gender. Reddy writes of the three-year-old child: "Sean began to say things that suggested he understood both race and sex as categories—as interrelated categories, in fact—and that he was trying to figure out the principles that govern those categories." This curiosity leads to his "jumbl[ing] everything up,"[21] hence the assumption that whiteness is always tantamount to having female genitalia. In a sense, this prepolitical, innocent mistake implicitly reinforces a message that is analogous to the assumption that Reddy's (black) friend makes when she mentions Reddy's successful assimilation into black community.

After Reddy notes that this conversation results in her epiphany, there is no further mention of the (black) woman who unwittingly evokes it. This invisible woman simply serves the purpose of allowing Reddy to see herself as "a white woman married to a black man, a white mother of black

children," and that is all.[22] This (black) woman lacks the potential to perceive, interpret, and critique the manner in which race and gender are
interrelated categories. Instead, Reddy herself demonstrates how white
womanhood is the site of inextricably feminist and antiracist perspectives.
Further, Reddy's infant son's remark that "white people have vaginas"—
and that this remark should become the point of extended deliberation—
indicates that in an incipiently multiracial era, the intellectual contribution of intersectionality is child's play.

In the Absence of Adult Interracial Intimacy: Imagining Childhood

Motherhood displaces the issue of interracial intimacy—which includes
same-sex friendships—and sexuality with the now-central matters of reproduction and child rearing. From the beginning, it is clear that *Crossing
the Color Line* does not make interracial sexual intimacy its central concern. Rather, it takes up the often-neglected component of the Richard
and Mildred Loving's case in legal commentary: the responsibility toward
and status of interracial children. In this way, Reddy extends the question
of justice beyond the canonical place that *Loving* has occupied as the ruling that dismantled antimiscegenation law. It wants to consider the difference between the rights adults have to privacy from the state and the lack
of guidance available for (white parents) functioning within an interracial
family. Reddy writes, "In the absence of direct testimony from the inside,
we *know* almost nothing about interracial marriages,"[23] yet her own testimony does not shed much light here either, except to describe that black
and white partners are equally linked (although not through a process of
assimilation) until children appear. In this way, the importance of interracial marriage—the aspect that requires revelation, and that perpetuates
the political relevance of the institution—is the production of children.
Here Reddy specifies most clearly:

> With children, the dynamics of interracial marriages entirely alter.
> Before the first child's birth, both partners share equally in violat-
> ing social norms: each has married a taboo person and each faces
> cultural consequences. . . . When as children we [Reddy and her
> husband Doug] imagined our adult futures, those fantasies
> included partners of our own races when any partners at all

appeared. . . . When our fantasies included children, mine were
white and Doug's were black. And that is where our adult realities
diverged: Doug's children *are* black, but so are mine.[24]

One might imagine that the legal insistence for equal protection—an
affront to white supremacist ideology—has heightened implications for
African Americans who have been routinely denied constitutional rights.
Yet here Reddy is clear about the similarity of risk that each black and
white partner takes when "violating social norms." Because legalism cannot fully extend into the realities of normative transgression, black and
white adults willingly and equally bear "cultural consequences."

An interesting aspect of Reddy's description is how the legal marriage
between herself and her husband, Doug, actually produces a divergence,
rather than a convergence, of temporal reality through parenthood. Their
prior convergence is psychological, facilitated by the concept of miscegenation (not contemporary, cultural assimilation), and overtly located in
the 1960s. Reddy writes: "In the mid-1960s, when we were children, we
each thought that the world's racial problems might be solved if *everyone*
was the same blended race. Apart from this simple solution to prejudice—
to which both of our mothers said, 'Yes, that might work'—neither of
us seriously considered crossing the line as a personal possibility."[25] The
subsequent divergence, therefore, is clearly not the one produced by de
jure segregation and the criminalization of interracial marriage. Despite
Reddy's whiteness and her husband's blackness, both have had strikingly
similar fantasy lives during their upbringings when de facto segregation
would have in fact separated them. Because segregation and antimiscegenation are the conditions through which racial discrimination was codified, this description still begs the question of why similar fantasy lives of
the white Maureen and the black Doug did not lead to a romantic or social
meditation on crossing the line, rather than an immediate consideration
of children, racial reproduction, and biological interracialism.

Because both Maureen and Doug were themselves children, and therefore too immature to fully imagine what adult romantic partnership was,
they were presumably more capable of incipiently devising a standpoint
on interracialism about children, being children themselves. This perspective from childhood—that racial equality is linked to the blending
of children—occurs in Reddy's narrative a few years after the *Loving*
decision. Their mutual incipience prevents them of actually imagining

(heterosexual?) partners, but both are able somehow to imagine having children. The civil rights era's imaginative conjuring of blended children implies that even when romantic interracialism is not prominent—Reddy and her husband were themselves children—interracial children can still provide the rationale for potential antiracist practice. It is as if the bridge between Maureen and Doug is solidified through the not-yet-emergent blended race.

What I would like to emphasize here is a paradox that emerges after the outcome of constitutional justice, the legality of interracial marriage, and the recognition that blacks and whites have similar fantasy lives, similar interiorities, and indeed similar historical trajectories. Just as this equity appears taken for granted in 1994, a new racial discrepancy is produced by the legal status of marriage and legitimate children. After *Loving,* this condition is revealed once we go behind the veil that Reddy symbolizes: *Loving,* and legal redress generally, is not only insufficient when it comes to undoing the intransigence of racism, but it actually displaces racial disparities to the domain of the private, the family, and motherhood. Having children, in other words, is precisely the condition that illuminates an ongoing political movement toward racial unity that has to be achieved through the family and through the claiming of black children. When Reddy claims that "Doug's children *are* black"—a condition that, apparently, was always already his destiny—she is distinguishing this from her particular challenge to claim their black children. What this moment implies is that as a child, Reddy thought as a child. The decidedly idealized potential of a blended race is not in fact possible, even in the context of interracial intimacy. In this schema, Reddy is establishing two things at once: first, Doug's black children do indeed belong to her according to multiple modalities that include legalism, biology, and affect; and second, and paradoxically, she is declaring that claiming black children will present an ongoing challenge that is not shared by her husband.

This is where the postlegitimated racial disparity occurs. Despite the foundational qualities that make children one's own, these foundational elements still leave an unaccounted form of illegitimacy when it comes to a white mother of black children. Doug and his children—black subjects, and in particular a black male subject, because she focuses most closely on her firstborn, a boy—seem unscathed by this emergent, unaccountable form of illegitimacy. In other words, an interracial, parental legitimacy establishes an emergent form of interracial illegitimacy that primarily impacts Reddy. Prior legal redress that centralized the social condition of blacks is distinguished from the present, in which the particular challenges white mothers have to claim their birthright to motherhood is at the center. In this way, Reddy makes a clear distinction between the secondary politics of her interracial marriage and the primary matter of becoming the mother of black/multiracial children who seem to be black.

Just to clarify: this is the opposite of what is foregrounded and backgrounded in the *Loving* decision. Mildred Loving is a seminal figure of the multiracial movement, yet she is virtually unaccounted for in contemporary discourses of multiracialism as a black mother of black/multiracial children. Instead, the *Loving* case is interpreted as central to the legitimizing of marriage that subsequently legitimates the interracial family. Reddy's (black, female) friend foregrounds the question of interracial marriage, although she is represented as an ameliorating presence who signals Reddy's social proximity to blackness without producing a treacherously critical distance between black and white subjectivities. In other words, the friend serves as the bridge figure enabling Reddy to cross over various historical gaps, voids, and absences (that is, Mildred Loving) to arrive at a white feminist, antiracist ethics. Here we have, finally, the manner in which Reddy and her black husband are disparately related to the condition of parenting black/multiracial children: Doug, unlike Reddy, represents an unexamined coherence between black identities of the past and present, current interracialism notwithstanding. Because blackness suggests a necessary absence, amelioration, or uncritical historical continuity, it is up to Reddy to describe a project through a metaphorical bridge—which, unwittingly, is her (black, female) friend—between older, black-centered racial politics, and the presence of mixedness as a racial formation that naturally ties racialized bodies with the whiteness of motherhood. In a sense, she discusses discrimination against interracial kinship as analogous to pre–civil rights–era racial segregation. White supremacy is still the problem in this new form of discrimination, but now the recourse is making white motherhood instrumental in the public or political exposure of the multiracial family's double consciousness.

It might be useful to note that Reddy is committed to joining an antiracist agenda with a feminist one. This raises the question of how a gendered politics relates to matters of antimiscegenation and interracialism, as well as the seemingly waning relevance of legal redress. As Reddy notes in the epigraph to this chapter, *Crossing the Color Line* "is not *about* black people," but at the same time, it is about "mothering black children." Is this to indicate something about the manner in which, up until now, motherhood had been left out of the patriarchal power/knowledge of racialized kinship? Notice that in Reddy's account of the "simple solution" that she and Doug devised to racial discrimination—presumably as children—black and white mothers provide affirmation. In a sense, the consensus between Doug's black mother and Reddy's white mother on the potential of crossing the color line through miscegenation possibly reveals a gendered commentary on the inefficacy of granting the family its coherence through racial separatism. However, although Reddy is foregrounding the similarities of black and white motherhood, one cannot help but speculate about the differences between these subject positions. If black motherhood cannot claim the same strategic illegitimacy that white motherhood can in this moment, then what distinguishes the previous moment of legal victory from the current moment of multiracial politics for black women?

In Reddy's final chapter, entitled "Mothers, Daughters, Sisters, Comrades," she meditates on the often troubled relation between black and white women. In a sense, this brings the memoir full circle. I have described an early scene in which Reddy (mis)reads her presumably black female friend's easy acceptance of her assimilation, but by the end, Reddy is openly aware of the skepticism black women have of her and of white women in general. She acknowledges the troubled history between black and white women over feminist politics but then gingerly refers to her own exceptional experience on this front. In her account:

> I have a number of close black women friends, as well as a very large circle of black women colleagues and acquaintances with whom I work on various political issues, ranging from electoral politics to school curricula.
>
> One common thread in these relationships is that all began with some point of mutual interest and slowly grew from there, in the case of friendships, or remained focused on one issue or cluster of issues, in the case of political alliances. That point of mutual interest has often been black children, a theme that I see repeated frequently in my life and in black women's imaginative literature.[26]

This is the chapter in which Reddy writes most overtly as a literary critic of African American literature, which she does by profession. Just as her actual social relationships are structured around political labor, which is an indicator of her commitment to an interracial feminist community, Reddy extends interracial feminist dialogue to her engagement with three particular texts written by black women: Alice Walker's *Meridian,* Sherley Anne Williams's *Dessa Rose,* and Toni Morrison's *Beloved.* All of these novels help Reddy explicate the manner in which white and black feminist collaboration has been politicized in the black feminist imagination.

I submit that Reddy not only conceptualizes a strategy for recapturing an opportunity missed by black and white feminists to develop a mutually beneficial analysis of the inextricability of gender, race, and class, but she also reveals the manner in which a subject mourns the loss of such an opportunity. The loss of such an opportunity seemed so profound by 1994 that the most viable approach to regaining social, black/white feminist reciprocity—indeed, to confronting an interracial feminist agenda as troubled terrain—was through the one mutual interest in the black child. This single touchstone eclipses the other forms of social and political engagement that Reddy lists at the start of the passage cited above. Although Reddy is attempting in this final chapter to expand the range of feminist social relationships and collaboration that had been constricted to the nuclear family since the 1960s, it seems that even this attempt at expansion is relegated to the time of childhood development. Such futurity is not necessarily implied in the broader projects simply identified here as "political issues, electoral politics, and school curricula"; but then again, in Reddy's account, all of these projects are most significant for the way in which they lead to the common ground upon which black and white women can move forward.

In this way, Reddy's vision is not unlike the outcome of the film discussed in the previous chapter, *Losing Isaiah,* in which interracial female engagement was made possible only by comothering a black child. The novels that Reddy focuses on all offer representations of black and white women sharing the labor of caring for black children, and this labor is seemingly the only potential for bridging the gulf between black and white women who failed to be sisters, might possibly be comrades, and perhaps can achieve this status as mothers. As Reddy notes, "Family models are problematic in all kinds of ways, but the one role in the family through which women might form enduring cross-racial alliances is the role of mother. Mothers are committed to preservation and to the future in ways that sisters are not, or at least do not have to be. Hence, the 'othermother' model may be especially useful."²⁷ This interpretation of familial time-lines—sisterhood does not lead to futurity—leads to the unspoken pre-condition of this moment. If feminists of an earlier generation understood their kinship in terms of sisterhood or as solidarity between women who shared and exchanged experiences and ideas within social networks such as the consciousness-raising groups that emerged during the 1960s and 1970s, then Reddy is suggesting that such intimacy was unsustainable. This implicit grief over the social ground underfoot "splintering to pieces" likely informs Reddy's most prominent strategy for reestablishing engage-ment, which is with the textual presence of black women.

As Reddy describes the overall importance of the novels she interprets, othermothering is significant. She writes, "The mothering that goes on in *Meridian, Dessa Rose,* and *Beloved* . . . offers white women a model of motherhood rooted in African-American experience, not privatized but cooperative and collective."²⁸ In her reading of *Beloved* in particular, Reddy focuses on the collaboration between Amy Denver, a white inden-tured servant in antebellum Kentucky, and Sethe, a black runaway slave who is about to give birth while traveling toward the free state of Ohio. Despite their differences, Amy helps Sethe deliver her daughter. Although Amy is seemingly dismissive of Sethe's subjectivity and thereby unable to understand the commonalities between her and Sethe, as Reddy explains, "Sethe, however, realizes that they are both runaways, 'two throw-away people, two lawless outlaws.' Naming her child 'Denver' is Sethe's acknow-ledgement of a link with the 'whitegirl,' as Morrison renders the descrip-tion throughout *Beloved*."²⁹ The politicized outcome of this representation is that the mutual goal of preserving a black child's life is what enables the differently raced women to work together, hence uniting them. Fur-ther, Morrison offers an example of a white woman who "nurses the black woman," because Sethe is close to death at the time of her encounter with Amy. However, this last observation—the care given to a black adult—is eclipsed by the takeaway contribution of all of the novels Reddy reads, which is that "in all three novels the only significantly positive connections between black and white women come about because of black children."³⁰ By the end of this final chapter, and hence the end of the memoir, Reddy acknowledges that mothering is most politically meaningful when it "pro-vides the opportunity first to acknowledge socially enforced weakness, and then to develop and capitalize upon mutual strengths."³¹ Reddy thus raises key questions derived from her vision of an interracial feminism based on collaborative mothering: "If we can be comrades only if we first are mothers, does supporting an interracial feminism require an implicit endorsement of precisely those attitudes that oppress all women? Does it also exclude women who are not mothers? And does it recapitulate white women's historic relation to objectified black maternal figures of fantasy?"[32]

These questions are essential, and while they are offered here primarily as conjectural, Reddy's bottom line is that motherhood is a starting point for an interracial feminism that is built on the foundation of love. For white women, mothering and loving their black/multiracial children builds a coalitional bridge between white communities and black communities. As she explains, "Loving blackness is about refusing to put whiteness at the center of everything, resisting white supremacist views of blackness, seeing the value of blackness. . . . Feminists should be in the vanguard of this bridge building [across the color line]."[33] Loving her black/multiracial children provides a stable ethics for an antiracist feminism, but what of the historical context that Reddy foregrounds in her moment of conjure? To go further, if children are signs of an interracial feminist future that has been historically denied, or as the bridges upon which black and white women move toward an antiracist horizon, then what do we make of the much earlier implication that Reddy's son bears a strange proximity to a "malevolent ghost"? Perhaps a question that once signaled a racist past of antimiscegenation is strangely appropriate here: but what about the children? This question that evokes both a racist past and the potential of an antiracist future is meant to emphasize how children do not simply signal the bridging of temporal moments, but rather reproduce the instability of a the political moment after *Loving*.

Interlude: A Precondition to Bridges

At this point, I would like to construct my own bridge between Reddy's memoir, which offers a particular ethics of motherhood, and Lazarre's memoir, which refuses a separation between her maternal identity and the identities of her children. This bridge will be my brief reading of *Beloved*, which problematizes both an ethics of maternal affect and a symbiosis between mothers and their children. Previously I suggested that *Beloved* is a pre-text to *Crossing the Color Line* that produces an ethical paradigm of cross-racial collaboration. Reddy supports the potential of Morrison's paradigm for multiracial politics over the memoir's ostensible privileging of mother authority when she speculates about the "malevolent ghost" that seems either to be in strikingly close proximity to her flesh-and-blood multiracial son, or to represent her son. It is therefore fitting that the section on *Crossing the Color Line*—and indeed the memoir itself—closes with Reddy's interpretation of *Beloved*. Whereas Reddy takes the text as an opportunity to explore the potential of a viable, interracial feminist project, I want to focus on what the text reveals about the lines of force between mother and child. Like the ghostly child that returns with malevolent vengeance in Morrison's *Beloved* and confronts her mother with the ethical groundlessness that was the very fabric of a mother's love, Reddy is unwittingly introducing doubt about the extent to which motherhood is naturally endowed with stable political agency.

In Morrison's novel, Sethe, once a runaway slave, has no morally stable choice when it comes to the fate of her daughter: either she has her child taken back into slavery in Kentucky, or she murders her own child to prevent this. The right decision is not only impossible to discern, but the murkiness of ethical mother work is implicated, if not consciously explored, in Reddy's suggestion that risk and malevolence is a shared possibility between the mother in the driver's seat and the child who lacks control. This would mean that this is one of the many places where crossing the line is fraught: the line between the authoritative mother and the infantilized child can be complicated by imagining different lines of force, or power relations, between the two. The important political question is not only how to mother "black children in a society that does not value . . . black children." There is also the question of how the child, as a separate subject with needs that may not only depart from those of the mother but in fact run counter to them, can become an actual driving force of multiracial discourse. Like Morrison's ghostly child who returns to her mother with an insatiable love and desire for her, but also with undeniable malevolence, the ghost that haunts Reddy is the emergence of a political question that has yet to be considered outside the realm of maternal power: what does the multiracial child want?

To further consider *Beloved* as a pre-text that represents the critical production of knowledge as opposed to the reproduction of racialist assumptions, in addition to the way in which the value of black children has been systemically denied and recuperated by black mothers historically, one might remember two significant moments. The first is when

Denver, Sethe's adolescent daughter with whom she lives several years after Emancipation in 1873, and Beloved, the embodiment of a ghostly daughter who returns from the dead, discuss what they know about their mother, and in so doing, they also unearth the complication between knowing and desire. I will quote at length in order to explore how this trend unfolds here. Denver asks:

> "Tell me, how did you get here?"
>   "I wait; then I got on the bridge. . . . It was a long time."
>   "All this time you were on a bridge?"
>   "No. After. When I got out."
>   "What did you come back for?"
>   Beloved smiled. "To see her face."
>   "Ma'am's? Sethe?"
>   "Yes, Sethe."
>   Denver felt a little hurt, slighted that she was not the main reason for Beloved's return. . . .
>   Denver was seeing it now and feeling it—through Beloved. Feeling how it must have felt to her mother. . . . And the more fine points she made, the more detail she provided, the more Beloved liked it. So she anticipated the questions by giving blood to the scraps her mother and her grandmother had told her—and a heartbeat. The monologue became, in fact, a duet as they lay down together. . . . Denver spoke, Beloved listened, and the two did the best they could to create what really happened, how it really was, something only Sethe knew because she alone had the mind for it and the time afterward to shape it.[34]

First, the exchange between Denver and Beloved evokes the possibility that Beloved is not simply the incarnation of Sethe's dead daughter, but also the return of multitudes who did not survive the Middle Passage. In the conversation above, Denver asks Beloved to describe what it was like "over there," and Beloved responds that it was "Hot. Nothing to breathe down there and no room to move in," which evokes the crowded and stifling conditions in which Africans were transported to the New World on cargo ships.[35] In this way, reference to being on a bridge may signal the manner in which this embodiment was once in fact on a slave ship in another time, and through a passageway is conjured into the world of postbellum Ohio. It would be a transportation from the spirit world into the world of the living.

In Morrison's response to this aspect of the novel, she claims that Beloved is also "another kind of dead which is not spiritual but flesh, which is, as survivor from the true, factual slave ship. She speaks her own language, a traumatized language, of her own experience, which blends beautifully in her questions and answers, her preoccupations, with the desires of Denver and Sethe. . . . The gap between Africa and Afro-America and the gap between the living and the dead and the gap between the past and the present does not exist."[36] This lack of distance in the various manifestations Morrison lists, along with the agency Beloved is granted in the novel to tell her own story while producing a mode of reciprocity—"questions and answers," shared desire for the missing beloved—sets up a particular ethical paradigm. Although Morrison emphasizes a variety of ways in which the "the gap" between subjects "does not exist," the paradigm here does not assume that an entanglement of past and present subjectivities is predicated on familiarity, which then produces knowledge and authority. The gap that does not exist, in other words, is not like a relationship that produces motherhood as a naturalized, driving force in shaping the political wants and welfare of their children. Rather, Morrison is referring to symbiosis between subjects that requires a responsibility to recognize what is unknown. Before one can account for the millions of subjects lost in the Atlantic slave trade, the subjectivities of Africans who survived and those who did not, one has to be accounted for, to become transformed, by this unfamiliar territory. Beloved, as spirit and flesh, signals the potential of symbiotic mystery, rather than an ethics of affect; the bridge is not shaky here, but neither is it to be taken for granted.

The child who this bridge implicates is a direct participant in its recognition. Denver and Beloved attempt to reshape what Sethe did and thought, providing an opportunity to reconstruct her motives and experience. This collaboration between children allows for an undercutting of the various ideologies about motherhood as either a moral or destructive role. If Beloved is the only one who has the authority to decide whether what Sethe did was right or wrong, then Sethe is in no position to develop an ethics that is built on the foundations of maternity. Reddy claims that love is a basis of empathy but not of a shared identity; she is clear that the refusal of white privilege does not make a white subject black. Yet she does not interrogate the essence of love as a basis for political analysis. Indeed, in this alternative reading of *Beloved,* love is not stable as an ethical ground. The spatial bridge upon which Beloved awaits for temporal beginning/continuity—which is both a presence in the New World and a return to an originating maternal presence—indicates that Sethe is a placeholder for a new knowledge project of which she is not the primary agent. Beloved does signal the time of mourning as she waits, and that version of time is malleable, because all we know is that "it was a long time." Sethe is desired, but as an unambiguous figure of what one lacks. To see her face is not necessarily to desire a normative relation between motherhood and childhood. Rather, it indicates a desire for either a foreclosed or not-yet version of human connection that has yet to be developed.

While Beloved and Denver collaborate to imagine what the connective tissue is between themselves, and between Sethe and themselves, Reddy's distinction between the uses of sisterhood and motherhood breaks down. Here sisterhood and motherhood are not oppositional; nor are they positioned in a generational grammar. It is not as if sisterhood is noncommittal with respect to futurity while motherhood is (over)committed. Rather, if Denver wishes to be the object of Beloved's desire, if Beloved participates in the duet of reconstructing the past, and if, ultimately, this collaboration undercuts the individuated initiative of narrating history, then futurity is about providing life to the past. It is about "giving blood to the scraps her mother and her grandmother had told [Denver]—and a heartbeat." In this way, temporality is about participants—sisters, strangers, and yes, mothers—fortifying a historiography that does not privilege any particular subject position and that does not take the hierarchies between familial subjects for granted or develop a timeline that takes generational progression as its natural logic. Sethe's overwhelming love for her Beloved daughter leads to the murder she commits: it is a murder done out of love. Sethe's love for Denver leads to the protective omissions in the long story of her engendering. This complication of maternal obligation leads to an alternative version of a racial ethics that would have to grapple with the manner in which love is operative both in the rationale for familial cohesion and in its splintering apart. Responses that foreclose the recognition of mourning for the losses of a past—whether it be for an interracial feminist movement, or for the incomparable destruction of human connection—do not require a substitution of affect (love), but a sustained deliberation on what is being foreclosed, and why.

Barriers versus Bridges: *Beyond the Whiteness of Whiteness*

When Jane Lazarre asks, "What is this whiteness that threatens to separate me from my own child?," she is signaling a very different approach to the visceral void left in the wake of legal redress and interracial feminist collaboration than that offered by Reddy or Morrison. Reddy attempts to revitalize an antiracist project that takes a feminist analytic as its basis, but in the process, she becomes mired in the ambivalence of how to bridge the present and future in the wake of vanishing historical conditions. Ultimately, a mutual interracial focus of black/multiracial children does not unequivocally lead to a future in which black and white women—and mothers specifically—revitalize social engagement that undercuts the privatization of the nuclear family. Instead, the conditions of motherhood, and the subjectivities of children, evoke a nonlinear temporality in which racial inequity and the denial of adult gratification perpetually haunt a new antiracist politics of affect. In contrast, *Beyond the Whiteness of Whiteness* attempts to figure the void left in the wake of a clear antiracist feminist movement as if it should be easily filled with the natural right a mother has to love her own children, despite a whiteness unshared by her black/multiracial sons. An evocation of the history of racial formation in the United States, and particularly the history of African Americans, is seemingly sufficient to suture the differences between her black family, her own Euro-Jewish heritage, and her multiracial children.

According to Lazarre's text, if there is a shaky ground upon which to build an antiracist project, it is due to a lack of broad recognition of the labor of love that occurs within interracial families and through interracial connections. Mother work is the privileged form of labor that does not simply bridge black and white women through a shared focus of children. Rather, maternity within multiracial families appears to have the capacity to transform the neutrality of whiteness into a racialization that is akin to multiracialism. Whereas Reddy's exploration of white maternity was inextricably linked to a concern for the future of feminist collaboration, Lazarre's exploration has a divergently gendered trajectory. When Lazarre questions what whiteness is and how it can possibly separate her from her differently raced child, or how race interferes with affect, she is also asking how whiteness can potentially separate her from her son.

This inquiry differs from the mode of memoir produced in Reddy's text, even as both texts signal an implicit problem with memoir as a political form. Both Lazarre and Reddy are indicating that political multiracialism has the potential to conceptualize the private experiences of motherhood and family as metonymic for a larger social sphere. Lazarre's prologue begins with a description of how memoir requires the individual to be contextualized socially and historically. As part of her life in academia, she "focus[es] on the rich tradition of African American autobiography as a reading curriculum."[37] Her professional specialization in African American literature and culture offers one approach to historicizing her own familial experience. As she explains her philosophy on "writing the self," Lazarre explains: "I believe that identity and the search for consciousness are profoundly linked to cultural meanings and the historical moment in which we live."[38] This is how Lazarre understands her first memoir, *The Mother Knot,* in which she explores "the experience of motherhood and the many ways in which that experience reveals, sustains, and constantly recreates my sense of connection to and responsibility toward a wider world."[39] However, this attempt returns us to one of the initial questions of this chapter: how, precisely, does one make the crossover from the legal unfettering of affective (heterosexual) relations irrespective of racial differences, to actually producing a trend of interracial intimacy, socially, outside of the privatized family? After *Loving* and *Palmore,* how, precisely, does one cross over from feeling maternal affect for children, irrespective of racial differences, to producing an antipatriarchal, antiracist politics outside of the privatized family?

For both Reddy and Lazarre, it seems that history—the void of what was, a sense of what has vanished—is the key to fortifying a public that has been enervated by the 1990s. There is a tacit acknowledgment in each memoir that fortifying public space is somehow the key to futurity. However, because both memoirs choose the idioms of motherhood and childhood to explore approaches toward producing new knowledge and analyses about race, social welfare, conditions of intimacy, and care, they become fixed within the scope of private life. In a sense, one potential problem with the memoir as a political form is the manner in which it relegates large sociopolitical concepts and phenomenon to individuated experience. As a result, Reddy cannot openly tangle with questions about which historical forms—which moments, which movements—haunt her meditation about interracial family. Lazarre, on the other hand, seems to lack even a visceral sense of being haunted, and this is likely because her maternal narrative attempts to explain the factual plight of black manhood, which was a salient concern of the 1990s.

The task of raising black/multiracial sons heightens Lazarre's sense of the social risks that exist for black men, and this heightened racialized–gendered awareness is conflated with what would otherwise be the naturalized task of mother work. This conflation is precisely why Lazarre finds the idea of a barrier—whiteness—that threatens to separate Lazarre from her children such an offense. Even a metaphoric bridge would fail here. For Lazarre, the process of fostering children who are differently determined in terms of gender and race entails a sharing of identity that makes the conceptualization of distance—temporally or spatially—difficult. In the first chapter's opening anecdote, Lazarre describes her visit to an exhibit entitled "Before Freedom Came," which includes photographs and artifacts that document the conditions of black enslavement. As she assesses her experience with this display of the national past of black dehumanization, she describes a realization that comes as a combination of seeing the "forgotten" vestiges of history and from living within a "Black" family: the "change" of perception that comes with the loss of false consciousness occurs slowly, as a result of absorbing small bits of "truth" at a time. So as one slowly recovers "small pieces of knowledge instantly 'forgotten,'" repeatedly and more fully each time, there is an accumulation of a shifted perception that one barely perceives.

As Lazarre begins to describe how the exhibit of American slavery had affected her, she conflates her encounter of historical artifacts with the experience of becoming a "member of a Black American family" twenty years before, a seminal moment marked by her first pregnancy: "Soon after I married Douglas and became a member of a Black American family, I became pregnant and, in the innocent, exultant power of the first day of a first and wanted pregnancy, I realized that I—my body and self—was no longer exactly white. . . . During the next twenty years I would undergo a transformation of consciousness as defining as any I have ever known."[40] This transformation facilitates her capacity to profoundly comprehend the significance of what she views at the exhibit: "Confronted with a sequence of rooms which recorded in stark, powerful visual images the story of American slavery, the *pattern* of my experience came into sharp and explicit focus. I saw my country, its history, and therefore myself differently, a difference that in key ways would change the way I saw everything and therefore the way I lived."[41]

The metaphor of transformation exploits a conception of racial embodiment that is repeated in various ways throughout Lazarre's memoir. While the ostensible project of explaining how historical memory can be literally cultivated in the body, and how (heteronormative) bodily attachments might allude to an unspoken risk that is involved with interracial intimacy, it appears to have the more overt purpose of inverting the manner in which history gains social relevance. While Lazarre describes viewing the exhibit as part of a group of other college instructors from across the country, the manner in which the egregiousness of nation building hits home is through the accumulated experience of gestating and birthing a black child, and through her place within a decidedly black family. Memory and its accumulated effects are individuated conditions that work outward and seem to have less force when construed as social phenomena that influence collective consciousness. Lazarre does allude to collectives— the black Americans of whom she has become a part, the Jewish Americans who are also her kin—but her intellectual and emotional investment in collectivity is most clearly derived from the immediacy of identification.

At the exhibit, Lazarre views a portrait of a man who is identified as a former slave of the Confederate general Robert E. Lee. The process of recognition begins with an understanding that she "cannot *know* this 'slave of Robert E. Lee' nor certainly claim his experience which is so different from [Lazarre's] own."[42] However, this recognition of historical distance becomes surmountable with a brief explanation that "autobiographical writing"—in the form of memoir, for instance—necessarily connects the writing subject's experience with others across time and space, so that she can begin to "imagine" how the formerly enslaved subject of the portrait "suffered." The next leap of identification entails a separate moment in which Lazarre hears a radio segment on General Lee. The segment emphasizes Lee's historical importance and underplays his role as a slave owner and proponent of slavery. This leads Lazarre to a brief meditation on how national historiography is naturalized, a speculative analogy between the valorization of German Nazi generals and American Confederate generals, and then "outrage" over the suppression of "the more important truth." Lazarre concludes this section of the memoir this way: "Listening to the profile on the news, for a moment I became my sons, Black Americans listening to the story of an American hero, Robert E. Lee."[43]

If what *Beloved* explores is the manner in which "the gap between Africa and Afro-America and the gap between the living and the dead and the gap between the past and the present does not exist," then we are

invited to think in terms of a multiplicity of racial timelines and subjectivities that continually tangle with each other. In Lazarre's account, the syn-
chronicity of events, the modes of violence, and the desired outcome to
combine her own subjectivity with those of her sons reveals the manner in
which she chooses not to negotiate the multiplicity of temporal times produced after civil rights, and indeed through a discourse that makes the
racialization of the family central. If Lazarre cannot retrieve a sense of linearity in which her own incipient understanding about racial difference or
gender equality leads to the promised future that arises after the civil rights
and women's movements have run their respective courses, then she
attempts this retrieval through her sons. Unlike in *Crossing the Color Line,*
Lazarre does not seem troubled by a "malevolent ghost" that might produce
a fragmentary perspective of the linear road ahead traveled by a mother
and her sons. Why does Lazarre choose not to identity with "Black Americans" generally, those who presumably know very well "the more important truth" of historical racial violence? Why must her sons be the proxy for
such a collective understanding? If Lazarre became her sons momentarily,
then this is all the more poignant since her sense of separation is so deeply
felt. Although her sons share her secular Jewishness, Lazarre is aware of
how their blackness overdetermines their social encounters with Jews and
others: "Black and Jewish, raised in a nonreligious home, coming of age as
young Black men at a time when their very lives are in danger from several
directions simply because they are young Black men, they had learned . . .
that most white Jews saw them as 'different' . . . always as Black."[44]
    Lazarre understands black masculinity as a condition mired in danger.
She does not choose this moment to deliberate on how the relative class
privilege of her black sons, parental protection, social recognition, resi-
dential location—in a word, various circumstantial elements that render
forms of danger contingent—are operative. They are black like other black
men, and perhaps they are black like Robert E. Lee's former slave was.
Endangered, black masculinity is always already recognizable to itself and
others. As Lazarre explains of her sons, "By the time they were in their
teens, they had come to know themselves as Black men, an identification
that seemed not only right to me but sane."[45] The sanity of synchronic-
ity allows Lazarre to understand her own process of transformation—of
consciousness, of becoming her sons—as the individuated and remarkable process of temporal movement. Her sons are black Americans. But
"meanwhile, negotiating the complex maternal roads that paralleled their

growth into manhood, overstepping boundaries between self and others as mothers so often do . . . I would come to see myself as an 'interracial' person in a family of Black Americans."[46]

Even when a transformation of awareness that Lazarre's sons have undergone is described, the emphasis is placed on the impact this process has on Lazarre. She describes a moment when one of her college-age sons explains that although he has a white Jewish mother, he identifies as black and not biracial. She accepts his declaration, but she describes her simultaneous sense of "exile":

> Perhaps even more than most mothers, I have identified with my children. Like other writers of my generation, I have used the experience of motherhood to try to comprehend the essential human conflict between devotion to others and obligations to the self, the lifelong tension between the need for clear boundaries and boundless intimacy. . . . What is this whiteness that threatens to separate me from my own child?[47]

The manner in which white motherhood has been mobilized around an emergent multiracial politics—through a "transformation of consciousness" for white women of black children—suggests that this agency is predicated on naturalized qualities of maternal affect and, less explicitly, white privilege. While both are posited as sites of political transformation, maternity, unlike the ostensibly disavowed sign of whiteness, is not offered as a ground for epistemological uncertainty. In the contemporary moment, the white female body is transformed into something no longer exactly white when it produces black children. However, by having black/multiracial children, white mothers can deliberate on their embodiment of whiteness, their familial proximity to blackness, and on their children's fraught racial identities. However, what might be actually transformative here is the manner in which Lazarre unwittingly describes an impasse fairly uncommon in the broad archive of multiracial narratives. She is describing the impossibility of configuring a melded identity with her children, a melding that is implicitly naturalized in mother relations. Although she identifies whiteness as that offending category that seems to prevent a naturalized and simultaneously politicized intimacy, I wonder whether whiteness here acts as a proxy for motherhood. What if, anti-intuitively perhaps, motherhood itself, in its capacity to advocate for the multiracial child and to devise a multiracial political agenda, was the threatening disjunctive agent between mother and child, two social subjects with divergent interests? What sort of relational schemes would need to be taken up in the wake of this?

In Lazarre's case, we get an intensified version of identification with blackness and with her sons, Adam and Khary, in particular. Even as she describes a sense of anxiety that is akin to Reddy's insofar as it is provoked by a lack of certainty over white maternal affect as the new vehicle for an antiracist project after civil rights, her response is to conceptualize a time-line that would foreclose a multiplicity of temporalities and subject positions. Even as she describes the threat of whiteness in haunting terms— "encircling me in some irresistible fog"—the historicity of racial formation is quickly resolved at the start of the next section: "A close friend, a Black man who grew up in North Carolina with [her husband] Douglas, has taken a special interest in Khary, and tells him one day: Your mother isn't really white. She's a Black person in disguise."[48] Although Lazarre refutes the comment about her hidden blackness, this close friend seems to serve the same function as Reddy's friend, which is to provide validation by a black subject of the memoirist's authentic relation to black people and black community. As it happens, these black subjects get it wrong; Lazarre is comforted by the validation, but she also knew "its message is false." She, like Reddy, rejects the ease with which they both seem to traverse the color line or the barrier of whiteness. However, both women desire to be recognized as the embodiment of an aberrant version of whiteness, and for both, it is motherhood that renders whiteness racially aberrant. In a sense, it is as if the desire at this historical moment is for recognition of the manner in which motherhood—rather than other categories of collaboration, such as sisterhood or feminism—is the most auspicious political category for reconciling interracial activist communities that formed at the incipience of the civil rights movement.

Whiteness, as historically manifested, including within the women's movements of the 1960s and 1970s, has served the functions of separating individuals from one another, producing inequities, and provoking violence. In Crossing the Color Line and Beyond the Whiteness of White-ness, motherhood ostensibly has no such history. Motherhood would not threaten to separate Lazarre from her own children. However, the insistence that we focus on a category that has been subjected to heightened degrees of contemplation but lesser degrees of theorization in these mem-oirs—motherhood—only stresses the question that these memoirs attempt to answer: why should motherhood be the central condition of an anti-racist project after the era of civil rights? Ultimately, both of these memoirs unwittingly posit motherhood as a starting place. According to Reddy's bottom line, maternity is a means to rebuilding the broken coalition between black and white women, and between racial communities in general. Lazarre, on the other hand, is decidedly less interested in the potential of a neofeminist community, the mutual interest of black/multiracial children notwithstanding.

At the end of her memoir, when she considers the manner in which autobiographical writing can textually construct only one version of personhood, Lazarre is comforted by textual collaboration. If this textual collaboration is not with the likes of Toni Morrison, Alice Walker, or Sherley Anne Williams, it does address Lazarre's desire "to make a bridge between solitude and the world."[49] Her son Adam has written a screenplay "about a young Black man falling in love with a Jewish woman," and her other son, Khary, has written a novel about "a young Black man coming of age in New York City, crossing and recrossing the borders between the security of home and the violent streets of the city."[50] While it is striking that narratives her sons write implicate Lazarre in a few ways—as the Jewish woman who had become a young black man's lover, as a mother who is highly concerned about what happens to her black sons once they leave the security of home—what interests me is open recognition that the black male voices of her family life fortify her expression of personhood. She and her sons "trad[e] manuscripts" while her husband does the work of "posing questions, [and] offering critique," and this engagement with "the absolute certainty of voices different from [her] own" provides Lazarre with confidence to publicly assert her own truth.[51] Is this confidence one develops around the promise of personhood just part of inhabiting a functional family? Or is there a tacit shift that occurs somewhere between Reddy's maternal politics and Lazarre's in how to approach gender analysis? By the late 1990s, when Lazarre's memoir is published, the historicity of gender politics continued to inhabit racial discourses. However, if white women were still taking the lead in terms of multiracialism politics, mourning for an interracial feminism that might have subtly given way to a decidedly different mode of remembrance. In the next chapter, I will take a look at multiracialism's disappearing acts: the textual return of racial passing, the resounding silences of political correctness, and overall, the paradox of seeing by virtue of concealment—the paradox of color-blindness.

CHAPTER 4 ·

Ambivalent Outcomes

Blackness and the Return of Racial Passing

These memoirs are part of the same broad cultural and academic movement that has produced so much recent interest in whites and whiteness; they also share a marked resonances with the most quixotic branch of that field, the group of writers aligned with the journal Race Traitor, *who agitate for the "abolition" of whiteness.*

—France Winddance Twine, "Review"

In representing the transgression of the categories through which subjects are socially compelled to "see" themselves, passing narratives render visible the contradictions of race as a locus of identification, even in cases when the subject's self-recognition conforms to that identity that is ascribed by racial discourse.

—Gayle Wald, *Crossing the Line*

THE PREVIOUS CHAPTER focused on the manner in which white motherhood had been mobilized through an emergent multiracial politics of the 1990s. In general, this mobilization occurred through several strategies: as mentioned earlier in this book, one was advocacy, as Project RACE cofounder Susan Graham suggested was necessary for the self-esteem and recognition of multiracial children. Another strategy was a thoroughgoing consideration about how motherhood itself facilitated a transformation of consciousness for white women of black/multiracial children, such as the one Jane Lazarre undergoes. The previous chapter focused extensively on this second strategy. Both strategies suggest that the agency of white motherhood is predicated on the condition of maternal affect and, less explicitly, white privilege. Motherhood and whiteness are posited as sites of political transformation. However, unlike the ostensibly

· 121 ·

disavowed sign of whiteness, maternity is not offered as a category marked by an insidious history of inequity. Whiteness is a formation one can disavow without accounting for the conditions of white racial formation that leads to enduring privileges of white femininity. Neither Reddy nor Lazarre fully account for the larger social and political context in which they write: white women were at the forefront of multiracial activism. Both Reddy and Lazarre fully recognize the relative privilege of whiteness, but they do not account for how this privilege is constructed in conjunction with their class and gender identities. Whiteness as a category can be disavowed once it is disarticulated from class and gender analyses. Yet the very impulse to disarticulate these three categories is not accounted for as an effect of white privilege.

In a short book review of the new literary genre that appeared during the 1990s, France Winddance Twine refers specifically to Reddy's *Crossing the Color Line* and Lazarre's *Beyond the Whiteness of Whiteness,* both of which I have discussed in the previous chapter.[1] Twine's framing of these narratives within a politics of those white writers attempting to disassociate from whiteness, a sign of historical domination, in order to dismantle racial privilege and hierarchy suggests collusion between antiwhiteness and multiracialism. During the 1990s, the simultaneous rise of whiteness studies and multiracial cultural politics implied that both discourses shared in part a strategy for addressing racialized inequities through an extended scrutiny of the contingencies of whiteness. Whiteness is a constructed form of privilege that can either be dismantled or extended to include multiracial kinship. Potentially, both strategies would alter how whiteness appears in racial discourse: it would become yet another version of nonnormative, historically constructed identity rather than a sign of racially neutral personhood.

In a sense, the instrumentalization of motherhood to produce analyses about the vicissitudes of whiteness is an effect of how an ostensibly gendered discourse came to foreground a racial one. Motherhood became useful for the articulation of two disparate impulses that together mark a rhetorical tendency used to address the racial future of the United States. The first impulse is conceptualized as affect, a natural, color-blind bond of kinship that can potentially be extended into a schema for civic belonging, as well as a schema for forgetting white anxieties of the nineteenth and twentieth centuries over making contact with and being in close proximity to the reproduction of black bodies.[2] The second impulse is the manner in which white maternal advocacy became a prominent discourse that yoked together the authority of maternity and race consciousness—two concepts that can potentially reinvigorate whiteness in a late twentieth-century context where white masculinity endured its own pop-cultural narrative of embattlement. One might think here of a ubiquitous cultural type during the 1990s: the angry white man. David Wellman describes this construction as part of a neo–minstrel show, staged to reaffirm white heterosexual American masculinities: "Quota queens, unqualified beneficiaries of preferential treatment, reverse discrimination victims, and angry white men" became the key players, and "rather than speaking in dialect, [angry white men] talk the language of 'fairness,' 'color-blindness,' and 'meritocracy.'"[3] In this context, the prominence of affective white motherhood in popular multiracial rhetoric is, at least in part, what made the politics of multiracialism vulnerable to neoconservative appropriation during the 1990s. Unlike her angry white male counterpart, the white maternal figure appeared to be at a neutral distance from contentious discussions on equality.

If what I've been referring to as the preconditions of the multiracial movement—feminist political and intellectual insights on personal and public life, civil rights and an expanded expression of personhood—have been so thoroughly missing—forgotten, consciously absent—by the middle and end of the 1990s, then this absence is worthy of further scrutiny. Thus I now turn to representations of absence, particularly the literary trope of racial passing, and the cultural and political ideologies of political correctness and color-blindness. The ways in which these phenomena emerge in the texts to be considered here all demonstrate the quandary that cultural producers are in when they write about identity during the 1990s. How does one grapple with the legacies of identity politics at a historical juncture when cultural and political sensibilities of both the neoconservative right and the mainstream have grown skeptical of the ongoing necessity to redress identity-based inequities, and racially based inequities in particular? This is a another version of how racial timelines that run from the 1960s—with the advent of identity politics—meet an impasse during the 1990s, and thereby reveal the ambivalence embedded within a moment that, ostensibly, was producing the ends of race discursively. This chapter will explore the manner in which the racial discourses of the 1990s—the enforcement of color-blind public policy and the emergent concern of politically correct speech, both with their accompanying cultural politics of racial neutrality—are curiously evoked through the decidedly more anachronistic phenomenon of racial passing. The salience of these idioms for exploring race in the 1990s has a direct connection to the manner in which multiracialism is politicized at the end of the twentieth century.

James McBride's best-selling memoir *The Color of Water: A Black Man's Tribute to His White Mother* (1996) and Philip Roth's novel *The Human Stain* (2000) share a preoccupation with a condition in which the visible and discursive presence of race in popular culture is worth continued thought, even as the relevance of race was seeming to wane in the public sphere. They both force a negotiation between adherence to the historical logics of racial categorization and the impulse to embrace a version of personhood that transcends these historical logics. However, they diverge when it comes to their conclusions of how the conditions of personhood are related to the formations of race and gender. Color-blindness and political correctness—meant here in the broadest sense, which includes the circumstances that determine appropriate speech (and silence)—are recognizable as two common approaches to addressing racial politics at this moment in time. The least likely topic to contextualize the discursive landscape of the 1990s is racial passing, which is a concept that is born out of the segregationist logics of earlier historical eras. Yet passing continues to be a useful idiom because of its ambivalence. On the one hand, it can provoke further consideration of racial consciousness in a post–civil rights era. On the other hand, it could facilitate an oppositional, color-blind approach to race. Therefore, this final chapter begins with passing.

Racial Consciousness: Passing in *The Color of Water*

When Twine discusses the work of Reddy and Lazarre, she considers another memoir that fits the genre of maternal self-revelation, although it is not written by a white mother of black/multiracial children. This work is McBride's memoir. In her review of the three memoirs, Twine explains that *The Color of Water* is distinguishable from the narratives by Lazarre and Reddy, which demonstrate an entrenchment of class privilege in contemporary deliberations of white antiracist politics. Unlike Lazarre and Reddy, who are relatively privileged by virtue of marriage and profession, the mother in this narrative, Ruth McBride Jordan, James McBride's mother, is a "working-class white woman." As Twine points out, this is a subjectivity that has traditionally been absent from the record of what she refers to as an "antiracist literary genre." A similar absence seemed to exist within the leading ranks of multiracial organizations. As Kim Williams notes, "Relatively affluent, suburban white women" were leaders of a multiracial agenda. The emphasis on such a working-class subject position highlights the various ways in which formations of whiteness, as race intersects with "gender, class, age," and so forth, are multiple and unevenly related to power.[4] Also, the fact that Ruth McBride Jordan does not write her own story reflects the silence of economically disempowered women more generally.[5] However, the provocation caused by what Jordan does not say, by the privacy and silence of her past, allows the narrative to figure passing, silence, and privacy as exactly the sites where questions about racial difference and the potential failure of racial normativity emerge. Although this particularly social form of silence can usefully be extended into a more thoroughgoing analysis of whiteness as Twine suggests, silence also suggests a key reversal of roles between white mothers and, in the texts discussed here, their multiracial sons in the archive of antiracist and multiracial rhetoric.

In *The Color of Water,* McBride's mother reveals to her now-grown black son that she is an Ashkenazi Jew who had been passing for black throughout his childhood. However, as McBride describes it, Jordan did not pass in the standard sense of willfully performing or assuming another identity. Unlike the subjects of modernist passing narratives like Clare Kendry in Nella Larsen's *Passing* (1929) or the unnamed protagonist in James Weldon Johnson's *The Autobiography of an Ex-Colored Man* (1927), Jordan does not feign an alternative identity in order to deceive others. Instead, McBride explains that his mother simply avoided discussing the subject of her upbringing with her children. The first line of the memoir explains: "As a boy, I never knew where my mother was from—where she was born, who her parents were."[6] Perhaps Jordan did not hide her Jewishness from her black husbands or her neighbors, but she does hide it from her children, and they assess her according to their own understandings of blackness. Although Jordan does not actually pass in the conventional sense, the concept is usefully applied here because the memoir resituates the focus from the subject who passes to the subject who observes the pass.

How can one see what is unobservable? As Gayle Wald points out, passing narratives activate the contradictions of racial identification, rather than neutralizing them. In this way, Jordan's eventual disclosure to an adult McBride that she is, in fact, an Ashkenazi Jew does not restore an order of racial discourse that has been destabilized by years of ambiguity. Conversely, if Jordan's children assumed their light-skinned mother to be black, then this assumption about blackness was rife with contradictions. This irresolvable quality of race becomes the impetus for McBride's memoir. To begin by thinking of Jordan as a passing subject is to relocate the site of the transgression: although Jordan does not willfully pass, a key focus of the memoir is what her children see, rather than what she does. In other words, once the significance of passing shifts from the act of racial performance to the observation that something tricky is going on, or that something is being concealed and simultaneously revealed, then our focus can shift from the adult passer who is in control to the juvenile, less empowered subjects who attempt to make sense of what they (are not) seeing.

McBride documents his mother's story in her own words, so Jordan's voice, along with McBride's, is equally present in the memoir. The narrative stages a dialogue between McBride's recollections of growing up black during the 1960s and 1970s in predominately black neighborhoods of New York City and eventually in Wilmington, Delaware, and Jordan's new disclosures of her Jewish girlhood in the American South during the 1930s. The daughter of a tyrannical rabbi father and a crippled, abused mother, Rachel Shilsky changes her name to the more Americanized "Ruth" and leaves her unhappy home life in Virginia at the age of nineteen. Her name change to Ruth as a precursor to her immersion in black community is ironic because Ruth means "truth."[7] She moves to New York City and marries Andrew Dennis McBride, a black man also from the South, and together, they have eight children. James McBride was the last. During her marriage to Andrew McBride, who was commonly referred to as Dennis, Ruth completely abandons Judaism and becomes a devout Christian. The two cofound the New Brown Memorial Baptist church in the Red Hook Housing Projects in Brooklyn. After Dennis dies, Ruth marries Hunter Jordan, who, like her first husband, is African American. Together, they have four more children, and after Hunter's death, Ruth McBride Jordan is left to care for all twelve children on her own.

Each in his and her own voice, McBride and Jordan tell their stories in alternating chapters. McBride writes, "Here is her life as she told it to me, and betwixt and between the pages of her life you will find mine as well."[8] Jordan reveals the secret of her past, and McBride simultaneously narrates the effects of her previous silences on him and his siblings. Jordan's passing—meaning her lack of disclosure about her Jewishness—is not so

much a successful act of rendering racial and ethnic difference unremarkable as it is a provocation for the young McBride, who perceives a discrepancy between his sense of blackness and his mother's identity. Jordan's
lack of disclosure neither neutralizes her difference nor prevents McBride's
emergent black identity. Instead, her silence becomes a placeholder for
a deferred interaction. This deferral further emphasizes the difference between Jordan's maternal identity and those of Reddy and Lazarre. By not
speaking about her racial and ethnic background at all until well into
McBride's adulthood, Jordan provokes a sense of her own difference for
her son, rather than presents a sense of racial coherence. The belatedness
of Jordan's disclosure serves to indicate what has already been implicated
by her refusal to talk about her history. As the narrative demonstrates, a
refusal to disclose one's historically oppressed, racial, or ethnic identity
does not automatically result in normative or coherent outcomes, and in
the visual economy of race, whiteness does not necessarily function as a
sign of racial neutrality.

In "Passing for What?" Phillip Brian Harper describes the way in which
Jordan's particular act of "reverse passing" from Jewish to black does not
rely on an adherence to a visual economy of black and white because she
does not darken her skin to assume blackness. Indeed, as he mentions,
"Ruth McBride Jordan never really *passes* at all, since, rather than 'pretend-
ing' to be other than the white person that her appearance suggests she
must be, Ruth McBride Jordan simply never lays claim to any racial identity whatever."[9] Jordan's mode of identification is based on a chosen association with black community, as opposed to a performance of identity
ownership or essence. Although Jordan bears a social affinity to blackness
rather than attempt to actively perform it, she openly disavows whiteness.
For instance, when a young James asks his mother whether she is white,
her response is, "No. I'm light-skinned."[10] James senses that this is not
true, yet Ruth McBride "refuse[s] to acknowledge her whiteness."[11]

Ruth McBride Jordan's eventual admission to being "born an Ortho-
dox Jew . . . in Poland" was understandably slow and was done more at
the behest of her adult son than "out of any desire to revisit her past"—or,
it would seem, to disassociate herself from black identity.[12] The disclosure is for McBride's benefit; as a result, he is motivated to learn more
about Jordan's Jewish family and heritage. However, as Harper points out,
this is only one of multiple outcomes: "Ruth McBride Jordan's 'passing'
has a social effect prior to this narrativized disclosure, too, in that, by

simultaneously bearing a white skin, nurturing a black identification, and remaining silent about the entire matter, Ruth prosecuted a repudiation of whiteness that also constituted for observers—foremost among them her own children—its very deconstruction as a normative identity."[13] Harper rightly suggests that what makes *The Color of Water* unusual is its description of passing as a method for subverting or reversing the trajectory of the European immigrant's transformation into normative whiteness. Jordan's assimilation—her "shedding of originary language, culture, and tradition"—aids her acclimation in a historically marginal realm of blackness, rather than into an unremarkable white identity.[14]

To extend Harper's focus on the genre of passing narratives, *The Color of Water* is remarkable insofar as it allows a child of the passing subject to actively participate in a deliberation of racial identity. In a traditional, or pre–civil rights–era, schema of black-to-white passing narratives, children are often absent because producing offspring that can potentially appear to be black presents the dangerous risk of exposure for black subjects passing as white. Or children are figuratively silent because they are not privy to any racial transgression. Examples include the previously cited *Passing* and *The Autobiography of an Ex-Colored Man*, but also Walter White's *Flight* (1926). As either absent or silent, children are represented as one among many complications that accompany adult negotiations with racial meaning, rather than as autonomous subjects who may stake their own claims to matters of identity. Also, McBride's memoir reverses how proponents of the multiracial movement have tended to narrate the relationships between multiracial children and their monoracial parents, particularly white mothers. Ultimately, McBride demonstrates how a continued engagement with racial and ethnic difference is facilitated by the very silences that would deem race and ethnicity unremarkable. In this text, encounters with these various forms of what is ostensibly commonplace enable continual deliberations on how to renegotiate an approach to such heavily laden concepts as race, ethnicity, and, as a site where matters of the personal bear an ambivalent relation to the social, family.

Maternal Privacy Is Political

In McBride's memoir, the realm of privacy is formulated as a disjunctive, uncertain space rather than as something that can facilitate the transformation of historical racial terror into the affective connection that leads to civic belonging.[15] The ambiguity of Ruth McBride Jordan's background is the force of the narrative; this white mother becomes the site for reflecting on the unknowable, on the uncertainty of a politics that, at least in part, is built on the rhetorical foundation of maternal affect. There are various moments in McBride's memoir that demonstrate how Ruth McBride Jordan's responses reflect interests that are not only mysterious, but also do not necessarily concern her children. For instance, although Ruth's decision to pass allows her children the ability to identify with blackness unequivocally (as opposed to questioning their own identities), the problem is still about why she makes the decisions that she does. Why does Ruth want to forget her past? Why does this mother want to appear as if she is without a history? This line of questioning emerges again and again in the memoir: "As a boy, I always thought my mother was strange. . . . Her past was a mystery she refused to discuss."[16] In another moment, McBride recalls this exchange about Ruth's familial estrangement:

"I'm removed from my family."
   "Removed?"
   "Removed. Dead."
   "Who's dead?"
   "I'm dead. They're dead too by now probably. What's the difference? They didn't want me to marry on the black side."
   "But if you're black already, how can they be mad at you?"
   Boom. I had her. But she ignored it. "Don't ask me any more questions."[17]

In a sense, Ruth McBride Jordan's responses simply offer the representational tendencies that are commonly used in traditional passing literature: the concepts of death and ambiguity often figure the passing of a subject from one life to another. Passing suggests a condition of liminal existence, of being transitional. Here, however, removal suggests a tightfisted attempt to obscure a historical narrative from James, who, while ignorant of that narrative, is absolutely implicated by it because he is the outcome of that history.

Yet there is never any indication of how or whether Ruth's withholding of information is intended to have a direct benefit for her children. This is not to say that her silence does not benefit them: as I note above, it allows them an easy identification with blackness and demonstrates a challenge to an unmarked, white identity. If she chooses to pass—or, more accurately, to not disclose the facts of her past—then it is primarily because of a personal, individuated discomfort with that past. It is not because her children do not wish or cannot make use of the opportunity to know about it. As McBride recalls, "Since she refused to divulge details about herself or her past . . . what I learned of Mommy's past I learned from my siblings. We traded information on Mommy the way people trade baseball cards at trade shows, offering bits and pieces fraught with gossip, nonsense, wisdom, and sometimes just plain foolishness."[18]

Affective attachment between mother and children in this case does not overshadow the way in which James and his siblings experience the profound limits of their connection to Ruth. Those limits of knowledge, like the figurative limits that the passing subject transgresses, are experienced by the McBride–Jordan children as a site of uncertainty but also of productivity. Fragments of information are collectively pieced together in a way that illustrates a keen awareness of the conceptual gaps as well as an active engagement with what is imagined as the past. This describes the form of memoir itself: it attempts to capture and describe the relevance of social history through a private deliberation of fragmented and subjective moments of experience and memory.

By stating that her family did not want her to "marry on the black side," Ruth is clearly describing a past that was defined by something other than black identity. More specifically, she is referring to a process of assimilation that could potentially differentiate the status of Jewish immigrants from African Americans, and that has allowed white ethnic groups to distinguish their group identities from the persistent subordination of blackness. Initially, this difference between racial ethnic groups is treated as an absence: "What's the difference?" Yet it is significant that at this very moment of absence, a surprising and key revelation occurs: "What's the difference? They didn't want me to marry on the black side." The two clauses hinged together illustrate that the act of silence or nondisclosure actually evokes, and therefore makes productive, the matter that is hidden. In this case, what this denial produces is an acknowledgment of what it refuses. For James, the moment produces an opportunity to open a space of doubt with regard to his mother's performance of racial passing. Ruth resists acknowledging what her children observe all along, which is that she is somehow white and her children are not, the bonds of kinship not withstanding. However, McBride's narrative raises the issue of how modes of silence and obscurity—racial passing, and by extension color-blind policy—can become the occasions for a renewed set of inquiries into the ways in which social and subjective experiences have been and continue to be determined. When a young James takes advantage of his mother's unwitting provocation—"But if you're black already, how can they be mad at you?"—there is no response that can adequately fulfill the insatiable need for answers or undo an awareness that something came before, something for which there is no resolution. It is the unspeakable itself, the performativity of omission, that begs for a constructive approach toward historical, social, and familial comprehension.

Unlike the rhetorical figure of the multiracial child, which at least in part gains its visibility and political relevance from its natural bond to white embodiment, Ruth's willful removal from a previous set of kin, from history, or from clear-cut racial and ethnic taxonomies, does not lead to an undoing of blackness; nor does it revitalize whiteness. Instead, her ambiguity continually produces questions about the nature of racial and familial allegiances. Her act of passing ultimately queries the natural foundations of political rhetoric—the bonds of kinship, for instance—and the epistemologies involved with reconstructing the past. Unlike the rhetorical function of the child, who requires advocacy to gain a stake in the public sphere, the young James McBride demonstrates an alternative approach to this position. Rather than acting as an innocent figure of an emergent nation space, where the possibility for race consciousness is conditioned by a competing, color-blind discourse of affect, James is the multiracial son who actively returns to the relevance of race and to the racial and ethnic vicissitudes of history.

Such a return to race is decidedly unexpected in *The Color of Water*. The memoir makes a deceptively earnest embrace of color-blindness, and it seems to illustrate this embrace in two ways. As the title of McBride's memoir suggests, God—the "all-powerful"—has no preference because "He loves all people. He's a spirit." This ubiquitous presence, through which all people are loved indiscriminately and equally, "doesn't have a color," as "God is the color of water. Water doesn't have a color."[19] This benevolent omnipresence, which transcends history, metaphorically describes the complications of defining and categorizing race and ethnicity. On the surface, *The Color of Water* seemingly makes use of two narrative strategies that are easily brought to bear in discourses that would support the ideal or spirit of color-blindness as a social arrangement, if not necessarily a legal criterion.

This first narrative strategy emphasizes how strict racial categorizations such as black and white are complicated by both the presence of mixed racialism and ethnic specificity. In other words, these identities are demonstrated to exceed the reductionism of black and white, rendering such a binary unviable. McBride is, as the memoir's subtitle announces, the black man who tributes his white mother, but we understand that the circumstances described in the narrative exceed the convenience of these categories. In a sense, the indiscriminate recognition of "all people" evoked in the first part of the title challenges the stressed taxonomies of the subtitle. The second strategy, extending from the first, is that race (blackness) and white ethnicity (Jewishness) are seemingly collapsed into a synonymous plane of injury in which dynamics of racial hierarchy are underplayed. Because both McBride and Jordan seem to be narrating their childhood stories simultaneously in alternating chapters, blackness and Jewishness take on historical symmetry. For instance, the symmetrical titles of their alternating accounts—"The Old Testament" (Jordan) and "The New Testament" (McBride), or "Shul" (Jordan) and "School" (McBride)— underscore the suggestion that McBride and Jordan are representing two minoritized groups of parallel status. This second strategy addresses an impulse to elide, or to willfully forget, the historical particularities of racial inequity. In this way, "What's the difference?" is an approach to reaching the conclusion that there is no justification for political or legislative redress to particular racial injury in the present moment.

If all minoritized populations have been discriminated against in similar ways, then a subsequent implication is the viability of racial–ethnic neutrality. One could take pains to recite the separate elements of identity, in all of their ethnic and racial particularity, and then submit that it all amounts to the same thing. Here, blackness and Jewishness can be narrated as separate elements and could be without any enduring relevance because, paradoxically, they amount to the same thing. Just as colorblindness, the refusal to take race and ethnicity into account, could easily suggest that there is no longer a need to highlight these forms of identity, the concept also enables the opposite. The separate elements of identity can be emphasized because they are nondifferential: blackness can be Jewishness, and race can be ethnicity. Race and ethnicity can appear in public in a way that refuses to account for all forms of historical legibility.

As mentioned earlier, the effect of Ruth McBride Jordan's passing for her children is not only the undercutting of unremarkable white identity, but also the production of questions on what identities mean. Jordan's performance—the site of the indeterminable, where white women, for reasons unknown, claim to be light-skinned blacks, or where white is black—opens a space for her son to profoundly interrogate what he knows. What James does know evokes all that the passing narrative of his familial life cannot adequately address, rather than glossing over the missing pieces of information. If color-blindness, as a set of cultural protocols, can be conceptualized as the attempt to foreclose any further opportunity to focus on, examine, or interrogate the historical dynamics of race and ethnicity, then McBride's memoir wants to deliberate on the outcomes of various encounters with this kind of shutting down. What the memoir resists is an informational avoidance that leads not only to a flattening or neutralizing of various relevancies ("What's the difference?"), but also reverts back to what is too easily knowable: the commonsense view of subjective experience. Just as a young James is provoked, rather than placated, by the foreclosing of general knowledge about the engendering of his family and is challenged by how this foreclosure impedes his ability to make proper sense of what he does understand, the memoir itself becomes a wider opportunity to revisit what we know well. We know, for instance, that white women are not the subjects who have passed racially, and that the interwar migration from the South to urban centers of the North was a phenomenon that affected African Americans.

Ruth McBride Jordan's account demonstrates how Jewish identity supplements and complicates these commonplace markers of Jim Crow–era history. While reflecting on an interracial romance she had as a girl in Klan-ridden Virginia, Jordan remarks, "You know, the thing was, I was supposed to be white and 'number one,' too. That was a big thing in the South. You're white, and even if you're a Jew, since you're white you're better than a so-called colored."[20] In a sense, what Jordan is emphasizing is not the synonymous quality of blackness and Jewishness, but instead the process through which whiteness engulfs some forms of cultural difference at the constant exclusion of supposedly nonmalleable black identity. Rather than commenting on how Jewishness has been alienated in the same way as blackness has, or pairing the two group experiences in a flattened plane of minoritization, an emphasis on the vicissitudes of whiteness highlights the particular and historically rooted way that black identity has been located on the outside of both white privilege and the malleable space of ethnicity.

Jordan is clear about the danger that both she and her boyfriend, Peter, faced in 1930s Virginia, but she emphasizes the disparity of risk between them. Although Peter had been kind to her, as she recalls, "He did it at the risk of his own [life] because they would've strung him up faster than you can blink if they'd have found out. Not just the Ku Klux Klan but the regular white folks in town would've killed him."[21] While blackness is alienated in relation to both whiteness and a pliable quality of ethnicity during an era of segregation in the twentieth century, this alienation is not drastically reduced by the middle and end of the century. As Rachel Moran notes, African Americans are currently least likely to intermarry with whites, and black/mixed racial children have the slightest ability to assume white privilege: "While other groups equate multiracialism with integration and assimilation, blacks have discovered that white parentage cannot fully shield them from racial isolation."[22] Indeed, near the end of the memoir, McBride's search for his mother's origins leads him to a synagogue in Suffolk, Virginia, which is the one Ruth had attended with her family. He worries about loitering outside: "Black males are closely associated with crime in America, not with white Jewish mothers, and I could not imagine a police officer buying my story as I stood in front of the Jewish temple saying, 'Uh, yeah, my grandfather was the rabbi here, you know.'"[23] Just as Peter does not demonstrate the potential of black assimilation through his association with Ruth but rather the opposite, McBride reinforces this particular form of alienation approximately sixty years later, mother–son kinship notwithstanding.

One condition that the memoir demonstrates is how generic whiteness can be particularized by the culture heritage of Jewishness, which, as an ethnicity, bears its own contradistinctive relationship to normative whiteness. Also, as a light-skinned (black) woman who eventually reveals her (white) Jewishness, Jordan potentially demonstrates that recognition of racial hierarchy and inequity is no longer sustainable because race becomes ethnicity, and because blackness is indistinguishable from minoritized whiteness. As Ian F. Haney Lopez argues, this conflation of race and ethnicity can be explained by a neoconservative shift in the interpretation of racism during the 1960s, which replaces a historical narrative of racial disparity with a framework of ethnic plurality that minimizes the relevance of racial hierarchy: "The ethnic analysis replaces the notion of dominant and subordinate races with a narrative of culturally defined groups in pluralistic competition, where culture rather than systemic racial advantaging or disadvantaging explained disparate group success."[24] To attribute this shift to 1990s-era multiracialism entirely would be to dismiss a prior and distinctive process through which political discourse is produced.

Overall, although the memoir seems to affirm a perspective that would deem attentiveness to racial hierarchy impossible, *The Color of Water* rejects this direction. The function of family to bear the potentiality of color-blindness, or the rhetoric of affect as an approach to interracial kinship, are complicated by the ways in which McBride's and Jordan's narratives challenge historical common sense. It is not primarily the relationship between mother and child—the affective, natural space of maternity, for instance—that guides the memoir's deliberation on race and ethnicity. Rather, it is how Jordan and McBride each demonstrate that the ultimate incommensurability of their stories can become productive within the private, intimate space of family. Unlike other figurations of this space, which at various moments champion the potential of racial–ethnic neutrality through either passing or amalgamation, or through the potential of love, here the family becomes the site where the tensions between socially determined and self-recognized identities can clash and evoke discrepancies.

Color-blindness: Passing in *The Human Stain*

I have just mentioned that color-blindness, or the refusal to account for race and ethnicity, could easily suggest that the separate elements of identity can be emphasized because they are nondifferential: blackness can be Jewishness, and race can be ethnicity. Race and ethnicity can appear in public in a way that refuses to account for all forms of historical legibility. If *The Color of Water* attempts to capture the historical vicissitudes of racial and ethnic formation, then the text I discuss next is decidedly less invested in developing the negative of color-blindness into a positive snapshot in which the distinctiveness of racial and ethnic differences show. If the manner in which light-skinned, Jewish Ruth Shilsky McBride Jordan had offered a provocation with this question—"what's the difference?"—then the next text implicitly poses the same question to foreclose the possibility that whatever difference matters.

In Philip Roth's *The Human Stain,* Coleman Silk—a sixty-nine-year-old classics professor and a black man passing for white and Jewish—finds

himself under attack by his colleagues for unwittingly and ironically making a racist remark in the classroom. This remark sets the novel's plot
in motion. As the incident goes, Silk takes attendance during the first
few weeks of the semester. Two of the fourteen students routinely never
respond when their names are called. Finally, at the start of one class ses-
sion, Silk asks the rhetorical question, "Does anyone know these people?
Do they exist or are they spooks?"[25] Because the absent students are both
African American, and because the term *spook* carries a historically racist
connotation when used to refer to African Americans even into the late
1990s, when the novel is set, charges of racism against Silk quickly gain
momentum and ultimately lead to Silk's public disgrace and his resig-
nation from Athena College. However, throughout the controversy, Silk
vehemently maintains that this speech could not have been racist because,
sight unseen, he could not have known that the absent students were
black. As Silk attempts to explain to the faculty dean, "I was using the word
in its customary and primary meaning: 'spook' as a specter or a ghost."[26]
Feeling unduly embattled and misaligned, Silk eventually decides that he
will set the public record straight by writing his own version of the incident; the nonfiction book Silk attempts to write is unambiguously entitled
Spooks. After his attempts to write his story prove to be woefully unsuccessful, Silk ultimately abandons the project altogether.

While *The Human Stain* is concerned with de-essentializing identities
(blackness and Jewishness especially), it is just as concerned with the
conditions of self-authorship. This second concern renders the irony that
racial passing enacts the timeliness and timelessness of two contemporary
discourses about race: color-blindness and political correctness. Coleman
Silk has always already been living the fantasy of late twentieth-century
policy makers who would like nothing more than to dismantle the state's
capacity to see race as a public issue. However, the irony is that while Silk
performs a neoconservative desire to keep quiet around race matters, he
actually has no voice of his own, particularly when he chooses to write
his own personal truth about how race matters. This is not simply to note
that Silk stubbornly refuses to disclose his latent blackness. Rather, it is to
mention that the book he is unsuccessful at writing, *Spooks,* is eventually
written by someone else after Silk's untimely death, with the new title *The
Human Stain* (which is, of course, the same title of Roth's actual novel). As
critic Derek Parker Royal usefully points out, most of what we learn about
Coleman Silk is someone else's speculation: "A close reading suggests that

much of what transpires is just as much a matter of the narrator's imagination as it is of recorded fact."[27] Hence, perhaps it would be apt to wonder about where exactly he is within the pages. Does Coleman Silk exist,
or is he a spook?—*spook* in the customary and primary sense of the word,
of course.

Although Silk is successful in passing, his task is somewhat too successful: because nobody at Athena College knows about Silk's true black
identity, and because it is presumed that he wishes to keep his blackness a
secret, he forfeits a potentially effective response to the charges of racism
that tarnish his image. In other words, passing, the act that would allow for
an extension of social freedom, actually translates into a more narrow set
of terms for social engagement. Perhaps more significantly in this novel,
and suggestively bearing reference to the actual life of *New York Times*
book critic Anatole Broyard, Silk's unwillingness to declare his blackness
leads to the failure of his writing. Initially, in the heat of his outrage, Silk
brings his story to Nathan Zuckerman, the novel's narrator and Roth's alter
ego, to write. Zuckerman is a sixty-five-year-old professional writer who
leads a secluded life in the Berkshires. When he refuses to make fiction out
of Silk's story, Silk works on the manuscript himself, only to realize eventually that he cannot adequately shape a self-image through narrative. As
he explains to Zuckerman, "Writing about myself, I can't maneuver the
creative remove. Page after page, it is still the raw thing. It's a parody of the
self-justifying memoir. The hopelessness of explanation."[28] The tasks of
publicly disclosing secret attitudes toward race—a secret racial affinity
or inappropriately racist attitudes—may be related to the total prevention
or incoherence of language. For instance, the erudite and otherwise productive Anatole Broyard was famously unable to write a novel that was
to be based on his own coming-of-age experience. As his daughter, Bliss
Broyard, writes in a recent memoir, "My dad was never able to write [the
novel] with the spontaneous elegance that was in his speech. Something
kept making him tongue-tied whenever he faced the blank page."[29]

With its concomitant concerns over a lived racial performance and
linguistic racial legacies, *The Human Stain* explores how personal agency
is either undercut or promoted by performance or language. There are
clear limits to what racial passing can deliver to an individual in terms of
social advancement, or as a potentially political act of transgression. Roth's
novel demonstrates the limits of passing as performance, but in doing
so, it also suggests that an alternative is writing, narrative, the shaping of

social discourses on the level of language. Racial passing prevents Silk's
participation in shaping a historical narrative that will endure beyond the
confines of his lifetime, and he is therefore stripped of agency as a historical subject. To see Coleman Silk historically is, in a sense, to not see Silk
as he understands himself. We have no access to Coleman as a subject
who can create a narrative self, or who can self-justify for the historical
record. All we have are the discursive ghosts of his black students and, as
it eventually becomes clear, Zuckerman's written speculation.

It is Zuckerman—not Silk himself—who eventually writes an enduring account of Silk's life, which is an amalgam of the facts he knows
about Silk and invention. In Zuckerman's account, Silk himself becomes a
presence who in one sense is not fleshed out, but rather a presence that
appears as a trace of the unknowable. Yet Zuckerman's narrative, and
Roth's actual novel, which it mirrors, situates the absence of black subjectivity in a narrative that empties the potential of reading the conditions
of American blackness historically. Instead, the narrative itself takes the
place of an earlier context with regard to Silk's life, just as the word *spooks*
takes the place of Silk's African American students, who never appear
in the flesh within the novel. Indeed, Silk's students are forever caught
between the two discourses that shape them: historic racism and political
correctness. It is impossible to retrieve these individuals—as subjects who
would tell their own stories—from the language used to speak about them.
Because Silk's decision to pass as white is what prevents his authorship
of his own narrative from being successful, racial passing in *The Human
Stain* acts as a defense for this substitution of narrative agency. What Silk
gains in performing a self, he loses in the ability to produce an identity in
writing, an account of himself. How historical accounts will be narrated
into the future, and for whom, are matters to be brought to bear on how
we understand the stakes of Coleman Silk's ultimately absent voice.

Silk's practice of racial passing, which implicitly indicts political correctness and champions color-blindness, does not actually privilege Silk.
A primary reading of the novel reveals its implication that today's emphasis on racial neutrality is the same as yesterday's black political and intellectual activism, and it is also significant how the ostensible end of white
male privilege becomes a useful discourse for interpreting the misfortune
of Coleman Silk. This reading would take into account a process through
which Jewish Americans have fashioned white identities. For instance,
Karen Brodkin argues that Jewish public intellectuals of the postwar era

constructed a "model minority" version of Jewish culture "that explained
the structural privileges of white maleness as earned entitlements." The
outcome was a Jewishness that was "male-centered" and "prefiguratively
white," but nonetheless a particularly Jewish form of whiteness.[30] If Silk is
unable to authorize himself through writing, then this marks a failure that
is as gender related as it is racially related. Not only does Silk fail in terms
of creating a textual self, but by failing at the public intellectual work of
textual production and dissemination, Silk also falls short of becoming a
race leader in his own right, or a masculine voice of intellectual authority
that more than just prefigures whiteness. We know that Silk is a professor
of classical texts, yet the novel begins with his inability to speak as either
an authority or critic of white culture. The Jewish intellectual is silenced
by the earned entitlement of whiteness.

Brodkin also argues that postwar Jewish public intellectuals were poised
to speak "as white Americans for white America" while, ambivalently, "also
as white critics of the culture of 1950s whiteness."[31] *The Human Stain* suggests that whiteness is no longer the central domain of American power at
the end of the twentieth century. Silk's persecution over the spooks incident—persecution resulting precisely from his whiteness—demonstrates
this. The novel comments on how white normativity becomes embattled
and particularized in the 1990s; therefore, it can no longer easily be understood as an empowering destination that one can assimilate or pass into,
as the case may be. The emergence of whiteness studies and the widening
dismantlement of affirmative action might testify, albeit tacitly, to this new
discourse of white political injury. Silk avoids oppression from the ways a
public continues to look and speak about black men, but ultimately, whiteness does not allow him to circulate in public untainted either.

However, just as political correctness, color-blindness, and in this case
passing foreground particular ideologies that effectively obscure the vicissitudes of historical perspective, understanding the embattled Jewish Silk
through the lens of white injury does not bring us any closer to seeing him
historically. Timothy Parrish suggests that Roth's novel reworks Ralph
Ellison's trope of invisibility within an exploration on public perception
of identity and personal agency. As he writes, "The 'invisibility' of [Silk's]
African American students is the narrative mechanism that will unleash
Zuckerman's exploration of Coleman's own 'invisible' African American
self."[32] Although Coleman's unfortunate speech propels the novel into an
exploration of Silk's secret black life, there is an imbalance between the

invisibility of Coleman Silk as a black man who negotiates with the limits and possibilities of self invention and the invisibility of the black students who are never heard or seen in the text. Perhaps this imbalance posits the suggestion of a splitting of black identity in Roth's novel where, on the one hand, black subjectivity is rendered as invisible in the sense that it is not simply misrepresented but dropped beyond the realm of representation and, on the other hand, blackness is mutable, or made to speak of the symmetry of identities. This difference within the field of blackness holds stakes for how blackness itself can be signified in a narrative that reads the conditions of identity at the end of the twentieth century, after the color line. The racial passing plot of *The Human Stain* becomes an ironic demonstration of how the linguist life of race exceeds the personal choices individuals make regarding race, including those choices regarding speech or narrative.

One way in which the novel attempts to restore historical and identity coherence is through narrative construction. Their semifrequent conversations notwithstanding, Zuckerman knows only of Silk's invented Jewish identity. He does not learn about Silk's blackness until after his death, when he meets Silk's sister, Ernestine, who is identifiably black, at his funeral. As Zuckerman learns of Silk's blackness belatedly, his interest in narrating Silk's life is also belated. He attempts to write a coherent narrative that would include in its trajectory the circumstances of Silk's upbringing, the conditions that lead to his decision to pass, and the interior life of someone who would make the decisions Silk had. By the end of the novel, we learn that the narrative that Zuckerman has been writing bears the same name as Roth's novel, *The Human Stain*. As Royal has pointed out, the logic of the novel(s) suggests that Zuckerman cannot possibly have all the facts of Silk's personal history. His narrative therefore fills in the gaps for what, with Silk's death, is irretrievable knowledge.

Zuckerman's narrative locates the question of racial identity on the level of his own attempt to invent a self as a writer. During Silk's lifetime, Zuckerman understands the symmetry between his experience and Silk's, as both men are around the same age, are originally from the East Orange section of New Jersey, and are Jewish. In a sense, the belated knowledge of Silk's blackness, along with a prior sense of shared identification, allows Zuckerman to invent in his narrative a method for reconciling the differences and similarities of the two racial ethnicities, blackness and Jewishness, which is posited in this description of Silk: "All in all, he remained a neat, attractive package of a man even at his age, the small-nosed Jewish type with the facial heft in the jaw, one of those crimped-haired Jews of a light yellowish skin pigmentation who possess something of the ambiguous aura of the pale blacks who are sometimes taken for white."[33] In Zuckerman's description of Silk, there is collusion between the misrecognition of both blackness and Jewishness as inscribed on the body. Under the sign of an "ambiguous aura," both identities are mutable, and therefore each identity has been constructed and influenced by historical contingencies rather than signifying antihistoric essences. Both Jewishness and blackness are posited in distinctive relation to whiteness, and both, in their mutually complicated connection to bodily legibility, resemble each other. This tacit reflection of the problem of how identities become legible—how one correctly deciphers and inscribes this "ambiguous aura"—enables Zuckerman's writing project. As Jewishness and blackness flow into each other through both Silk's inherited and performed identities, but also through Zuckerman's sense of the familiar mixed with a sense of the uncertain, the ambiguous combination of the two allows Zuckerman space in which to write.

Self-made Men and Racial Neutral Individualism

By focusing on either Zuckerman's interpretation of Silk or Silk's struggle with self-authorship, one thing seems certain: the collaboration between McBride and Jordan that facilitated a race-conscious dialogue is replaced in *The Human Stain* with a marked individualism. Yet individualism is yet another dimension of passing literature in general. In his treatment of passing as a literary theme, Werner Sollors points out that passing implies both a sense of self-made individualism and a persistent notion that one's racial identity can be either real or fake: "The paradoxical coexistence of the cult of the social upstart as 'self-made man' and the permanent racial identification and moral condemnation of the racial passer as 'impostor' constitute the frame within which the phenomenon of passing took place."[34] Within this frame is a wide range of thematic and literary representations that include not only independence and individual courage, but also communal betrayal and social critiques of a system of racial categorization that are simultaneously inequitably hierarchical and fundamentally arbitrary. As a narrative device, racial passing can have a multitude of functions that are contingent on social and cultural context. For instance, it has been influentially argued that passing functions as a narrative code for the more dangerous subplot of black female sexuality in the modernist era,[35] or as a framework for identity politics that reveals the contestation of situated knowledges in the postmodern era.[36] Passing in *The Human Stain* signals the difficulty of establishing a logical foundation for a postracial politics. Passing not only skips an engagement with leftist racial politics after the civil rights era to elide the perspectives of yesterday's civil rights activism and today's neoconservative policies, but it also represents this elision as a sort of silence or incoherence around race. The passing subject—as a figure who cannot talk openly about race matters—is perfect for an era in which many would rather end all public conversations about race.

To evoke what W. E. B. Du Bois famously referred to as the problem of the twentieth century—in public and private, violently and strategically—serves the purpose of distinguishing black modernist novels of passing with *The Human Stain*. Roth's treatment of passing shows little concern for the negotiations or interactions a passing individual might have with a black community. The novel does not consider in a sustained manner the discourses or the cultural and political experiences that define community. Johnson's *Autobiography of an Ex-Colored Man* posits the unnamed protagonist's decision to pass in a manner that seemingly relates to Coleman Silk's desire for raceless individuality: "I finally made up my mind that I would neither disclaim the black race nor claim the white race; but that I would change my name, raise a mustache, and let the world take me for what it would."[37] This refusal to claim or disclaim seems analogous to Coleman Silk's first apparent experience with racial passing.

A young Coleman is told by his boxing coach simply not to mention his race in a situation where being colored might disqualify him. As the white and Jewish coach puts it, "You're neither one thing or the other."[38] However, for Johnson's protagonist, the decision to pass is not only an attempt to demonstrate individual capability in a playing field leveled by color-blindness. Instead, it is also the immediate fear of bodily destruction: while in the South, the protagonist witnesses a lynching in which a black man is burned to death. The protagonist identifies acutely with the individual who is literally destroyed for being black, and the double element of danger is that as he stands amidst the murderous mob, he is momentarily passing for white. In other words, the actual murder clarifies the stakes of simultaneously identifying as black while passing for white.

The protagonist's seemingly noncommittal decision to let the world peg him for either "one thing or the other" is tied to a sharp recognition that black Americans "could with impunity be treated worse than animals."[39] Here we might think of a final moment in *The Human Stain,* in which Silk's sister, Ernestine, recalls explaining to their brother, Walt, the meaning of context when thinking of Coleman historically: "Coleman couldn't wait to go through civil rights to get to his human rights, and so he skipped a step."[40] The central difference between passing in Johnson's Jim Crow–era novel and Roth's much later one is that the former is profoundly clear about the instrumentality of law to realize human rights. In Johnson's *Autobiography,* the individual's decision to live as if race is mutable is, presumably, a less effective solution than one that is rooted in law, and that recognizes the need to prevent race-based inequality. In contrast, the suggestion in Roth's novel is that civil rights—the social demand that the state redress historical, race-based inequities through legislative reform and public programs—ultimately achieves an emphasis on personal responsibility. The individual—not social movements, not state legislation—is responsible for attaining successful public and private life. This historical view skips a step to resemble a current tendency to undercut claims that racial inequality continues to persist decades after legal segregation is dismantled.[41]

Jim Crow–era passing and late 1990s-era color-blindness are not the only metaphors for racial time that haunt Roth's novel. As I just mentioned, the young Coleman Silk had a boxing coach. Boxing frequently provides the occasion for Silk to think historically about the vicissitudes of individuality. Silk chooses to pass permanently from the 1950s onward in a context that includes the influence of Doc Chizner, the aforementioned Jewish boxing coach at the Newark Boys Club. Before a fight at West Point, Doc encourages the young Coleman "not to mention that he was colored": "You're neither one thing or the other. You're Silky Silk. That's enough." Chizner is a figurative father who had "as good as adopted" Coleman through fight training.[42] An equally important influence is Coleman's actual father, Clarence, who upheld high educational and cultural standards for his children: "In the Silk family they had read all the old classics. In the Silk family the children were not taken to prizefights, they were taken to the Metropolitan Museum of Art in New York to see the armor."[43] This is as close as the novel comes to representing a black communal origin for Silk. Significantly, the cultural cues that accompany Silk's upbringing in a black family are a careful attempt to signify high culture according to a neutral standard of value. Indeed, all the old classics would be defended decades later during the culture wars in academia, when the perceived onslaught of multiculturalism appears to politicize—and therefore weaken—the standards for academic quality. In this pre–civil rights scene of black family life, culture is ostensibly not political: the black subject engages the breadth of Western culture to contribute to a broadly cosmopolitan, undifferentiated economy of ideas.

When Silk initially decides not to succumb to a group identity, he does so in terms that are borrowed from both of his black and white fathers. He evokes the lines of *Julius Caesar* as quoted by his biological father ("What can be avoided / Whose end is purposed by the mighty gods?"[44]), but he evokes the name granted by Doc: "*This* had been purposed by the mighty gods! Silky's freedom. The raw I. All the subtlety of being Silky Silk."[45] An erstwhile black subject who simultaneously chooses a secular Jewishness and whiteness bears commentary on a liberal collaboration between African Americans and Jews during civil rights–era activism, which is eventually fractured by separatist, identity-driven political stances typified by the rise of black cultural nationalism during the late 1960s. The 1950s-era collaboration, if unintentional, between a black father and a Jewish father with regard to shaping Silk's personality suggests another way in which Silk skips the identity-driven excesses of the 1960s and 1970s, to arrive at the end of the twentieth century with a set of neutral values for public survival. The ability to fight strategically and skillfully as a singular individual is a metaphor for public self-determination; such self-determination runs against "the coercive, inclusive, historical, inescapable moral *we*."[46] Similarly, the armor at the Met, *Julius Caesar,* and other classics are represented in the novel as part and parcel of Silk's black inheritance.

The Human Stain wishes to foreclose a concerted consideration of why identity politics should be granted any legitimacy in public discourse by rendering the concept as either intellectually vacuous or undeniably invidious in relation to unfettered personhood. However, such representation is less clear when one focuses on the schema of two paternal figures for Coleman—one black, the other white/Jewish—to ask why such an interracial and interethnic parity of men is simultaneously granted with significance and denied overt recognition. When *The Human Stain* puts an emphasis on fatherhood, rather than on formations of racialized masculinity in political discourse, the result is a conflation of blackness and Jewishness that fortifies culture and kinship. The conflation between black/Jewish paternities produces a quintessentially singular individual, or a son who manages to achieve successful personhood in a hostile United States. Ideally, this son will mature into an exceptional role model—the "raw I" of Silky Silk, Cablinasian, or "the skinny kid with a funny name." Little does anyone know that the freedom of the "raw I" will become the failure of self-authorization. As mentioned previously, Silk will lament in the future that he cannot tell his own story because "page after page, it is still the raw thing." The rising of a multiracial son is already setting here.

Entanglements between black and Jewish paternities (and histories of U.S. marginalization) notwithstanding, the fallback position of *The Human Stain* is that men go it alone. It is fitting, therefore, that Coleman's coming of age is represented through his autonomy in the boxing ring. Michele Elam notes the significance of boxing as a metaphor for racial passing in *The Human Stain,* and she describes how notions of performance are crucial for revealing the sort of labor passing does in the novel. Boxing as metaphor combines a masculinist response to racial inequity—especially when aggression is between differently racialized men—with the appearance of neutral, fair play. She refers to a scene in which Solly Tabak, a white boxing promoter, asks the ostensibly white Silk to extend his match with his black opponent Beau Jack "in order to put on a show." Rejecting this request, Silk defeats Jack in the first round. When the frustrated Tabak asks Silk why he ended the match so abruptly when he was specifically asked not to, Silk's response is, "I don't carry no nigger."[47] This scene, along with the previous moment in which Silk's manager deems Silk "neither one thing or the other" racially, provides the context for how passing nominally produces Silk's whiteness through the logic of merit. Elam writes,

> Passing requires actively staging himself inside and outside the ring as unequivocally white in part by self-consciously rendering "impassable" the distance between Beau Jack and himself. Earlier in the narrative, Silk is called the same epithet and the "impact was devastating." . . . It is no accident, then, that the same expression from Silk's lips—as casually and cruelly rendered—becomes a speech act (re)creating the racial divide and securing his chosen side on it.[48]

Elam's analysis here evokes the national staging of racialized caricatures that David Wellman discusses in terms of the figurative angry white men of 1990s-era political culture. Silk's whiteness comes into being through the mobilization of anger. Although such anger ostensibly results from his own experience of racial cruelty—"Silk is called the same epithet and the 'impact was devastating'"—this prior experience becomes reinterpreted as a reversal of discrimination: the ostensibly white Silk is wrongly pressured literally, by being asked to downplay his own skill inside the ring, as well as metaphorically, outside the ring on the national stage. The show is a false demonstration of racial equality, which is only possible if the white Silk carries his black opponent.

The impassable distance between Silk and Jack occurs through "a speech act that (re)creates the racial divide," as Elam asserts. Yet it also occurs through a more subtle, implicit conversion that the novel itself enacts: the conversion is between the devastation that Silk felt from previously being the target of antiblack racism, to the embattlement he experiences by potentially having his white masculinity—and the aptitude that is the unspoken condition of this identity—undermined by a black subject. Indeed, as Elam claims, it is no accident that the pass in this textual moment is provoked by Silk's earlier interpellation as a nigger. However, it is curious that the fulfillment of the pass occurs through a transhistorical set of emergent discourses, in which Silk goes from feeling himself to be a Jim Crow–era victim of antiblack discrimination to closely resembling the angry white man of 1990s-era popular and political culture. Elam's comments help to illustrate that Silk achieves an idiosyncratic sense of selfhood through a conversion from racial neutrality ("neither one thing or the other") to unequivocal whiteness ("I don't carry no nigger"). To be more precise, Silk's process of becoming unequivocally white is equated with his becoming complicit in the cultural politics of white supremacy.

The Return of Maternal Affect and the Death of Black Motherhood

Elam explains that "Silk's iconoclasm, his autogenesis . . . occurs through, not despite, this participation in racism."[49] Suddenly, the collaborative influence of Coleman's two fathers disappears as a determinate for Silk's development. Instead, antiblack racism exists as a precondition for the "raw I," which is a proxy for unquestionable whiteness and racially neutral, idiosyncratic personhood. Indeed, the novel means to emphasize this connection between whiteness as race neutrality and the achievement of personhood. In light of how passing is staged as a battle royal between American masculinities, what commentary has *The Human Stain* to offer in terms of racial passing, individual freedom, and maternity? Which mode of affect—if not anger—facilitates the narration of maternal desire with regard to the "raw I," toward unfettered personhood, toward social entitlement based on individual freedom?

Elam pinpoints a curious detail that is embedded within the precondition of (white) personhood: after a discourse that has been generally masculinist and that has made prominent the significance of paternity, the condition of Silk's freedom suddenly focuses on maternity. On the conditions of Silk's individualism, Elam explains that Silk's participation in racism "is not just the cost of individualism; in the novel, it is what makes individualism possible. Silk quite consciously decides he must metaphorically 'murder' his mother 'on behalf of his exhilarating notion of freedom!,' to 'live his life on the scale he wants to live it.'"[50] In a clear sense, Elam is identifying a common convention within the genre of passing narratives, which is that the passing subject must sever ties with one's family of origin and one's racial community. To some degree, the manners in which Coleman's fathers figuratively fade away in order for the adult, iconoclastic Silk to emerge might be one example of this convention. It is less clear, however, why this severing is directed toward motherhood specifically, and why this severing is so metaphorically violent. Interracial fatherhood, in both literal and figurative manifestations, leads the way for Silk's achieved sense of personhood. Conversely, black motherhood ostensibly offers no formative function for the raw individual and thus must be exorcised as the origin of identity. The convention of passing narratives that insists on a clean break from the past is utilized in Roth's novel as a mechanism for ridding black motherhood from a history because such a role inexplicably yet forcefully threatens the fulfillment of American personhood. Such a role, therefore, is implicitly the negation of what American personhood is.

What, precisely, would black motherhood want? The most striking aspect of *The Human Stain* with regard to this question is the manner in which the novel completely disregards it. Silk—having passed for white and Jewish for the last few years—decides to marry the secular, "non-Jewish

Jewish" Iris Gittelman. He goes back to East Orange, New Jersey, to tell his mother, and his intention is to sever ties with his family of origin in order to begin his new family. Although Silk obviously initiates the discussion, his mother's voice defines it:

> He had prepared himself. The important thing was to . . . let her speak, let her find her fluency and, from the soft streaming of her own words, create for him his apologia.
>   "You're never going to let them see me," she said. You're never going to let them know who I am. 'Mom,' you'll tell me, 'Ma, you come to the railroad station in New York, and you sit on the bench in the waiting room, and at eleven twenty-five A.M., I'll walk by with my kids in their Sunday best.' That'll be my birthday present five years from now. 'Sit there, Mom, say nothing, and I'll just walk them slowly by.'"[51]

Ironically, when Coleman's mother speaks, she renders herself ghostly and silent. This metaphorical murder is accomplished through collaboration between mother and son. While *The Color of Water* also illustrates collaboration between a mother and a son, the outcome is an exploration of what the limits and conditions are for asserting one's agency and for producing knowledge about social and personal histories. In the case of this scene, the only future that Gladys Silk has is outside of the fold of kinship relations and extended family. She can imagine her proximity to family as either a spook—in the customary and primary sense—or, by extension, a domestic laborer who is allowed to make contact with her son's future family only by relinquishing public recognition of her subjectivity and her selfhood.

In the voluntary apologia that she creates for son, Gladys Silk imagines herself passing as the help: "You tell me the only way I can ever touch my grandchildren is for you to hire me to come over as Mrs. Brown to baby-sit and put them to bed, I'll do it. Tell me to come over as Mrs. Brown to clean your house, I'll do *that*."[52] As a false identity, "Mrs. Brown" is an obvious reference to how Gladys Silk would be seen once she is relegated to the quasimaternal but nonfamilial role of caregiver. The name is purposely generic; it evokes a long history in which women with brown skin have been most prominent to members of white families only when they are tending to the needs of white familial households. Once Mrs.

Brown—who could easily be any black woman—is done with the work
of putting someone else's children to bed and cleaning someone else's
house, she seemingly disappears into an unseen and unfathomable family
life of her own. It is as if the metaphorical murder refers to the death of
Gladys Silk's legitimate maternity. It is a death she paradoxically contributes to by virtue of being a loving mother to Coleman, and by for-
giving him with her self-negating speech. As Coleman reminds himself,
"It was not a moment to allow himself to be subjugated by the all-
but-pathological phenomenon of mother love."[53] In this case, the near
pathology of maternal affect is implicitly racialized; "mother love" loses
its connotation as a racially and politically neutral, natural condition. In
this case, "mother love" verges on the pathological when it threatens to
suppress that "exhilarating notion of freedom" from black identity. In
this case, (black) mothers have to be murdered so that their sons are
finally free. And (black) mothers will participate in their own murders if
it means—all but pathologically—that they can still play a role in the lives
of their sons.

However, the tragedy here is that Coleman understands Gladys's narrative as an actual apologia for his behavior. Furthermore, he understands
that what he is doing by ridding himself of a (black) mother is completely
final: "Once you've done a thing like this, you have done so much violence
it can *never* be undone—which is what Coleman wants."[54] Yet the irre-
versibility of death, or the finality of it, is not what Gladys is describing.
While Coleman understands his version of passing to require the total
extermination of (black) motherhood, Gladys is describing an alternative
version of passing that is akin to Beloved's existence in Toni Morrison's
novel. As the living subject, Gladys Silk, she may never be able to know
or touch her familial descendents. She imagines herself as the ghostly figure that haunts a railroad station—itself a metaphorical site of passage—
where fading ancestral black mothers share a passing glance with emergent and privileged white sons turned fathers. When Mrs. Brown babysits
those potential (white) (grand)children, would they notice a curiously
familial resemblance, and formulate their own unspeakable and unan-
swerable questions? As a son, Coleman wants to be freed of the maternal
bond. Such freedom—such violence—eventually returns as that which
disastrously descends on the white nuclear family, maternity, and, ultimately, Coleman's substitute for black motherhood: a white, non-Jewish
Jewish wife.

Public Suppression of Personhood: Political Correctness

If the passing novels of the early twentieth century consistently deliber-
ated on how the passing, self-made individual is always in proximity to
very real dangers, then it is possible to imagine how *The Human Stain* sets
up a similar relation. However, instead of angry lynch mobs and racist husbands, the danger that Silk is in closest proximity to is the white liberals
and African Americans that comprise the thought police of leftist campuses. By virtue of his entanglement with a possibly racist discourse, but
also with a new social climate of political correctness, Silk, passing as a
white Jew, runs the risk of being exposed as an invidious racist. He does
not risk being exposed as black. This is not to claim that exposure in passing narratives refers to the revealing of an essential identity that exists
underneath the appearance of things. Again, passing takes place at the risk
of real danger. Hence, in the context of social threat, being exposed means
signifying an ideological problem that requires violent, painful defeat,
rather than revealing something essential. In the context of the 1990s, the
question of whether African Americans have access to various civic spaces
is not the ideologically embattled issue for neoconservatives. Instead, the
actual, primary issue is the silencing of normatively white men by the
dogmatic left.

Or so we have been told in the 1990s. This silencing is so egregiously
inequitable that it is not only Coleman Silk who suffers from the tyranny.
During the fallout of the spooks catastrophe, Silk's wife, Iris, dies suddenly
of a stroke. Outraged, Silk cries out at one point, "These people *murdered*
Iris."[55] According to the logic of the novel, Iris's actual death shares less
of an affinity with Gladys's metaphorical death than it shares with the
lynched black body in *Autobiography of an Ex-Colored Man,* as a testimony
of social injustice. By "these people," he includes "the college's small black
student organization and . . . a black activist group from Pittsfield."[56] Of
this tumultuousness, Jay Halio writes, "Not since David Mamet's *Oleanna*
has there appeared so powerful an indictment of political correctness
and a travesty of student rights and faculty vulnerability in higher education."[57] The grotesque distortion of the public's reaction to Silk's speech
in the novel not only implicates the (black) students and their bid for
recognition of rights, but also the involvement of black activists from the
surrounding community.

According to the novel's perspective, which greatly favors Silk's point
of view and on this matter resembles a neoconservative stance, the travesty,

the tragedy, is the wrongful tie that academia maintains with identity-driven politics developed outside of its ivory towers. Such an indictment suggests that the politicized world passes into the academy during the late 1960s and 1970s when black studies and women's studies programs arise on campuses across the country. When the denunciation of political correctness begins at the start of the 1990s, multiculturalism passes as scholarly criteria for reconstructing curriculum. Indeed, political correctness becomes a salient phenomenon in American cultural consciousness as it is directly related to academia. As Marlia Banning traces in a late twentieth-century genealogy of political correctness, by the early 1990s, "'PC' is presented in counter-leftist discourse as a widespread phenomenon primarily occurring in U.S. universities. U.S. universities are represented as riddled with the special interests of women, minorities, gays, lesbians, and various other 'isms,' thus threatening tradition, including the universal truth and knowledge that universities have been entrusted to produce and protect."[58]

As it is represented in the novel, political correctness refers to "the ideology and programs of the cultural left," but also to the neoconservative trend of the 1980s and 1990s to ridicule the excesses of New Leftist politics, with one effect being, as Andrew Ross has claimed, to "empty" those politics "of all meaning."[59] Richard Feldstein notes that many latter-day neoconservatives, who as policy makers realize right-wing decisions, "were originally members of the Democratic Party and heirs of the Truman Doctrine. . . . These 'reformed' socialists and New Deal liberals . . . turned on their younger counterparts during the contentious Vietnam era."[60] Not only has there been a reversal of those formerly within the ranks of the left as leftist politics were generally transformed during the 1960s, but uses of the term *political correctness* had also been reversed. The term had initially been bandied through a longer history of "left-on-left self-criticism."[61] However, according to Feldstein, "the mythic version of *political correctness* concocted by right-wing neoconservatives partially suppresses the previous meanings of the term [. . . and] political correctness is stripped of its historical significance before being filled with a newly manufactured meaning."[62]

The concept of racial passing, as it is taken up in the context of late twentieth-century indictments of political correctness, might be viewed as bolstering the production of ahistorical, manufactured meaning. The question is no longer about the right wing denying the liberties of the disadvantaged, as Coleman Silk seems to do when he (inadvertently) refers to African Americans with a racist slur. Instead, it is a matter of the left misunderstanding the right as the enemy, when in fact the right is one of their own. For instance, the overly zealous liberal contingent mistakes Silk for a white invidious racist, when in fact he is a victimized African American, not unlike his students and the community activists. If the conversation is no longer about history—which identities have been historically privileged, which ones have been disempowered—then what is at issue is present-day tyranny, in this case tyranny imposed by an ironically color-blind left. Silk understands the overwhelming reaction to his politically incorrect speech as "shenanigans . . . so much jockeying for power. To gain a bigger say in how the college is run," or as "a way to prod . . . the administration into doing what they otherwise would never have done. More blacks on campus. More black students, more black professors. Representation—that was the issue. The only issue."[63] Identity politics, which produces the issue of representation, does not account for what really happened in Coleman Silk's classroom because identity politics cannot address the "customary and primary meaning" of Coleman's speech. Although Coleman's speech supposedly conforms to the straightforwardness of the situation at hand—two students never appear and are therefore unknown—the politicizing of speech effectively distorts this main sense of meaning. An identity politics of representation in this way misrepresents the true intentions of speech and attitude of white/Jewish men like Silk in order to endlessly invoke the injuries of the past: the primary definition is concealed by a political (or politically incorrect) definition, which then strong-arms the academy into admitting and hiring more African Americans. Supposedly, a leftist allegiance to representation—the bodily appearance of the historically underrepresented—distorts the present set of circumstances in public life. To understand the enduring absence of African Americans in some social spaces is to misunderstand the customary and primary crisis of democracy currently: the tyranny of the identity-divisive left is enacted by a wayward recasting of facts and meaning, which effectively and undemocratically silences the white male subject in public. Indeed, from the perspective supported by the novel, the absence of African Americans is not the result of embedded state or institutional practices; it is a matter of black individuals deciding not to show up as public participants, to render themselves nowhere to be seen.

   One might take this opportunity to point out the manner in which the term *spooks* is already an example of "customary and primary meaning" politicized and distorted to become a derogatory term for African Americans. Indeed, this production of new meaning was not the work of African Americans or present-day leftists. There is a perpetual process by which, as Feldstein has put it, language is stripped of historical meaning and filled with new meaning. To see discourse historically, as a terrain of strategic shifting, is to understand that primary meanings become useful alibis for the production of new signification. In this way, new racist neutrality is viable only because of its seeming distinctiveness from old racist protocol: color consciousness and its effects, segregation, open discrimination. Color-blindness—as it is meaningful in neoconservative discursive practices of the late twentieth century—makes earlier leftist strategy an alibi for the current arguments against a color-conscious politics of difference. That Silk does not address the public outrage over his spooks comment by openly revealing his own blackness suggests that racial neutrality or color-blindness is part and parcel of academic integrity. This is say that Silk's decidedly antiquated performance of racial passing in 1996—and the individualism that motivates it—is profoundly compatible with the new ideology of color-blindness, and by extension new policies against racially conscious politics. The Jim Crow–era phenomenon of racial passing as an anachronism for individual choice demonstrates a schema in which the historical past and the neoconservative present can reasonably be collapsed into each other.

The primary racial crisis revolving around Coleman Silk allows Roth's novel to deliberate on a few salient matters couched in the popular consciousness of the late 1990s: the vicissitudes of public and private life (a concern heightened by Bill Clinton's affair with Monica Lewinsky, which the novel repeatedly references); enduring obligations to somehow categorize race and ethnicity; and the mounting inefficiency and presumed anti-intellectualism of identity politics. The novel's focus on a racial specter that is by definition not there demonstrates the problem of how race is to emerge in public discourse in a post–civil rights era in which an anxious fear of reviving or provoking the antiracist challenges of the past gives way to a pervasive, and perhaps wishful, silence about the state of racial politics in the post–civil rights era. As Eduardo Bonilla-Silva argues in a study on the rhetorical strategies of what he terms "color-blind racism," "post–Civil Rights racial norms disallow the open expression of racial views," which is the reason why "whites have developed a concealed way of voicing them."[64] Concealment is a necessary strategy in an era when, for example, no one wants to appear to be racist in public. While the new protocols of color-blindness in the 1990s indicate mainstream sensitivity toward historical forms of bigoted behavior, they also demand that historically racist atti-tudes and their critique now become cloaked in the language of neutrality, such that racism becomes impossible. In this way, the specter of racial inequity passes as that which cannot be said and known, or which can no longer be properly publicized or understood as racism.

Yesterday Is Today: The Racial Time of Skipping a Step between Jim Crow and 1990s Postracial Politics

The consistent plea of *The Human Stain* is that Silk cannot be compre-hended as part of a racial, political, or religious formation because he is the revival of the individual, with a sense of selfhood that exceeds any racial or ethnic category, or any group-driven ideology. Instead of real-izing a fluid individualism by the end of the twentieth century, Silk ex-presses an unfulfilled desire for the promised fluid individualism of the civil rights movement, feeling himself coerced into still identifying with rigid categories or politics. In a sense, this was the anticipated outcome of the symbolic entanglement between black and white/Jewish fathers who unwittingly shared a vision of the future in which the neutrality of culture could undercut the distinctiveness of race and ethnicity. The novel seems to ask whether, in private, we are defined less by public identities than by personal fears and desires.

As a late twentieth-century discursive strategy, color-blindness allows racist individuals to pass in public as nonracists because it conceals private attitudes that are informed by deeply entrenched, historically racist per-spectives. While the discursive premise of color-blindness is that a form of public concealment is a necessary step toward the abolition of racism, the paradoxical resistance to political correctness indicates that PC con-cealment, or the regulation of speech, impinges on the quality and truth-fulness of public communication. Advocates of color-blindness pose the right to have one's racist speech protected against and above the right of people of color to be protected against its damaging effects. This para-dox demonstrates a problem for the rationality of postracial discourse: the insistence that racial color-blindness is the route toward a collectively desired end to racism that entails an undesired restriction of personal lib-erty: the freedom of speech. *The Human Stain* does its best to bypass this complicated knot in the paradigmatic scene that began my discussion of this novel. The politically correct outcry over Silk's speech—a public concern for racialized communities and for two black students in particular— is rendered inappropriate because Silk literally had no way of seeing the people he called spooks. Color-blindness, in this way, is not a discursive strategy that bumps up against the rationality or ethics of political correctness. Indeed, it is not discursive at all but rather a matter of natural perception. The PC outcry is beside the point because the students, the ostensible victims of racism were, in fact, not to be seen.

Both color-blindness and the controversy around political correctness entail a process of co-optation from early twentieth-century liberalism to the neoconservatism of the 1980s and 1990s. These strategies notwithstanding, the most obvious trope for deliberating on the relationship between private and public in the novel—racial passing—is also the most anachronistic, in the sense that it does not have a function that is consistent in current political discourse. Racial passing, as a social phenomenon among African Americans, is posited in the novel as a sort of historical remnant. Indeed, as someone who continues to pass well into the late 1990s, Silk is an utter anomaly and utterly singular. Elaborate speculation aside, the reason why he clings to a decades-old performance without revising his approach is never quite clear. In contrast, color-blindness, as a 1990s-era political ethos, has an obviously current function in the dismantlement of affirmative action. In a varying but nonetheless significant way, charges of political correctness 1990s-era indictment of leftist cultural politics function most saliently in reference to speech codes, curricula, and cultural changes in academia. As Marilyn Friedman notes, academic political correctness "emerged as a national news media preoccupation" precisely at the beginning of the decade, "in the fall of 1990."[65] While the academic left of the 1980s and 1990s challenged the masculinist, heterosexist, and Eurocentric bias in traditionalist curricula and institutional practices, opponents claimed that the push toward diversity and multiculturalism threatened scholarly impartiality and would lower academic standards. In contrast, racial passing is conceptually rooted to an age before such widely influential leftist reforms, and therefore evokes the persistence of racial difference even as it challenges it.

Yet it is because of this anachronistic quality of a black subject passing for post–de jure segregation that makes racial passing so suitable for illustrating the vicissitudes of contemporary racial politics. In this way, racial passing, as a trope in *The Human Stain,* provides ahistorical support for contemporary attempts to undercut what might be called identity politics or a politics of difference in public. In varying ways, both political correctness and color-blindness emphasize anxiety over the enduring publicness of race in the 1990s; racial passing, as evoked here, attempts to make the analogous case that African Americans (before the divisively nationalist 1960s and 1970s) have historically been anxious about the publicness of race and have perpetuated their own form of neutral individualism in the name of liberation. If we think about blackness historically, we understand that black desire has actually been in sync with that of the neoconservative agenda decades later. When we begin to think historically, today's color-blindness is yesterday's racial passing.

Toward the end of *The Human Stain,* after Silk's death, his sister, Ernestine, recalls urging their brother, Walt, to forgive Coleman by recognizing his decision to pass in terms of its broader significance: "Coleman couldn't wait to go through civil rights to get to his human rights, and so he skipped a step. 'See him historically,' I say to Walt. 'You're a history teacher—see him as a part of something larger.'"[66] However, seeing Silk historically is also to see him ahistorically, as a figure of the past that could curiously be situated at any time at all.

Colorless Stains: Seeing Race through Privacy, Color-blindness, and Love

Ernestine—herself a retired educator—provides her own commentary on current disciplinary and political framings of history, in her own voice: "Here in America, as far as I can see, it's just getting more foolish by the hour. . . . In East Orange High they stopped long ago reading the old classics. . . . Youngsters were coming to me the year I retired, telling me that for Black History Month they would only read a biography of a black by a black. What difference, I would ask them, if it's a black author or it's a white author?"[67] If we think historically, the past of black activism—a civil rights movement and ensuing legislation, a cosmopolitan intellectual tradition—is in tandem with the neoconservative, postracial impulse of today. Race consciousness loses all of its coherence, as if it belongs to a moment that never was. Indeed, Black History Month has no history whatsoever in this context. The fact that Roth's novel conveys this most clearly through the speech of a black woman bears an eerie resemblance to an earlier

moment when another black woman, Coleman's mother, voluntarily narrates her own ghostly disappearance. The irony of this passage is that ultimately, the question that looms large in Roth's *The Human Stain* is, "What
difference . . . if it's a black author or it's a white author?" What difference
if it's Coleman Silk or Nathan Zuckerman who wrote this (auto)biogra-
phy? If only the question issued a starting point for conjecture, for speculation on why some subjects disappear, are rendered silent, or seem not
to exist in either word or action. Instead, a current color-blind ethos would
have it that there is no difference, just the ghosts of an excessively racialized history.

Conversely, one discourse on the enduring history of racial hierarchy
and the specific terms of racial disadvantage is rendered visible in *The
Color of Water*. McBride's memoir wants to tell a fairly conventional story
about an individual woman who passed across the color line, idiosyncrasies notwithstanding. However, the memoir itself enacts a decidedly
postmodern attempt at passing between these two modes of discourse—
enduring history and speculative potential that reach beyond the optic
conventions of race and ethnicity—that effectively complicates an assessment of racial and ethnic recognition at the end of the twentieth century.
Like a palimpsest, the two modes of discourse—which could also be described as race consciousness and color-blindness—pass through each
other; any gesture toward one meaning renders the presence of the other.
Although traditional representations of passing treat the concept as a secret
transgression, one that relies on concealment for its effectiveness, passing
as described in *The Color of Water* is reconceptualized as a consideration
of how seeing—visual or historical consciousness—can occur through
paradoxical or inconsistent means, rather than of whether one sees forms
of identity that are already socially legible. This sort of deliberation suggests that the liminal space between any of the rhetorical oppositions
that are readily available to talk about race and ethnicity, or the systems
of power and resistance that animate these categories—black and white,
color-consciousness and color-blindness—is where new approaches to
and knowledge about these fraught categories can be devised.

Just as the memoir reworks the trope of racial passing to deliberate
on emergent ways to recognize race and ethnicity, it also reinvigorates the
rhetorical dimensions of mixed racialism. McBride's narrative suggests that
although he is keenly aware of his mother's racial indeterminacy, his own
sense of identity remains steadily unambiguous. This sets up a reversal in

the usual schema of representations on mixed racial subjectivity, where the crux is often a commentary on the complications of being multiracial and is properly recognized as such. Here, multiracialism, like passing, becomes an opportunity to rework the rhetorical dimensions of the concept, particularly as it circulates in the late twentieth century. If matters over multiracial identity have gained their public and political salience in part from their connection to matters of family and kinship, then *The Color of Water* takes this connection as an object of inquiry. Significantly, the memoir reverses the gaze between the white mother and her mixed racial, emergently social child.

Through James McBride's young perspective, multiracial subjectivity does not posit multiracialism itself as a marker of difference or crisis. Instead, it holds up the often naturalized qualities of motherhood and affect as sites for questioning the terms of social normativity and of personal (and, implicitly, political) agency. Indeed, motherhood is posited as a site where questions over the terms of social normativity, and personal and political agency can emerge, rather than as a site where familial bonds are unremarkable and therefore where maternal dominance (in matters of advocacy, for instance) is beyond doubt. In some of the rhetoric that surrounds the politics of multiracialism, motherhood or maternal love articulates two disparate impulses: color-blindness (a desire to turn a blind eye to a racialist, national past) and color consciousness (the insistence that race and ethnicity, particularly their new multiforms, matter). While *The Human Stain* challenges maternal authority and the naturalness of maternal affect, it does so by joining the ranks of many a politician, public policy maker, and cultural producer to target black motherhood specifically and exclusively. Comparatively, in *The Color of Water,* maternal love—love in its most natural form—acts as the impetus that translates the personal (and private and familial) into the political and social.

The Color of Water calls into question of the terms of this translation. While love is the ethos that binds this tribute together—the title names a spirit of love—the narrative does not easily accept or take for granted the epistemologies that underpin available strategies for recognizing matters of racial and ethnic experience. Ultimately, the question is not whether color-blindness can be regarded as a more viable strategy than color consciousness, but rather how to determine the ongoing and potential effects of these strategies. Multiracialism is not necessarily a privileged perspective for this task, although one might imagine its possibility: what if multi-racialism, rhetorically, was unmoored from the authority of both older racialist scripts and from a more recently devised political schema? What sort of questions might it facilitate? Through the narration of a son who, out of curiosity, takes a look at his mother, and the narration of a mother who, in turn, invites her son to take a look, McBride's memoir does not simply rely on the realm of the indecipherable—love—to fill in the gaps, but also imagines how encounters with what we don't know can be productive. Ruth Shilsky McBride Jordan becomes a willing partner—not an advocate, a political strategist, or a privileged authority—in cobbling together the disparate fragments of a complicated and mutual history, with all the fissures and fault lines betwixt and between.

Dreams of the Father and Potentials Lost

Obama's ability to speak bilingually . . . (the language of both white and black America) is not a product of his biraciality per se. Had his background been the reverse, had he been fathered by an absent white man and raised within the context of an African American, working-class, maternal family, Obama would not have been allowed the same intimate entrance into the white world and could not have emerged versed in the biculturalism needed to respond to a culturally segregated America.

— Cherríe Moraga, "What's Race Gotta Do with It?"

We are now in a moment when our very capacity to question the fact and power of nationalism is jeopardized precisely because of the identity and charisma of the president, and because of the ways in which power has managed to make minority difference shine in hues we never thought imaginable.

— Roderick Ferguson, "An American Studies Meant for Interruption"

IN 2007, THE MULTIRACIAL SENATOR FROM ILLINOIS, Barack Obama, emerged as a strong candidate with the potential to become the first black president of the United States. The viability of multiracialism had become mainstream since Tiger Woods's pronouncement in 1997. By 2007, it was possible for Obama to recognize his white mother while simultaneously identifying—and being identified—as black. *Troubling the Family* opened with a racial/gender paradigm that arose in 1997, and it now closes in 2007 by discussing a symbol of multiracial personhood ostensibly attained. If *Troubling the Family* began with an anecdote that described how a race man became a Cablinasian, then the story of Obama's campaign might describe a reversal of sorts, or how a postracial candidate—someone who signaled the end of racial relevance because of his mixedness—became identified with blackness. Whereas Tiger Woods's negotiation with race became a lightning rod for proponents of mixed racial designation, Obama's negotiation, including the constant references to his white mother, became a sign of the unprecedented advances of black citizenship. How did mixedness come to conjure blackness once again in the nation's history?

As a representative of racial politics, Obama produced both celebrations of transcendent multiracial identity and black (masculine) advancement. As Charles E. Cook Jr. explains, the "Obama phenomenon" was a recipe partially made up of the following ingredients: (1) calls for transformation signaled by "the future," "new ideas," and "change"; (2) "the power of a handsome, young, charming, charismatic, even glamorous figure, a modern-day Kennedy"; (3) a collective rejection of "familial dynasties," namely "the Bush, Clinton, or Dole families"; and (4) "the symbolism and historic nature that many Democrats see in nominating and potentially electing Obama as president of the United States, particularly in the fortieth year after King's assassination."[1] Taken together, these elements provide a snapshot of two ideologies that are ostensibly distinct, yet work to support one another with the celebrations of Obama. One is a postracialism ideology in which transformation is simply a social abstraction, and personal idiosyncrasies like being handsome or charming are recognizable because race is neutral. The other is the endurance of a distinctly black racial lineage, which is most recognizable when gendered as implicitly masculine. In a sense, the celebrations of Obama's election not only brought together two ideologies that apparently seem at odds with one another—postracialism and black identitarian politics—but used the two to support one another.

In a postracial era, race is neutral, and in a historiography where blackness is implicitly associated with masculine achievement, gender is neutral. To a degree, one might imagine that multiracialism functioned at this historical juncture to facilitate a curious version of racial time that neutralizes the past and present significance of racial and gender subjugation. The future and new ideas are yoked together with a neutral representation of Dr. Martin Luther King Jr.'s place in history. This version curiously intertwines a current will to obscure the historically racial dimension of statist and capitalist oppressions with an earlier black radical and nationalist will to obscure the historically gendered dimensions of statist and capitalist oppressions. It is this current relinquishing of race-based inequities in public and politics, in combination with the ossification of yesterday's civil rights activism, that likely became the temporal conceptualization of Obama's publicity.

So Obama's election as our decidedly first black president is implicitly the long-awaited fulfillment of King's dream for all of us. Obama, in this way, is positioned as a successor of King's civil rights activism, and therefore commemorates and perpetuates the historical conception of black political interests as gender neutral. However, such neutrality ideologically obscures the significance of gender and sexual difference within black communities. As Robin Kelley has explained with regard to black radical activist movements of the 1960s and 1970s, little concern was granted to the specific forms of oppression experienced by black women because black community as a whole was treated as a monolithic site of experience. He writes: "This ostensible gender-neutral conception of the black community (nothing is really gender neutral), presumes that freedom for black people as a whole will result in freedom for black women. Oppressions of sex and gender went unacknowledged or were considered the secondary residue of racial capitalism that would eventually wither away."[2] While analyses of how sex and gender-based oppressions are inextricably linked to the violences of racial capitalism have proliferated since the early stages of black radical activism, such revelations have not completely undercut the manner in which black leadership still presumes that black masculinity stands in for black community generally.

Perhaps ideological gender neutrality was not only the precondition for how black radical activist movements understood racial oppression back in the 1960s and 1970s, and how we remember their contributions—and the contributors—today. The ideology of gender neutrality as it was experienced during the 1960s and 1970s was a precondition for how Obama's transcendence was experienced forty years later. As Cook reminds us, the country might have lost its tolerance for a certain strain of familial dynasties, yet it seemed ready and willing to symbolize the perpetuation of black leadership in terms of paternal progenitors and progenies. If, a decade earlier, Jackie Robinson had been the symbolic forefather of the incipiently successful Tiger Woods, then Martin Luther King Jr. was similarly posited in relation to Obama. Even when the forefather/progeny paradigm is challenged, it remains intact, as in Ricky Jones's polemic on what he terms "Obamamania." Jones registers considerable concern about how today's black leadership is markedly inadequate when compared to the black leadership of previous generations. He asserts that despite the proliferation of wealthy and publicly prominent African Americans in the post–civil rights era, black American public life has been voided of its former cultural and political richness: "This is our new world—the new landscape of black America. It is less progressive, more nihilistic and numb. In many respects, it is closer to a post–civil rights nightmare than King's dream. Black leadership in this new reality has definitely expanded in quantity, but its quality and commitment trouble many."[3]

Jones argues that Obama is a likely example of this "new world" context, which then means that he's no Martin Luther King Jr. However, this lack of resemblance only intensifies what troubles so many, because what is being mourned is a symbolically paternal kinship that has been lost. In his final remarks on Obama's then-potential victory as president, Jones claims that Obama "is no Frederick Douglass, Charles Hamilton Houston, or Martin King Jr. For good or ill, he is not a 'race man.' He is not a black leader but an American leader who happens to be black."[4] In this last distinction, in this transhistorical turn—progressive legacies aside— we find a key, albeit unwitting tautology: Obama is not a race man because he is not a black leader, and black leaders happen to be black men.

Unable to beat him and unable to join him by 2008, the white and female Democratic opponent Hillary Rodham Clinton—running her own historic race—attempted to undercut the perception of Obama's racial neutrality by rendering the leadership of black men transhistorical rather than simply generational. She "compared Obama to Martin Luther King and herself to Lyndon Johnson, saying, 'Dr. King's dream began to be realized when President Lyndon Johnson passed the Civil Rights Act of 1964 . . . but it took a president to get it done.'"[5] Perhaps the most obvious—and unfortunate—aspect of these comparisons is the manner in which they obscure and oversimplify conditions of political leadership. Just as King's assassination implicitly marks the emergence of a new (racial) leader forty years later, Dr. King's dream also evokes a sort of death: it ends when President Johnson passes the Civil Rights Act. The resulting notion is that the temporality of King's dream is reducible to the racial time of rights-based activism, which has been rendered over-with and obsolete by a (white) liberal political establishment (represented by Johnson) and by new, more inclusive cultural standards of the nation more generally.

The manner in which Hillary Clinton's analogy is racialized—white America loses its racial bias through the neutral logic of the law, black identity politics therefore loses its leverage and relevance—is curious because the analogy serves two distinct functions. On the one hand, it trades in the specifically personal identities of Clinton and Obama because it is putting race exclusively at the forefront. As Michael Tesler and David Sears remind us in their account of the presidential campaign, *Obama's Race,* the analogy was part of a trend to code Obama as unequivocally black during the later stages of the campaign. Rather flat-footedly, Clinton is like the white democratic President Johnson (who gets the job done), while Obama is like the black civil rights dreamer Dr. King. Clinton is like a political pragmatist who remedies racial inequity through presidential power, while Obama is like a political idealist who has dreams and vague grievances, but no statist force with which to act. On the other hand of its dual function, the analogy conjures political identities that are transhistorical.

The King/Johnson analogy works because it conceals the manner in which Clinton and Obama are entangled in alternative historical moments. As subjects to come out of the second-wave feminist and post–civil rights eras, both Clinton and Obama could have represented personal sensibilities that would have disrupted what was posited as polarized political positions. Instead, much in the way that Jones mourns the quality of contemporary black leadership, rather than take to task the very conception of race men as a transhistorical sign of black communal vitality, the stories about history during the 2007–8 presidential campaign reveal that we had arrived at an impasse. In part, what comprises this impasse is the perfunctory way in which individuals must become aligned with transhistorical narratives, identities, rote political affiliations, and social practices that do not—cannot—account for alternative, complicated, and perhaps unrecognizable versions of personhood. However, the risk of publicizing such alternative versions of personhood is to seem outside of historical time, and therefore severed from historically determined constituencies and communities. Ideas of transhistorical political identity and personal identity as marked by Obama reveal a problem in history. Which versions of history—other than versions the nation coerces subjects to tell about itself and its citizens again and again—can help us make better sense of what Obamamania was tapping into? What is the role of history in describing and determining the political meaning of race as identity?

The problem of history was ostensibly resolvable in two ways. I've discussed the first way above: this moment—the current role of race and gender—will always already belong to a transhistorical story about political identities. The second way still suggests that the past is determinative. However, this historical determination emphasizes the significance of self-recognition and personal identity. In a brief essay published in 2008 entitled "Obama, the Instability of Color Lines, and the Promise of a Postethnic Future," David Hollinger argues that Obama's then-potential election would help render blackness, as the central site around which American racial identity politics operates intellectually and institutionally, untenable. According to his account, the reason for this untenability is to some degree owed to Obama's ambivalent self-definition "as the candidate of a particular ethnoracial group," which distinguishes him from previous race men who sought presidential election, specifically Jesse Jackson and Al Sharpton. Unlike his predecessors, Obama didn't derive his political relevance from reifications of color lines. As Hollinger imagines the future, as ushered in by Obama's prominence, "ethnoracial categories central to identity politics would be more matters of choice than ascription; in which mobilization by ethnoracial groups would be more a strategic option than a presumed destiny attendant upon mere membership in a group; and in which economic inequalities would be confronted head-on, instead of through the medium of ethnorace."[6] This last point is significant, insofar as it sets up Hollinger's later explication on how categorical "ethnorace" obscures the cultural differences within such categories that allow us to notice that not all individuals within such a categorical block experience economic inequities in the same way.

A key example he provides is the manner in which African immigrants suffer from such inequalities less systemically than people of African descent who have longer familial histories in America. It is for this reason that blackness per se cannot be the sign from which to identify inequality and its solutions. Overall, Hollinger makes his large point this way: "A postethnic social order would encourage individuals to devote as much—or as little—of their energies as they wished to their community of descent. . . . Hence, to be postethnic is . . . to reject the idea that descent is destiny."[7] Hollinger has sought to make a question of racialization, explicitly the possibility of being black and/or multiracial, a matter of individual choice. He suggests that in the future, race could be a matter of personal volition rather than coercion: "No public figure, not even Tiger Woods, has done as much as Obama to make Americans of every education level and social surrounding aware of color-mixing in general and that most of the 'black' population of the United States, in particular, are partially white."[8]

Color mixing notwithstanding, Hollinger's suggestion that Obama is a harbinger of a postethnic future primarily relies on a historical distinction between African-descended immigrants to the United States and African-descended subjects born in the United States to explain an achievement gap among blacks in America generally. He places considerable significance on the fact that Obama's black father was an immigrant from Kenya, arguing that black immigrants tend to be more economically and socially successful than black Americans who have a long legacy in the country. Although he goes on to explain that a more viable approach to addressing inequality is to consider economic disparities in conjunction with migration trends, he does little to unpack, ultimately, just how "Obama's illustration in his own person of the contrast between immigrant and nonimmigrant black people, and of the reality of ethnoracial mixing, presents a compelling invitation to explore the limits of blackness especially."[9]

So "descent is [not] destiny" when it comes to race and ethnicity, and yet Obama's Kenyan father was, according to Hollinger, a determining factor in Obama's success. However, what is so curious about this assessment—that Obama's success is an outcome of having an African father, rather than an African American one—is that he neglects to explain how this is so in light of Barack Obama Sr.'s absence from the future president's life. In Hollinger's account, there is something about Obama's having a black immigrant father—as absent as he may have been—that determined an exceptional mode of personhood, a mode that is exceptionally capable of negotiating socially based differences. Finally, because Hollinger is ostensibly concerned with the vicissitudes of blackness, he is therefore ready to point out that "many studies tell us that black immigrants and their children do better educationally and economically than do the descendants of American slavery and Jim Crow."[10]

Curious still is that Hollinger has virtually nothing to say about Barack Obama's wife, Michelle, in light of this. Unlike her husband, Michelle Obama is a black subject with deep familial roots in the United States, a "descendant of American slavery and Jim Crow," if you will. Still, she shares with Barack a high degree of educational and economic accomplishment. According to Hollinger's revelations about the contingencies of blackness—and placing ironic generalizations about nonimmigrant blacks aside—Michelle's success should be worthy of exploration because, presumably, it can't be attributed to nationhood, an originating presence, an immigrant parent, an influential father. So in an essay that calls for the destabilization of identitarian destinies, why doesn't the focus ever settle on what Michelle illustrates in her own person?

A cynical response to this question is that any account of Michelle's personhood—historical, cultural, social—is always already foreclosed by destiny. As the precondition for how we have traditionally understood U.S. formations of blackness, she is virtually unremarkable and indistinguishable, simply part and parcel of the generally dire outcomes of slavery and Jim Crow. If Hillary Clinton and Barack Obama Jr. traded in transhistorical political identities in order to become knowable in public, Michelle Obama, in the context of Hollinger's argument, is a sort of historical impasse personified. She can't instrumentalize the language of transhistorical national politics; nor can she account for herself as anathema to the nation's concealments of personhood. She is always already nowhere and knowable as nothing.

According to Tesler and Sears, the early stages of Obama's campaign in 2007 were generally racially neutral, insofar as they deemphasized Obama's blackness and connection to black community. In their account of the election coverage in 2007, "the media had predominately portrayed Obama as the post-racial candidate who transcended the divisive identity politics of the post–civil rights era. It was perhaps inevitable, though, in a country with such a long history of pernicious race relations, that Obama's racial background would not remain dormant forever."[11] This latter statement refers to what was to come in the following year: his opponents' use of clearer, stronger racial rhetoric (as Clinton's analogy illustrated), and even more obviously, Obama's affiliation with Reverend Jeremiah Wright and the protest tradition of black churches. In both cases, the rhetoric of racial neutrality or unequivocal blackness were two sides of a Janus head that indicated the historically unprecedented potential of resituating race and national power.

In his response to Kevin Gaines's presidential address to the American Studies Association, Roderick Ferguson points to the manner in which "Dr. King's dream," as it is vaguely referred to, ought not to be reducible to Obama's version of politics. King's activism was not reducible to the civil rights movement or to making appeals to the state for legislative change. Ferguson argues that Obama does not indicate a commensurable representation of King's broader and more radical "peace mission"; rather, he becomes an occasion to recognize how racial minoritization can "mobiliz[e] progressive traditions and histories for hegemonic leverage" at this particular historical moment. The hegemony refers to state power as perpetuated by the U.S. presidency, often against our interests. Ferguson turns to Dana Nelson's scholarship here: "Nelson reminds us that there is a structural asymmetry between the offices of the state and the communities those offices claim to represent." While Hillary Clinton evoked "Dr. King and President Lyndon Johnson" with the intention of representing two antithetical figures in the context of state power, the irony is that both can be mobilized to extenuate the power and violence of the state, by the state, today. Although the comparison between King and Obama was meant to mark a black and marginal political lineage, ultimately, the position of the presidency can absorb blackness (as masculine)—and womanhood (as white)—without being transformed by the absorption of such historical marginalization. Obama's masculine multiracialism is just another hue that shines in the fantasy of transgression.

Still, it shines. *Troubling the Family* concludes that what was actually being celebrated—what we were celebrating—was a revitalized sense of our own public and private potential. We celebrated the seeming realization of a long-standing dream: to have the idiosyncrasies of our personhood—in all of their racial, gendered, and sexual inappropriateness—overcome the normative epistemologies that still determine which sort of individuality can appear in public. Yet this version of personhood achieved actually undercuts the potential of granting personal experience with political significance. If Obama signals the promise of personhood we've been dreaming of, then the question remains what potentials are lost when we dream away the challenges that still exist to expanding our lives in public. "The personal is political" has become commonplace as we move through the twenty-first century. However, does the promise of personhood still generate various, complicated, and imaginative approaches to becoming political? What becomes of this promise when the mystifying role history plays in attaching personhood to politics seems to rely on deference to state power, and the compartmentalization of identitarian categories that obscure the complications and contradictions within them?

In a short piece published in the feminist journal *Meridians*, Cherríe Moraga discusses the manner in which she and her family—a "Chicana-lesbian-headed household" with teenage children—responded to the election-night victory of Barack Obama. Cutting across generations, the family's overall response was ambivalent. While Moraga's children were "ecstatic" about the new president-elect, Moraga and her partner, Linda, were skeptical that Obama's victory signaled the promise of equity, or, as Obama mentioned in his victory speech, that "America is a place where all things are possible."[12] Moraga begins her discussion within familial activity on election night, ranging from attending a public celebration in which predominately white liberals of the Bay Area recognize Obama's likely victory through faux indigenous performances to the more private act of watching the election results on television, at home. The two locations demonstrate how subjects might find themselves embedded within two opposing versions of racial time. The first demonstrates a travesty of multicultural celebration, facilitated by an implicitly violent lapse of public, historical memory. Predominately white participants performing a quasi-indigenous ritual raise the specter of theft, genocide, and entrenched disempowerment. Conversely, the second demonstrates a rare occasion for the "politically marginalized" to finally experience a "sudden sense of public membership in mainstream politics of the day."[13] Moraga explains that her "fifteen-year-old son . . . just wants for once in his young life to feel good about his president and his country."[14]

The home space and its extension—the celebratory phone calls by other family members—are represented here as the opposite of what has been traced throughout this book. The private lives within a particular family, and the affect produced by a sense of civic recognition finally achieved, do not facilitate the neutralization of the public sphere as that which fortifies the politics of the marginalized in multifaceted ways. Instead, the notable aspect of Moraga's account is that both versions of national temporality—the one that signals a public teleology of violent forgetfulness and the other that signals a teleology of marginalization finally overcome—fail to capture the moment of Obama's victory. If anything, the failure she identifies requires an alternative response, an alternative temporality.

For Moraga, this is where the personal becomes political. Moraga uses the autobiographical mode to reveal two conditions about the historical juncture that Obama's victory marks. First, it reveals the manner in which the often-used slogan reconceptualizes how temporality, in addition to private/public space, is experienced. "The personal is political" offered a strategy for women to see the underlying value systems that were operative in their everyday lives and to wage their resistance within institutions of patriarchal power. The temporal implications of this insight emerge as Moraga begins to unfold the way in which one ideology is facilitated through the other. The timeline of conquest (the public celebration by white liberals of multiculturalism) is connected to the timeline of civic and political exclusion of marginalized subjects (the private celebration by aberrant subjects of achieving full citizenship). Both versions are so persistently at cross-play with one another, and underpinned by an ideological centrality of nationalism, that Moraga's discussion begins to identify the problem of Obama's victory as a further obscuration of what, precisely, we gain by submitting our hopes and dreams at the feet of the nation.

Second, along with the implicit insight that "the personal is political" provides an analysis of temporality, Moraga's skepticism is part of a foundational antagonism to various modes of nationalism and their violences. Her discussion indicates how feminist movements of the 1960s and 1970s could be remembered still as the "occasion, the vehicle, of our hopes, and our dreams" at the very moment when such a memory seems irrelevant to the successful election of the country's first black/multiracial president. The timeline of 1960s- and 1970s-era feminisms extends from what seems like a bygone period of utopic, unsustainable liberationist projects to the current moment in which our primary challenge is to broaden our collective sociopolitical imagination. The overtly domestic situation is Moraga's springboard for returning the relevance of this particular election to a careful assessment of the public sphere, where various forms of economic and racially gendered inequities abound. Unlike her teenage children, Moraga and her partner retain a long historical memory of various activist analyses and aims. If Moraga's publication troubles the family, insofar as it begins with a divergence of perspective between mothers and their children, it does so in order to pan away from a tight focus on the nuclear family and the well-being of children, and toward the audacity of disenfranchised collectives who are currently the sign of how the meaning and practices of liberation cry for expansion.

Moraga offers a litany of nationalist violence to reveal the various ways in which injustice operates: not by simply relegating subjects to the margins of civil belonging, but by literally dehumanizing them, criminalizing them, and refusing to recognize their personhood. The breaches of justice that routinely occur within the nation's borders are many: "Indigenous American workers (from México, El Salvador, Guatemala) [are] hunted down like dogs in the night . . . ordinary immigrant Muslims are still held

in detention camps as never-tried would-be/could-be terrorists ... a geno-
cidal death rate within Native America ... a detained and pregnant un-
documented worker [wearing] an electronic ankle bracelet" illustrate her
point.[15] The manner in which the nation not only refuses to recognize
but also overtly attempts to destroy personhood for domestic labor, neo-
imperialism, and the perpetuation of its own identity is not limited to
indigenous populations, Muslims, women. At the heart of women of color
feminist activism was the contention that the personal lives of women
were bound to the lines of power that determined how public resources
were to be distributed, which services were to be made available, and what
counted as social equality. This broad view encompassed the manner in
which the category of womanhood, or female gender subjectivity, was
connected to a vast array of public and private practices that impacted the
lives of the historically dehumanized and disempowered. Women of color
activists yoked together a number of issues that ranged from domestic
violence to labor organization and better health care in black neighborhoods.[16] For black feminism in particular, the enrichment of personhood
meant revealing the intersections of identity and oppression, and demanding that the health, safety, and liberty of socially underprivileged persons
be made a public priority.

Moraga explains that her own participation during "the brief and minor-
scale heyday of the women of color feminist movement" continues to in-
form her political sensibilities. The way in which she understands the conditions of the "the disempowered poor (especially women and children
of color)" as "the litmus test for democracy" indicates that a short-lived
movement of the 1970s helped create the analytical architecture for what
social equality means today.[17] It moves toward a deliberation on how the
acknowledgment of our various relations to social history—from an incipient version of racial time to a more experienced, multivalent version—
undercut the optimism of Obama's victory, and introduce the question of
what, exactly, we were celebrating when we celebrated this victory.

While Moraga undercuts the nuclear family as the central site from
which to identify which aspects of private life ought to be political or public, she simultaneously comments on how the family has played a key
role in the making of a president. Moraga insists that Obama's ability to
speak the language of biracialism—or multiracialism—is contingent on
the absence of an alternative family narrative, in which white paternity
is missing and a black, working-class, maternal family is the privileged

domain of subjective development. In other words, there is no Obama—
or no leader with the capacity to reconcile America's racial divide—if
black motherhood is historically salient. In a sense, this presupposition
evokes Hollinger's silence about Michelle Obama, as if there is no version
of transhistorical political identity, or a counternational personal identity through which she can become publically recognizable, since black
womanhood is already the transhistorical absence against which other
identitarian forms become seen. In another sense, black maternity, or the
black maternal family, is ostensibly antithetical to the notion of us sharing
a national dream.

　　This returns to the multiple ways in which this particular racialized
version of motherhood, or a racially gendered version of the family, has
historically been pitted against the norms of American functionalism and
identity. From Patrick Moynihan's tangle of pathology in 1965 to the
mythical welfare queen of the 1980s, black mothers (and especially those
who are the single parents of black children) have been rhetorically central to what America can't be or want—to what we would never hope for.
Yet Moraga's assessment of what made Obama possible as a multiracial
man of the people—the condition of black maternal absence—also ex-
poses the contradictory necessity of black womanhood to become objects
within a normative historiography of racial and gender progress.

　　On this point Moraga marks a crucial moment in Obama's victory
speech, as she is concerned not only with how he became able to speak at
all, but also with his "oratory in both style and in substance." Moraga
describes a key moment during Obama's victory speech in 2008, in which
he historically contextualizes his personal success through the life of
Ann Nixon Cooper, an elderly black woman who had previously been
denied the right to vote. Presumably, the promise of full citizenship is
finally obtained with her role in electing the first black president. Here is
Obama's account:

> This election had its many firsts and many stories that will be told
> for generations. But one that's on my mind tonight's about a
> woman who cast her ballot in Atlanta. She's a lot like the millions
> of others who stood in line to make their voices heard in this
> election except for one thing: Ann Nixon Cooper is 106 years old.
> She was born a generation after slavery; a time when there were
> no cars on the road or planes in the sky; when someone like her

couldn't vote for two reasons—because she was a woman and because of the color of her skin. . . . And this year, in this election, she touched her fingers to a screen, and cast her vote, because after 106 years in America, through the best of times and the darkest of hours, she knows how America can change.[18]

Moraga identifies the reason why this focus on the one woman's life is so effective: it signals the end of inequity. Obama had previously addressed the endurance of systemic racism, but this emphasis wanes until the cornerstone story of Cooper's life. She writes, "Through the story of Ann Nixon Cooper, the issue of racism finally reemerges in Obama's campaign, but this time we have triumphed over it. Through the election of Obama, all of us—black, white, Asian, native—are absolved of its past inequities, its unspeakable violences, its requisite rage."[19]

While Moraga does not explicitly say so, the all of us who are now absolved of history's violences might feasibly include women among the triumphant masses. To some degree, this is not a negligible addition. To use his personal victory as the opportunity to narrate the story of one woman's life offers a substitution of sorts. Obama's idiosyncratic set of experiences and achievements is momentarily obscured by the idiosyncrasies of some one who may not live within the intersections of biculturalism but does occupy the particular intersection of blackness and womanhood. Why does Obama make this substitution? Why choose to have a black woman be the central object within a historical trajectory? Why single out the experience of one person, render the life of Ann Nixon Cooper exceptional, only to emphasize the manner in which that particular life is paradoxically anonymous? In another words, why offer this historic moment—this historic victory—as one in which equity is achieved for all of us, but individual recognition and personal agency become vaguely weakened and constricted in the process? Why have black womanhood be the conduit through which "past inequities, its unspeakable violences, its requisite rage" are eventually transformed into a moment of triumph for all of us today?

Perhaps this substitution is apt here if black womanhood already signals the beginning and the end of historical inequity. If, by the start of the twenty-first century, blackness in general offered a fraught version of liberalism's teleology—which is the insistence that black subjects accept a horizon of neutrality and move toward it while under the shadow of racial history—then black womanhood in particular offers a yet more fraught version. Black womanhood signals in particularly pronounced ways how what seems like a teleology produces its own logical other, which is immobility. Once again, Moraga implies that Obama's success is predicated, to some extent, on the absence of black women, and more specifically black maternity. However, in the extended story of Cooper that Obama tells, we not only get a version of temporality in which we all reach the end of historical inequities, but we also get a version of racial time in which black womanhood is somehow a sign of historical progress and, for being such, is curiously bereft of any specificity as a historical subject.

In a sense, the elderly Cooper is the black maternal figure who had been missing until now, and has been missing in this book, because she appears to be a mother to us all. She emerges at what seems to be the inception of modernity, at "a time when there were no cars on the road or planes in the sky," and comes to illustrate how the state has changed in a culmination of technological, political, and social practices. Even as personhood is the final achievement—for we understand the value of what Cooper knows and what she can choose to do—this person is strangely held captive by the statist insistence that she be individuated for the purposes of extenuating the state. This is not the same as utilizing the conditions of the personal as a litmus test for the health of a democracy. Rather, the personal is the beginning and the ending of all liberation struggles.

Perhaps Obama's prominence is not what it seems: he signals the manner in which the shifting operations of power make the lines of force difficult to recognize. In a sense, Moraga and Ferguson are assessing the significance of the Obama era from differing historical vantage points. Two timelines overwrite the emergence of the charismatic, multiracial leader, one that adheres to a long history of black and white racial and gender logics, in which black maternity is dysfunctional or impossible, and another that acknowledges that we cannot really be sure how such racial history has been co-opted for the uses of the nation at present. Although in this book I have argued that the precondition for the multiracial movement that emerged at the end of the twentieth century was the unfinished business of second-wave feminism—the mournful loss of black/white feminist collaboration—and the masculinist legacy of black nationalism, the presence of Barack Obama casts other ghostly shadows, or other potentials for recasting racial and gender historiographies.

This book began with a paradigmatic anecdote about the rise of Tiger Woods. It described how his place in popular culture demarcated one older racial lineage—the family of black race men and, by extension, the family of black community—from a newer lineage of the multiracial family, which was most ostensibly identified with white motherhood. At the time of this writing, however, the prodigious young athlete that Oprah Winfrey once referred to as America's son has become a fully grown man in public. His fall in 2009 occurred as a result of the public revelation that Woods had been human all this time.[20] This Woods—this version of personhood— was not only aberrant, but decidedly hostile toward normative family life: extramarital sexuality abounded with astounding frequency and variety. If he was no longer America's son, he came to resemble America's native son: beneath the skin, was there not something lurking, something latent, that would eventually make what Woods did the same as who Woods is? In 2012, neither Woods nor Obama exemplifies the lineages from which we come, or the promise of obtaining livable lives in public. However, it may be useful to downplay an approach to comprehending how anyone troubles the family in order to consider when—and for whom— family matters.

Acknowledgments

This book began in earnest six years ago as a minor irritant that eventually developed into a full-blown fixation. Completing this project would not have been possible without generous funding from the University of Washington. I'm grateful for receiving the Junior Faculty Development Award; a grant from the Institute for Ethnic Studies in the United States (IESUS), through the Graduate School Fund for Excellence and Innovation (GSFEI); the Walter Chapin Simpson Center for the Humanities Society Faculty Research (Society of Scholars) Fellowship; and research retreat support from the Helen Riaboff Whiteley Center.

At the University at Albany, I had the pleasure of sharing numerous conversations and roughly written drafts with fellow graduate students Menoukha Case and Josephine Huang. Bret Benjamin challenged and encouraged me in equal measure. Mike Hill was a careful and tireless reader of my early work; his swan song to whiteness studies left a subtle resonance that became increasingly louder. Sharon Holland helped me to imagine a home in this profession; her Black Cultural Studies seminar was an introduction to a scholarly world I wanted to inhabit. Mark Anthony Neal, who had more confidence in me than I deserved, makes the heavy lifting look easy like nobody else. Lisa Thompson is still one of the most generous mentors I have had the good fortune to know; she did me the great favor of lifting the veil. Valerie Smith paved the way and brought me into the fray of family.

The English department at the University of Washington in Seattle has been an exceptionally friendly and intellectually exciting environment in which to belong; I thank all of my colleagues for creating such a comfortable community. Carolyn Busch, Annee Fisher, Martha Mestl, Karla Tofte, Rob Weller, and Susan Williams are owed a large debt of gratitude for all that they do. Several colleagues deserve special mention, more than I can name here: Carolyn Allen, Jessica Burstein, Eva Cherniavsky, Louis Chude-Sokei, Laura Chrisman, Kate Cummings, Gary Handwerk,

Tom Lockwood, Colleen McElroy, Suhanthie Motha, Alys Weinbaum, and Kathy Woodward.

Of those colleagues who have enriched my life in Seattle during the past several years, very few are owed a bigger expression of my gratitude than Gillian Harkins, Chandan Reddy, and Caroline Simpson, who helped me bring this project into focus. From the moment of my arrival at the University of Washington, each one has been a gracious mentor, colleague, and friend. For their generosity, I am deeply indebted.

With regard to university-wide collaboration, I've had the good fortune to be a part of the interdisciplinary research and professionalization group Women Investigating Race, Ethnicity, and Difference (WIRED). There are more WIRED scholars than I can thank here individually, but I offer a hearty thanks to all the members for their collective wisdom, humor, and support. WIRED would not have been possible without the shared vision and labor of Janine Jones and Ralina Joseph, two founding "mamas." Ralina Joseph, LeiLani Nishime, and Tyina Steptoe have inspired and challenged me during our writing group sessions. A small selection of key contributors include Rachel Chapman, Alexes Harris, Michelle Habell-Pallan, Trista Huckleberry, Sonnet Retman, Ileana Rodriguez Silva, Stephanie Smallwood, Wadiya Udell, Manka Varghese, and Joy Williamson-Lott. Naomi Murakawa has been a wonderful colleague and friend during the long, sometimes painful, process of bringing this project to a close.

I have great appreciation for the colleagues across the profession who have been troubling, and expanding the concerns with, mixed-race studies: Heidi Aridizzone, Michele Elam, Jared Sexton, Rainier Spencer, and Catherine Squires. Roderick Ferguson and Grace Hong have been ideal editors of the series Difference Incorporated, and I am glad to be a part of their intellectual vision. Ruby Tapia was a thoughtful, careful, and kind reader of my manuscript for the University of Minnesota Press. Richard Morrison, editorial director, has been exceedingly supportive, and I thank him for seeing the potential of this project.

A word of thanks to those who have made the journey sweeter: to Danielle Elliott, Zohra Saed, and Simone Williamson for being thoughtful junior colleagues as we developed our nascent feminism of color poetics at Brooklyn College. To Larin McLaughlin, whom I've often relied on for sharp and judicious feedback. Grace Norman, Brian Patterson, Jennifer Manzelli Patterson, Jon Sequeira, Amanda Snellinger, and Jason

Roseler were warm and welcoming in a city known for its freeze. To Ian Duncan for his impeccable timing and potential. To Kristie Metcalf, whose style and ambition I greatly admire. To Rachael Dillman, who called my attention to Grey Villet's beautiful photograph of Mildred Loving and her daughter Peggy. Shelley Halstead was the very first person to welcome me to Seattle and had opened her warm and fuzzy home to me on more occasions than I can count. The pleasant Mr. Spaulding has never let me down. And to Shahrul Ladue, who was there at the start of it all. For everything, I thank you.

A special thank-you goes to Michael Swailes, who has been remarkably generous, kindhearted, and patient while awaiting the completion of this book. Thank you for making me at home. Finally, I thank my family, my parents, and especially my mother, Amina Ibrahim. She is the person who taught me more than she'll ever know.

Notes

Introduction

1. A few notable examples include the following: Rainier Spencer, *Spurious Issues: Race and Multiracial Identity Politics in the United States* (Boulder, Colo.: Westview Press, 1999); G. Reginald Daniel, *More than Black? Multiracial Identity and the New Racial Order* (Philadelphia: Temple University Press, 2002); Heather Dalmage, ed., *The Politics of Multiracialism: Challenging Racial Thinking* (Albany: SUNY Press, 2004); Kim Williams, *Mark One or More: Civil Rights in Multiracial America* (Ann Arbor: University of Michigan Press, 2006); Kimberly McClain DaCosta, *Making Multiracials: State, Family, and Market in the Redrawing of the Color Line* (Palo Alto, Calif.: Stanford University Press, 2007); Catherine Squires, *Dispatches from the Color Line: The Press and Multiracial America* (Albany: SUNY Press, 2007); Jared Sexton, *Amalgamation Schemes: Antiblackness and the Critique of Multiracialism* (Minneapolis: University of Minnesota Press, 2008); and Michele Elam, *The Souls of Mixed Folk: Race, Politics, and Aesthetics in the New Millennium* (Palo Alto, Calif.: Stanford University Press, 2011). Anthologies published in the last decade include the following: Yvette Alex-Assensoh and Lawrence Hanks, eds., *Black and Multiracial Politics in America* (New York: New York University Press, 2000); Kerry Ann Rockquemore and David Brunsma, eds., *Beyond Black: Biracial Identity in America* (Thousand Oaks, Calif.: Sage, 2002); Kevin Johnson, ed., *Mixed Race America and the Law* (New York: New York University Press, 2003); David Brunsma, ed., *Mixed Messages: Multiracial Identities in the "Color-blind" Era* (Boulder, Colo.: Lynne Rienner, 2006); and Mary Beltrán and Camilla Fojas, eds., *Mixed Race Hollywood* (New York: New York University Press, 2008). This continuously expanding list does not include the many recent autobiographical, biographical, and ethnographical works that address multiracialism.

2. Bruce Berlet, "Woods' First Major Title a Sports Masterpiece—This Performance Is Much More than Another Victory," *Hartford Courant*, April 14, 1997.

3. Quoted in Larry Dorman, "Woods Tears Up Augusta and Tears Down Barriers," *New York Times*, April 14, 1997, http://www.nytimes.com/.

4. Quoted in Larry Dorman, "Elder Proudly Watches Quest Fulfilled," *New York Times*, April 14, 1997, http://www.nytimes.com/.

5. Quoted in Dorman, "Woods Tears Up Augusta."

6. "Here's to You, Jackie Robinson," *Chicago Tribune,* April 15, 1997, http://articles.chicagotribune.com/.

7. Hazel Carby, *Race Men* (Cambridge, Mass.: Harvard University Press, 2000), 12–13.

8. Ibid., 14.

9. Cathy Cohen, *The Boundaries of Blackness: AIDS and the Breakdown of Black Politics* (Chicago: University of Chicago Press, 1999), 10–11.

10. Ibid., 14.

11. Henry Yu, "How Tiger Wood Lost His Stripes: Post-nationalist American Studies as a History of Race, Migration, and the Commodification of Culture," in *Popular Culture: A Reader,* ed. Raiford Guins and Omayra Zaragoza Cruz (Thousand Oaks, Calif.: Sage, 2005), 200.

12. Ed Sherman, "Tiger Woods Plays Golf with Michael Jordan, Tapes *Oprah Winfrey Show,*" *Chicago Tribune,* April 22, 1997.

13. Hiram Perez, "How to Rehabilitate a Mulatto: The Iconography of Tiger Woods," in *East Main Street: Asian American Popular Culture,* ed. Shilpa Davé et al. (New York: New York University Press, 2005), 231.

14. Sherman, "Tiger Woods Plays Golf."

15. Maurice O. Wallace, *Constructing the Black Masculine: Identity and Ideality in African American Men's Literature and Culture, 1775–1995* (Durham, N.C.: Duke University Press, 2002).

16. Yu, "How Tiger Woods Lost His Stripes," 205.

17. Perez, "How to Rehabilitate a Mulatto," 234.

18. Ibid., 225.

19. Ibid., 235.

20. Yu, "How Tiger Woods Lost His Stripes," 207.

21. Robert Reid-Pharr, *Once You Go Black: Choice, Desire, and the Black American Intellectual* (New York: New York University Press, 2007), 33.

22. Sujata Moorti, "Cathartic Confessions or Emancipatory Texts? Rape Narratives on *The Oprah Winfrey Show,*" *Social Text* 57 (1998): 83.

23. Ibid., 87.

24. Ibid., 83.

25. Janice Peck, "Talk about Racism: Framing a Popular Discourse of Race on Oprah Winfrey," *Cultural Critique* 27 (1994): 90.

26. Ibid., 91.

27. Ibid.

28. "Tiger Woods: April 24, 1997," *Oprah: The Oprah Winfrey Show* (Chicago: Harpo Productions, 1998). Transcript prepared by Burrelle's Information Services. I refer to the written transcript to cite dialogue here, but I supplement the transcription with my descriptions of the video telecast. This approach is especially

useful for capturing the set design, the mannerisms and gestures of Winfrey and Woods, and audience reactions. See *The Oprah Winfrey Show: 20th Anniversary Collection* (Chicago: Harpo Productions, 2005).

29. "Tiger Woods: April 24, 1997," *Oprah.*

30. Daryn Kagan, "Interview with Corporate Trainer Steadman Graham," *CNN Live Today,* May 13, 2002, http://transcripts.cnn.com/.

31. Hortense J. Spillers, "Mama's Baby, Papa's Maybe: An American Grammar Book," in *African American Literary Theory: A Reader,* ed. Winston Napier (New York: New York University Press), 257.

32. Ibid., 260.

33. Ibid., 261.

34. Ibid., 278.

35. Ibid., 257.

36. "Wendy Williams, Boyce Watkins to Discuss Oprah Winfrey's Relationship with 50 Cent, Ice Cube with Paula Zahn on CNN," *Hip Hop Press,* December 6, 2006, http://www.hiphoppress.com/.

37. Kerry Ann Rockquemore, "Deconstructing Tiger Woods: The Promise and the Pitfalls of Multiracial Identity," in Dalmage, *Politics of Multiracialism,* 132.

38. Ibid., 133.

39. Yu, "How Tiger Woods Lost His Stripes," 200.

40. Rockquemore, "Deconstructing Tiger Woods," 134.

41. Perez, "How to Rehabilitate a Mulatto," 222.

42. Richard Sandomir, "Media Overlooked Zoeller's News," *New York Times,* April 25, 1997, http://www.nytimes.com/.

43. Joe Drape, "Woods Meets Zoeller for Lunch," *New York Times,* May 21, 1997, http://www.nytimes.com/.

44. Quoted in Rockquemore, "Deconstructing Tiger Woods," 137.

45. Ibid., 133.

46. Williams, *Mark One or More,* 87.

47. Daryl Lindsey, "The Stakes Are a Bit Higher for Us," *Salon,* February 16, 2000, http://www.salon.com/.

1. Multiracial Timelines

1. See Rachel Moran's notable study, *Interracial Intimacy: The Regulation of Race and Romance* (Chicago: University of Chicago Press, 2001). Moran explores how assumptions about the transformative nature of romance or affect, and the legal legitimization of intimacy across racial and ethnic categories are not commensurate with actual practices. Moran's study is one useful beginning point for me because it establishes that affect and legality are both inadequate foundations from which to explain how interracialism (between couples) and multiracialism

(as the subjective outcome of interracial intimacy) can potentially deliver prom-ises of racial transcendence.

2. Theresa Man Ling Lee, "Rethinking the Personal and the Political: Femi-nist Activism and Civic Engagement," *Hypatia* 22, no. 4 (2007): 163.

3. Nancy Isenberg, "The Personal Is Political: Gender, Feminism, and the Politics of Discourse Theory," *American Quarterly* 44 (1992): 449–58.

4. Louis Althusser, *Lenin and Philosophy* (New York: Monthly Review Press, 1971), 144–47.

5. SanSan Kwan and Kenneth Speirs, eds., *Mixing It Up: Multiracial Subjects* (Austin: University of Texas Press), 4.

6. Moran, *Interracial Intimacy*, 9.

7. Johnnetta Cole and Beverly Guy-Sheftall, *Gender Talk: The Struggle For Women's Equality in African American Communities* (New York: Ballantine, 2003), 4.

8. See the Combahee River Collective's 1977 "A Black Feminist Statement," in *The Black Feminist Reader,* ed. Joy James and T. Denean Sharpley-Whiting (Malden, Mass.: Blackwell, 2000), for a description of how radical women of color feminism expanded the feminist movement's charge to understand "the personal is political."

9. See Joy James, "Radicalizing Feminism," in *Race and Class* 40 (1999): 15–31, for an extended conversation on the importance and difficulties of distin-guishing the ideological differences between black feminisms that developed from the civil rights era on.

10. Combahee River Collective, "Black Feminist Statement," 269.

11. See Lisa Duggan, *The Twilight of Equality: Neoliberalism, Cultural Politics, and the Attack on Democracy* (Boston: Beacon Press, 2003). Duggan provides an ex-tended explanation of how 1990s-era neoliberalism entailed an ideological separa-tion of cultural politics, which were ostensibly antiracist or race neutral, from the economy. This neoliberal separation lead to the impoverishment of cultural pol-itics, mystification of how party politics are unified in support of free markets, and the weakening of the public sphere as a site where social justice projects can expand.

12. DaCosta, *Making Multiracials*, 34.

13. "About Project RACE: Mission Statement," *Project RACE,* http://www.projectrace.com/.

14. Ramona Douglass, "The Evolution of the Multiracial Movement," in *Mul-tiracial Child Resource Book: Living Complex Realities,* ed. Maria P. P. Root and Matt Kelley (Seattle: MAVIN Foundation, 2003), 14.

15. These organizations included the National Association for the Advance-ment of Colored People (NAACP), the Mexican American Legal Defense and Education Fund (MALDEF), and the National Coalition for the Accurate Count of Asian and Pacific Americans. Ibid., 15.

16. Ibid.

17. Heather Dalmage, *Tripping on the Color Line: Black–White Multiracial Families in a Racially Divided World* (New Brunswick, N.J.: Rutgers University Press, 2000), 137.

18. Cynthia Nakashima, "Voices from the Movement: Approaches to Multiraciality," in *The Multiracial Experience: Racial Borders as the New Frontier*, ed. Maria P. P. Root (Thousand Oaks, Calif.: Sage, 1996), 81.

19. Ibid., 82.

20. Naomi Zack is the author of *Race and Mixed Race* (Philadelphia: Temple University Press, 1993) and the editor of *American Mixed Race: The Culture of Microdiversity* (Lanham, Md.: Rowman & Littlefield, 1995).

21. Naomi Zack, preface to Kwan and Speirs, *Mixing It Up*, xi–xii.

22. Joan Wallach Scott, *Gender and the Politics of History* (New York: Columbia University Press, 1999), 42.

23. This refers to the title of Winifred Breines's history of black and white radical feminisms of the 1960s to the 1980s.

24. Judith Halberstam, *In a Queer Time and Place* (New York: New York University Press), 5.

25. Peter Wallenstein and Erin Mooney, "*Loving v. Virginia* (1967)," in *The Public Debate over Controversial Supreme Court Decisions*, ed. Melvin Urofsky (Washington, D.C.: CQ Press, 2006), 260. The elision between "adulthood" and "childhood" at the site of those "[adult] children with multiracial identities" reveals the organizational centrality of motherhood for agents of multiracialism's cultural and political projects.

26. Hershini Bhana Young, "Black 'Like Me': (Mis) Recognition, the Racial Gothic, and the Post-1967 Mixed-Race Movement in Danzy Senna's *Symptomatic*," *African American Review* 42 (2008): 290.

27. Williams, *Mark One or More*, 105.

28. Ibid., 103.

29. DaCosta, *Making Multiracials*, 187. Williams makes a similar assessment in her study: "These white women [who took the primary lead in multiracial organizations] helped set an optimistic tone for multiracial activism; many believed that American racial polarization could be overcome by their example. Most of these women were looking for community—not for a census designation." *Mark One or More*, 112.

30. DaCosta, *Making Multiracials*, 187–88.

31. Winifred Breines, *The Trouble between Us: An Uneasy History of White and Black Women in the Feminist Movement* (New York: Oxford University Press, 2006), 12.

32. Ibid., 14.

33. Quoted in Spencer, *Spurious Issues*, 180.

34. Rockquemore and Brunsma, *Beyond Black,* 114.

35. Spencer, *Spurious Issues,* 181.

36. Rockquemore and Brunsma, *Beyond Black,* 114.

37. Dorothy Roberts, *Killing the Black Body: Race, Reproduction, and the Meaning of Liberty* (New York: Vintage Books, 1997), 215.

38. Moran, *Interracial Intimacy,* 105.

39. Kimberlé Crenshaw, "Demarginalizing the Intersection of Race and Sex: A Black Feminist Critique of Antidiscrimination Doctrine, Feminist Theory and Antiracist Politics," originally published by the University of Chicago Legal Forum (1989). Crenshaw points out how mainstream feminism and civil rights activism have each developed political critiques that delineate gender and racial issues respectively. She writes, "This adoption of a single-issue framework for discrimination not only marginalizes Black women within the very movements that claim them as part of their constituency but it also makes the elusive goal of ending racism and patriarchy even more difficult to attain." In James and Sharpley-Whiting, *Black Feminist Reader,* 219. Because this decidedly paradoxical condition of marginalization and inclusion has been the historical experience of black women within various political movements, it is instructive to ask whether this condition was produced within the multiracial movement, and to what effect.

40. Tavia Nyong'o, *Amalgamation Waltz: Race, Performance, and the Ruses of Memory* (Minneapolis: University of Minnesota Press, 2009), 176.

41. Ibid.

42. Avery Gordon, *Ghostly Matters: Haunting and the Sociological Imagination* (Minneapolis: University of Minnesota Press, 2008), 19.

43. Ibid., 190.

44. Carisa Showden offers another version of this in her explanation of how postfeminists and third-wave feminists misconstrue the contributions of second-wave feminism, and "the personal is political" in particular: "Girlie third-wavers, following Naomi Wolf, sometimes adopt an etiolated version of the slogan that says, in essence, 'whatever I do personally is political because I am a feminist.'" "What's Political about the New Feminisms?," *Frontiers: A Journal of Women Studies* 30 (2009): 174.

45. Sexton, *Amalgamation Schemes,* 161.

46. Robyn Wiegman, "Intimate Publics: Race, Property, and Personhood," *American Literature* 74 (2002): 869.

47. Ibid.

48. Ibid., 867.

49. Kathleen Odell Korgen, *From Black to Biracial: Transforming Racial Identity among Americans* (Westport, Conn.: Praeger, 1999), 22.

50. The Combahee River Collective notes how black feminist politics emerges from other political movements of the 1960s and 70s: "Many of us [black feminists]

were active in those movements (civil rights, Black nationalism, the Black Panthers). . . . It was our experience and disillusionment within these liberation movements, as well as experience on the periphery of the white male left, that led to the need to develop a politics that was antiracist, unlike those of white women, and the [*sic*] antisexist, unlike those of Black and white men" ("Black Feminist Statement," 262). Also see Michele Wallace's influential polemic on the sexism of black nationalist politics, *Black Macho and the Myth of the Superwoman* (1978; reprint, New York: Verso, 1999).

51. Wahneema Lubiano, "Don't Talk with Your Eyes Closed: Caught in the Hollywood Gun Sights," in *Borders, Boundaries, and Frames: Cultural Criticism and Cultural Studies,* ed. Mae Henderson (New York: Routledge, 1994), 188.

52. Revolutionary Action Movement, "The African American War of National-Liberation" (1965), reprinted in William L. Van Deburg, ed., *Modern Black Nationalism from Marcus Garvey to Farrakhan* (New York: New York University Press, 1997), 252.

53. Amiri Baraka, "It's Nation Time," included in his "Speech to the Congress of African Peoples" (1970), in Van Deburg, *Modern Black Nationalism,* 145–57.

54. Sexton, *Amalgamation Schemes,* 147.

55. Mike Hill, *After Whiteness: Unmaking an American Majority* (New York: New York University Press), 54.

56. Ibid.

57. Hill offers an alternative account: he wryly refers to multiracialism as a "dissensus nationalism," which indicates its paradoxical appearance as an approach to national collectivity even as it generates an uncontainable multiplicity of racial identities.

58. Charles Michael Byrd, "Speech," Multiracial Solidarity March I, *Interracial Voice,* July 20, 1996, http://198.66.252.234/speech1.html.

59. Ibid.

60. Norma Quarles, "Behind Million Men, Black Women," CNN, October 16, 1995, http://www-cgi.cnn.com/US/9510/megamarch/10-16/women/index.html.

61. Dalmage, *Tripping on the Color Line,* 142.

62. Lauren Berlant, *The Queen of America Goes to Washington City: Essays on Sex and Citizenship* (Durham, N.C.: Duke University Press, 1997), 7, 5.

63. Ibid., 6.

2. Legitimizing the Deviant Family

1. Angela P. Harris, "*Loving* Before and After the Law," *Fordham Law Review* 76 (2007–8): 2826.

2. Ibid., 2837.

3. Robert Pratt, "Crossing the Color Line," *Howard Law Journal* 41 (1997–98): 236.

4. Randall Kennedy, *Interracial Intimacies: Sex, Marriage, and Adoption* (New York: Pantheon Books, 2003), 273–74.

5. Quoted in ibid., 274.

6. Pratt, "Crossing the Color Line," 237.

7. Ibid., 230.

8. Warren, *Loving v. Virginia*, 388 U.S. 1 (1967), in Johnson, *Mixed Race America and the Law*, 63.

9. Kennedy, *Interracial Intimacies*, 272.

10. Carlos Ball, "The Blurring of the Lines: Children and Bans on Interracial Unions and Same-Sex Marriages," *Fordham Law Review* 76 (2007–8): 2747.

11. Daniel Patrick Moynihan, "The Negro Family: The Case for National Action" (known as the Moynihan Report), United States Department of Labor, March 1965, http://www.dol.gov/oasam/programs/history/webid-meynihan.htm, chap. 1.

12. Ibid.

13. Pratt, "Crossing the Color Line," 234.

14. From E. Franklin Frazier, "Problems and Needs of Negro Children and Youth Resulting from Family Disorganization," *Journal of Negro Education* (Summer 1960): 276–77. Quoted in the Moynihan Report, chap. 5.

15. Moynihan Report, opening remarks.

16. Moynihan Report, chap. 2.

17. Dorothy Roberts, *Shattered Bonds: The Color of Child Welfare* (New York: Basic Books, 2002), 176.

18. Ibid., 176.

19. Moynihan Report, chap. 3.

20. Siobhan Somerville, "Queer *Loving*," *GLQ: A Journal of Lesbian and Gay Studies* 11 (2005): 335–70.

21. Ibid., 347.

22. Ibid., 348.

23. Ibid., 349.

24. Ibid., 357.

25. Quoted in ibid., 355.

26. Madhu Dubey, *Signs and Cities: Black Literary Postmodernism* (Chicago: University of Chicago Press, 2003), 5.

27. Ibid.

28. "Washington's Black Majority Is Shrinking," *New York Times*, September 16, 2007, http://www.nytimes.com/.

29. Moynihan Report, chap. 3.

30. Peter Wallenstein, "Interracial Marriage on Trial: *Loving v. Virginia* (1967)," in *Race on Trial: Law and Justice in American History*, ed. Annette Gordon-Reed (New York: New York University Press, 2002), 179.

31. William Julius Wilson, *More than Just Race: Being Black and Poor in the Inner City* (New York: Norton, 2009), 98.

32. Ibid., 99.

33. Loïc Wacquant, "Deadly Symbiosis: When Ghetto and Prison Meet and Mesh," *Punishment and Society* 3 (2001): 95–103.

34. Ibid., 103.

35. "Trinidad Then and Now," Trinidad Neighbor Association, November 6, 2009, http://trinidad-dc.org/joomla/index.php?option=com_content&task=view&id=21&Itemid=88888895.

36. Wacquant, "Deadly Symbiosis," 103.

37. Ibid., 105.

38. Thomas Meehan, "Moynihan of the Moynihan Report," *New York Times,* July 31, 1966, http://partners.nytimes.com/books/98/10/04/specials/moynihan-report.html.

39. Wallenstein, "Interracial Marriage on Trial," 189.

40. Dubey, *Signs and Cities,* 26.

41. Roberts, *Shattered Bonds,* 176.

42. Ibid.

43. Ibid., iv.

44. Crenshaw, "Demarginalizing the Intersection of Race and Sex," in James and Sharpley-Whiting, *Black Feminist Reader,* 227.

45. Patricia Hill Collins, *Black Sexual Politics: African Americans, Gender, and the New Racism* (New York: Routledge, 2004), 131.

46. As Williams points out in *Mark One or More,* "It turns out that the multiracial movement at the grass roots was predominately led by white, middle-class women living in the suburbs" (86). Also, one of the effects of politicizing multiracial identity through the interracialism of families is that "many white women implied or stated outright [in their conversations with Williams] that race had been little more than a passing thought until they married a black man and had children" (99). The further effect is that multiracial identity, again according to Williams, is "the impossibility of disentangling the needs of parents from those of their children . . . the facts suggest that interracial family life is at least as challenging for parents as it is for children" (103). This challenge, as Williams frames it, has much to do with the loss of status and estrangement from white relatives that being a part of black, interracial families caused for the white women would become activists as a result of their chosen kinship relations. However, I suggest that the destabilization of white privilege through the process of having nonwhite children demonstrates a pervasive attempt to codify an ethics that constructs the whiteness of motherhood as a post–civil rights activist position that need not theorize the racialized dynamics of motherhood in order to conduct an ethical antiracist practice.

47. Ruth Feldstein, *Motherhood in Black and White: Race and Sex in American Liberalism, 1930–1965* (Ithaca, N.Y.: Cornell University Press, 2000).

48. According to the section in chapter 4 of the Moynihan Report entitled "The Tangle of Pathology," "In essence, the Negro community has been forced into a matriarchal structure which, because it is to out of line with the rest of the American society, seriously retards the progress of the group as a whole, and imposes a crushing burden on the Negro male and, in consequence, on a great many Negro women as well."

49. Williams, *Mark One or More,* 103.

50. Spillers, "Mama's Baby, Papa's Maybe," 84–85.

51. Ibid., 85.

52. Ball, "Blurring of the Lines," 2733.

53. Ibid., 2734.

54. Ibid., 2760.

55. Claudia Card, "Against Marriage and Motherhood," *Hypatia* 11 (1996): 16.

56. Dorothy E. Roberts, "Mothers Who Fail to Protect Their Children: Accounting for Private and Public Responsibility," in *Mother Troubles: Rethinking Contemporary Maternal Dilemmas,* ed. Julia Hanigsberg and Sara Ruddick (Boston: Beacon Press, 1999), 36–38.

57. Mary Lyndon Shanley, "Lesbian Families: Dilemmas in Grounding Legal Recognition of Parenthood," in Hanigsberg and Ruddick, *Mother Troubles,* 178–207.

58. DaCosta, *Making Multiracials,* 87.

59. Williams, *Mark One or More,* 87.

60. Ibid., 112.

61. Michel Foucault, "Friendship as a Way of Life," in *Ethics: Subjectivity and Truth,* ed. Paul Rabinow (New York: New Press, 1998), 136.

62. Judith Butler, "Is Kinship Always Already Heterosexual?," *differences* 13 (2002): 19.

63. Ibid.

64. Ibid., 19–20.

65. Ibid., 20.

66. Roberts, *Shattered Bonds,* 41.

67. Ibid., 38.

68. Ibid., 43.

3. The Whiteness of Maternal Memoirs

1. Moran, *Interracial Intimacy,* 125.

2. Peter Wallenstein, *Tell the Court I Love My Wife: Race, Marriage, and Law—An American History* (New York: Palgrave Macmillan, 2004), 6. My emphasis.

3. R. A. Lenhardt, Elizabeth B. Cooper, Sheila R. Foster, and Sonia K. Katal, "Forty Years of Loving: Confronting Issues of Race, Sexuality, and the Family in the Twenty-First Century—Introduction," *Fordham Law Review* 76 (2007–8): 2678.

4. Moran, *Interracial Intimacy*, 15.

5. M. M. Slaughter, "The Legal Construction of 'Mother,'" in *Mothers in Law: Feminist Theory and the Legal Regulation of Motherhood,* ed. Martha Fineman and Isabel Karpin (New York: Columbia University Press, 1995), 82. As Slaughter explains, the use of the capital letter M in Mother is "to indicate the person who rears children, rather than the person who bears them. In this usage, there is nothing in nature that requires women to Mother, or prevents men from doing so" (73).

6. Ibid., 110.

7. Wallenstein, *Tell the Court I Love My Wife*, 238–39.

8. Ibid.

9. Moran, *Interracial Intimacy*, 104.

10. Maureen T. Reddy, *Crossing the Color Line: Race, Parenting, and Culture* (New Brunswick, N.J.: Rutgers University Press, 1994), xiv.

11. Ibid., 3.

12. Ibid.

13. Ibid., 5.

14. For an extended analysis on racial divisiveness between black and white feminist projects of the 1960s and 1970s, see Breines's *Trouble between Us.*

15. Ibid., 5.

16. Ibid.

17. Ibid., 6.

18. Toni Morrison, *Playing in the Dark: Whiteness and the Literary Imagination* (Cambridge, Mass.: Harvard University Press, 1992).

19. Reddy, *Crossing the Color Line,* 35.

20. Ibid., 45.

21. Ibid., 45, 47.

22. Ibid., 5.

23. Ibid., 13.

24. Ibid., 15.

25. Ibid.

26. Ibid., 154.

27. Ibid., 168–69.

28. Ibid., 169.

29. Ibid., 158.

30. Ibid., 162.

31. Ibid.

32. Ibid., 167.
33. Ibid., 173.
34. Toni Morrison, *Beloved* (New York: Knopf, 1987), 88, 90–92.
35. Ibid., 88.
36. Toni Morrison, *Conversations with Toni Morrison,* ed. Danille K. Taylor-Guthrie (Garden City, N.Y.: Doubleday, 1990), 247.
37. Jane Lazarre, *Beyond the Whiteness of Whiteness: Memoir of a White Mother of Black Sons* (Durham, N.C.: Duke University Press, 1997), xviii.
38. Ibid.
39. Ibid.
40. Ibid., 3.
41. Ibid.
42. Ibid., 4.
43. Ibid., 5.
44. Ibid., 20.
45. Ibid.
46. Ibid.
47. Ibid., 24.
48. Ibid., 24, 25.
49. Ibid., 134.
50. Ibid.
51. Ibid., 134.

4. Ambivalent Outcomes

1. France Winddance Twine, "The White Mother: Blackness, Whiteness, and Interracial Families," *Transition* 73 (1998): 144–54, 144.
2. As Patricia Hill Collins discusses with relation to the significance of blood ties of family and the maintenance of separate racial categories, "White women play a special role in keeping bloodlines pure. Historically, creating White families required controlling White women's sexuality, largely through social norms that advocated pre-marital virginity. By marrying White men and engaging in sexual relations only with their husbands, White women ensured the racial purity of White families." "It's All in the Family: Intersections of Gender, Race and Nation," *Hypatia* 13 (1998): 69. This discussion points to the intersectional scheme of white racial purity and patriarchy that animates the ideal of family. In a sense, the family of popular multiracial rhetoric displaces the dominance of patriarchy and white purity without disrupting an enduring necessity for hierarchy in imagining ideal family organization.
3. David Wellman, "Minstrel Shows, Affirmative Action Talk, and Angry White Men: Marking Racial Otherness in the 1990s," in *Displacing Whiteness:*

Essays in Social and Cultural Criticism, ed. Ruth Frankenberg (Durham, N.C.: Duke University Press, 1997), 313.

4. Twine, "White Mother," 154.

5. Ibid.

6. James McBride, *The Color of Water: A Black Man's Tribute to His White Mother* (New York: Riverhead Books, 1996), xvii.

7. I thank Caroline Chung Simpson for this insight.

8. McBride, *Color of Water,* xvii.

9. Phillip Brian Harper, "Passing for What? Racial Masquerade and the Demands of Upward Mobility," *Callaloo* 21 (1998): 383.

10. McBride, *Color of Water,* 21.

11. Ibid., 23.

12. Ibid., xvii.

13. Harper, "Passing for What?," 385.

14. Ibid.

15. Jared Sexton, "The Consequence of Racial Mixture: Racialised Barriers and the Politics of Desire," *Social Identities* 9 (2003): 241–75.

16. McBride, *Color of Water,* 9.

17. Ibid., 99–100.

18. Ibid., 21–22.

19. Ibid., 51.

20. Ibid., 113.

21. Ibid., 111.

22. Moran, *Interracial Intimacy,* 174.

23. McBride, *Color of Water,* 220.

24. Lopez, "'A Nation of Minorities': Race, Ethnicity, and Reactionary Color-blindness," *Stanford Law Review* 59 (2007): 986.

25. Philip Roth, *The Human Stain* (New York: Vintage, 2001), 6.

26. Ibid.

27. Derek Parker Royal, "Plotting the Frames of Subjectivity: Identity, Death, and Narrative in Philip Roth's *The Human Stain,*" *Contemporary Literature* 47 (2006): 118.

28. Roth, *Human Stain,* 19.

29. Bliss Broyard, *One Drop: My Father's Hidden Life—A Story of Race and Family Secrets* (New York: Little, Brown, 2007), 431.

30. Karen Brodkin, *How Jews Became White Folks and What That Says about Race in America* (New Brunswick, N.J.: Rutgers University Press, 2000), 139.

31. Ibid., 140.

32. Timothy L. Parrish, "Ralph Ellison: The Invisible Man in Philip Roth's *The Human Stain,*" *Contemporary Literature* 45 (2004): 433.

33. Roth, *Human Stain,* 16.

34. Werner Sollors, *Neither Black nor White Yet Both: Thematic Explorations of Interracial Literature* (New York: Oxford University Press, 1997), 250.

35. Deborah McDowell, introduction to *Quicksand and Passing,* by Nella Larsen (New Brunswick, N.J.: Rutgers University Press, 1986), ix–xxxi.

36. Amy Robinson, "It Takes One to Know One: Passing and Communities of Common Interest," *Critical Inquiry* 20 (1994): 715–36.

37. James Weldon Johnson, *Autobiography of an Ex-Colored Man,* in *Three Negro Classics* (New York: Avon Books, 1965), 499.

38. Roth, *Human Stain,* 98.

39. Johnson, *Autobiography of an Ex-Colored Man,* 499.

40. Roth, *Human Stain,* 327.

41. See Michael K. Brown et al., *Whitewashing Race: The Myth of a Color-blind Society* (Berkeley: University of California Press, 2003). The authors classify those who hold this view as "racial realists" and specifically identify Jim Sleeper, Tamar Jacoby, Dinesh D'Souza, Shelby Steele, and Stephen and Abigail Thernstrom as belonging to this category (5).

42. Roth, *Human Stain,* 98.

43. Ibid., 88.

44. Ibid., 94.

45. Ibid., 107–8.

46. Ibid., 108.

47. Ibid., 117.

47. Ibid.

48. Michele Elam, *The Souls of Mixed Folk: Race, Politics, and Aesthetics in the New Millennium* (Palo Alto, Calif.: Stanford University Press, 2011), 106–7.

49. Roth, *Human Stain,* 111.

50. Elam, *Souls,* 138, 136.

51. Roth, *Human Stain,* 137.

52. Ibid., 137–38.

53. Ibid., 138.

54. Ibid., 139.

55. Ibid., 12.

56. Ibid., 13.

57. Jay L. Halio, review of *The Human Stain, Shofar* 20 (2001): 174.

58. Marlia E. Banning, "The Limits of PC Discourse: Linking Language Use to Social Practice," *Pedagogy* 4 (2004): 195.

59. Irvin Lewis Allen, *American Speech* 70 (1995): 112; and Andrew Ross et al., "A Symposium on Popular Culture and Political Correctness," *Social Text* 36 (1993): 1.

60. Richard Feldstein, *Political Correctness: A Response from the Cultural Left* (Minneapolis: University of Minnesota Press, 1997), 46.

61. Ibid., 57.
62. Ibid.
63. Roth, *Human Stain,* 17.
64. Eduardo Bonilla-Silva, *Racism without Racists: Color-blind Racism and the Persistence of Racial Inequality in the United States* (Lanham, Md.: Rowman & Littlefield, 2006), 57.
65. Marilyn Friedman, "Codes, Canons, Correctness, and Feminism," *Political Correctness: For and Against,* ed. Marilyn Friedman and Jan Narveson (Lanham, Md.: Rowman & Littlefield, 1995), 1.
66. Roth, *Human Stain,* 327.
67. Ibid., 329.

Conclusion

1. Charles E. Cook Jr., "The 2008 Presidential Primaries: What in America's Name Is Going On?," *Washington Quarterly* 31, no. 3 (2008): 202–3.
2. Robin Kelley, *Freedom Dreams: The Black Radical Imagination* (Boston: Beacon Press, 2002), 137.
3. Ricky Jones, *What's Wrong with Obamamania? Black America, Black Leadership, and the Death of Political Imagination* (Albany: State University of New York Press, 2008), 7.
4. Ibid., 123.
5. Quoted in Michael Tesler and David Sears, *Obama's Race: The 2008 Election and the Dream of a Post-racial America* (Chicago: University of Chicago Press, 2010), 30.
6. David Hollinger, "Obama, the Instability of Color Lines, and the Promise of a Postethnic Future," *Callaloo* 31 (2008): 1033.
7. Ibid., 1033–34.
8. Ibid., 1034.
9. Ibid., 1037.
10. Ibid., 1034.
11. Tesler and Sears, *Obama's Race,* 29.
12. Cherríe Moraga, "What's Race Gotta Do with It?," *Meridians* 9 (2008): 163.
13. Ibid., 165.
14. Ibid., 163.
15. Ibid., 168.
16. Combahee River Collective, "Black Feminist Statement," 269.
17. Moraga, "What's Race Gotta Do with It?," 170.
18. "Transcript: 'This Is Your Victory,' Says Obama," CNN.com, November 4, 2008, http://edition.cnn.com/.
19. Moraga, "What's Race Gotta Do with It?," 169.

20. According to journalist Buzz Bissinger, "It wasn't until after the early-morning hours of November 27—when Tiger Woods got into his Cadillac Escalade closely trailed by a golf club carried by his likely very furious wife, drove his car far less distance than he putts a golf ball, and hit a fire hydrant—that the tens of millions of us who admired him suddenly came to a realization: this was the first time we had ever seen him do something human." "Tiger in the Rough," *Vanity Fair,* February 2010, http://www.vanityfair.com/.

Index

academia: identity politics and, 151; multiculturalism and, 144, 151, 155; political correctness and, 136, 151, 155. *See also Human Stain, The* (Roth)

ACLU, 61

advocacy strategy, 10, 77, 118–19, 121, 122–23. *See also* multiracial organizations

affect: ambivalent forms of, 41; of denial and revulsion between blackness and multiracialism, 36, 40–41; liberal personhood and modes of, 28–33

affirmative action, 24, 25

Afrocentric nationalism, 37

agency: limits and conditions of asserting, in McBride's *Color of Water,* 148, 158; maternal, 83, 90, 109, 118, 121; possibility of, in historical construction of blackness, xvi; undercut or promoted by performance or language, in Roth's *Human Stain,* 137–38, 139, 148; women as primary agents of racial discourse, 16, 18

AIDS crisis, black political responses to, xi–xii

Aid to Dependent Children (ADC), 51

Aid to Families with Dependent Children (AFDC), 50–51

Alchemy of Race and Rights, The (Williams), 21

Alex-Assensoh, Yvette, 181n.1

alienation: of blackness in relation to whiteness and pliable quality of ethnicity, 134; as conduit for challenges to social injustice to go from public activism to private concerns, 39–40, 73; fostering inclusive communities to prevent, 12–13; in Reddy's *Crossing the Color Line,* 91, 98

Allen, Irvin Lewis, 194n.59

All the Women Are White, All the Blacks Are Men, Yet Some of Us Are Brave, 5

Althusser, Louis, 7, 184n.4

ambiguous aura, identities mutable under, 141

American Civil Liberties Union (ACLU), 61

angry white male, 1990s cultural type, 123, 146

Anna J. v. Mark C, 31

antimiscegenation laws: concomitance of immigration policy and, 54; dismantled by *Loving* decision, 9, 44–45, 47, 51, 60, 68–69, 81–82, 101; political forcefulness for people of Jim Crow era, 85; in Virginia, 46–47, 49, 56, 59

antiracism, neoliberal era of (1980s), xxvi–xxviii

potential, xxi, xxiii; excessive burden of signifying multitude of investments, xx; historical conditions of marginalization, 5–6, 8, 28, 36–38, 163, 186n.39; in neoliberal teleology, 38; outmarriage by, 27, 89–90, 97–98; racialized sexual imagery of, 89–90; "superwomen," 27; as transhistorical absence against which other identitarian forms become seen, 173, 175. *See also* black feminism; black motherhood

Bonilla-Silva, Eduardo, 153–54, 195n.64

Boutilier, Clive Michael, 53

Boutilier v. Immigration Service, 53

Breines, Winifred, 22–23, 185n.23, 185n.31

Brodkin, Karen, 138–39, 193n.30

Brown, Michael K., 194n.41

Brown v. Board of Education (1954), 47, 48

Broyard, Anatole, 137

Broyard, Bliss, 137, 193n.29

Brunsma, David, 24, 181n.1

Butler, Judith, 75, 190n.62

Byrd, Charles Michael, 11, 36–37, 38, 187n.58

Cablinasian, Woods's transformation from race man to, xix–xxiv, xxv; backlash from black community, xxiii–xxiv

Calvert, Mark and Crispina, 31

capitalism, racial, 58, 163

Carby, Hazel, xi, 182n.7

Card, Claudia, 70, 190n.55

caste distinctions: built into immigration laws, 54; built into marriage law, 44–45, 54; establishment of,

44, 49; as natural and therefore legal, 45, 46

childhood, ideal potential of, 28

children: in black-to-white passing narratives, 128; current conditions for denial of legal protection, 70; family time and, 19–20; as proxies for not yet visible or emergent mediation between adults, 22, 39. *See also* multiracial child

citizenship: affective dimension of, policing, 45, 46; family as affective space connected to, 68; ideological dimension of, 45; marriage and natural foundations of, 44–45; potential of kinship beyond family and, 73–80; during and after Reagan era of 1980s, 39; shifting discourse on conditions of legitimate, 53–54

city(ies): de facto racial segregation in northern, 55, 58; as dumping ground for expendable labor, 52, 59; ghettos, 52, 57, 58–59, 60; as holding place for deviance, 56, 58; intranational migration to, 54–60; moral panic about African Americans as prime threat to urban security and national community, 60; race riots of 1960s, 55; social dislocations in inner, 57; urbanization and racialization of geography, 56, 58, 62

Civil Rights Act (1964), 48, 55, 164

civil rights era: black women marginalized in, 186n.39; as foundation for 1990s-era multiracialism, xxvii, xxviii, xxix, 3; imaginative conjuring of blended children during, 102–3; interracial feminist collaboration during, nostalgia for lost, 22–23;

"How to Rehabilitate a Mulatto" (Perez), xv

Human Stain, The (Roth), xxx, 124, 135–56; black communal origin for Silk in, 143–44; boxing as metaphor for racial passing in, 142–43, 145–46; color-blindness in, 135–41, 153, 155; commentary on current disciplinary and political framings of history, 156–57; conditions of self-authorship in, concern with, 136–39; controversy over racism in, 135–36, 137, 139, 152–53, 155; emphasis on fatherhood in, 143–45; invisibility trope in, 139–40; political correctness in, 136, 138, 150–54, 155; racial time of skipping step between Jim Crow and 1990s postracial politics in, 154–56; return of maternal affect and death of black motherhood in, 146–49, 158; self-made men and racial neutral individualism in, 141–46; Silk's first experience with racial passing in, 142–43, 144; Silk's loss of agency as historical subject in, 137–38, 139, 148; Zuckerman's account of Silk in, 138, 140–41

hybrid criticality, development of, 75

hypodescent, rule of (one-drop rule), vii, 37

"idealized motherhood," myth of, 76, 79

identity: Hollinger's destabilization of identitarian destinies, 166–68; key approaches to framing notions of, 20–21; rise of multiracial identification, 31–36; transhistorical political and personal, 165, 166

identity politics, 31, 36, 144; academia and, 151; black, 162, 165; ethno-racial categories central to, as matters of choice, 166; legacies of, 123; maternal multiracialism neutralizing, 25–26; Obama as postracial candidate transcending, 166, 168; of representation, 152; in Roth's *Human Stain*, 142, 144, 151, 153, 156

illegitimacy: disjuncture between legitimacy and, 75; emergent form of interracial, in Reddy's *Crossing the Color Line*, 103–5; unstable status of interracial child and, 68–74, 77, 80

Immigration and Nationality Act (INA), 53

immigration policy, 53–54

impostor, condemnation of racial passer as, 141

individualism: fluid, unfulfilled desire for in civil rights movement, 154; neoliberal or individualist theory of racial justice, xxvi; racial neutral, in Roth's *Human Stain*, 141–46

integration, sense of lost ideal of, 23

interracial feminism: based on motherhood, 106–8; during civil rights era, nostalgia for, 22–23; imagined in Reddy's *Crossing the Color Line*, 95–101, 105–8

Interracial/Inter-Cultural Pride (I-Pride), 9

interracial intimacy: building bridges for, 84–91; challenge for both parents and children, 189n.46; children and dynamics of marriage, in Reddy's *Crossing the Color Line*, 101–5; long history of, 27, 46, 49;

81–82; as originating moment for
1990s-era discourses on multiracialism, xxix, 67, 81; paradox
performed by, 56; political business
left unfinished by, xxx, 82; privileges of heterosexuality consoli-
dated in, 53–54; responsibility
toward and status of interracial
children as often-neglected component of, 101; state control demonstrated in, 45–46
Lubiano, Wahneema, 32, 187n.51
lynching, stakes of racial passing
clarified by, 142

Malcolm X, xi, xix
"Mama's Baby, Papa's Maybe"
(Spiller), xx
Mamet, David, 150
Manpower Development and Training Act of 1962, 48
marginalization: of black women,
historical conditions of, 5–6, 8, 28,
36–38, 163, 186n.39; politics of the
marginalized, 170–71; racialized,
56, 89, 169
Mark One or More (Williams),
189n.46
marriage: contingent on profound
racialization of geography, 56;
normalized as tacitly white, heterosexual enterprise, 54; as state
institution, distinction of castes
embedded in, 44–45, 54; tendency
to render analogous interracial and
same-sex, 53–54. *See also* interracial
intimacy; *Loving v. Virginia* (1967)
masculine intimacy, rechanneling into
racial antagonism, 37
masculinity: centrality in racialized
communities, viii; emasculating

potential of black women, xxi, xxiii;
masculine lineage of race leadership stemming from civil rights era,
40; masculinist ideology underlying
founding texts of black American
history, xi; masculinist response to
racial inequity, 145–46; status of
racial hero implicitly functioning
through account of, x. *See also* black
manhood/masculinity
Masters Tournament (1997),
Woods's victory at, x
maternal memoirs. *See* memoirs,
whiteness of maternal
McBride, Andrew Dennis, 126
McBride, James, xxx–xxxi, 124–35,
193n.6; sense of identity of, 157–
58. *See also Color of Water, The: A
Black Man's Tribute to His White
Mother* (McBride)
McCabe, Jewell Jackson, 37
McDowell, Deborah, 194n.35
McLaughlin v. Florida, 47
Meehan, Thomas, 189n.38
memoirs, whiteness of maternal, xxx,
81–120; *Beloved* (Morrison) as
bridge between, 108–12; *Beyond
the Whiteness of Whiteness*
(Lazarre), xxx, 81, 82, 91, 113–20,
122; contextualizing individual
socially and historically in, 114;
*Crossing the Color Line: Race
Parenting and Culture* (Reddy), xxx,
81, 82, 91–109; memoir as political
form, potential problem with, 114.
*See also Color of Water, The: A
Black Man's Tribute to His White
Mother* (McBride)
Meridian (Walker), 106, 107
Meridians (journal), 169
Mfume, Kweisi, xxiii

ideological rift between, 10–13, 23–24; objectives of, balancing, 12–13; reasons for joining, 73

Multiracial Solidarity March (1996), 36–37

multiracial transcendence, desire for, 29

Nakashima, Cynthia, 14, 24, 185n.18

National Coalition of 100 Black Women, 37

national historiography, naturalization of, 116

nationalism: Afrocentric, 37; black, 4, 9, 32–33, 34, 36, 38, 175; black cultural, 144; Moraga on nationalist violence, 171–72; nationalist politics of intimacy invested in family, 39

nation time, 33–38

"Negro Family, The: The Case for National Action." See Moynihan Report (1965)

Negro revolution, Moynihan Report on achievements of, 48–49

neoconservatives/neoconservatism, 136, 142, 155; appropriation of politics of multiracialism, 123; color-blindness in discourse of, 2, 153, 155, 156; Gingrich as, 25, 27; origins of neoconservatives, 151; political correctness concocted by, 151; shift in interpretation of racism during 1960s, 134–35; silencing of normatively white men as issue for, 150, 152; trend of 1980s and 1990s to ridicule excesses of New Leftist politics, 151, 155

neoliberalism, xxvi–xxviii, 38, 184n.11

neutrality: neutralized space of family, 6, 14; new racist, 153; politically neutralized ideal of personhood, 18; racial, 81, 123, 127, 132, 135, 138, 141–46, 147, 153, 162, 164, 168; state, appearance of, 54; temporality of multiracialism and promise of, 2–3, 6; of whiteness, 113. See also color-blindness; racial neutrality

New Leftist politics, 151

Newton, Huey, xvi

New York Times Magazine, 1994 roundtable discussion on black manhood in, xv

Nike, xiii, xiv, xix; hidden Third World labor involved in, xiv–xv

Nyong'o, Tavia, 28–29, 186n.40

Obama, Barack, xxvi, 161–76; ability to speak language of multiracialism, 172–73; ambivalent self-definition of, 166; campaign for presidency, 165, 168; Clinton's comparison of King and, 164–65, 169; family's key role in making of president, 172–73; gender neutrality as precondition for transcendence of, 163–64; as harbinger of postethnic future, 166–67; identification with blackness, 162; Kenyan father of, 167; Moraga family's response to election of, 169–75; negotiation of race, xxxi; as no race man, 164, 166; "Obama phenomenon," 162; as representative of transcendent multiracial identity and black advancement, 162; victory speech of, 173–75

Obama, Barack, Sr., 167

Obama, Michelle, 167–68, 173

Sears, David, 165, 168, 195n.5
segregation, de facto racial, 55, 58
self-authorization, failure of, 145
self-authorship, racial passing and
   conditions of, 136–39
self-determination: black, 32, 57, 58;
   public, passing as, 144
self-esteem of multiracial children, 25,
   40, 67–68, 77, 78, 85–86, 88;
   antiliberatory connotation of, 89
self-made man: cult of social upstart
   as, 141; racial neutral individualism
   and, 141–46. *See also* racial passing
self-reflexivity, lack of, 27–28
separatism: black, 37, 144; racial, 86,
   98, 105
Sexton, Jared, 29, 30, 34, 35–36,
   181n.1, 193n.15
sexuality: complicit with one's
   impact on childhood caretaking,
   77; downplaying race as mechanism for excluding nonheterosexual
   modes of, 53–54; illicitness of, drug
   abuse and, 63; interracial, 29–30;
   racialized sexual imagery, 88, 89–
   90; of white women, racial purity
   and control of, 192n.2
Shanley, Mary Lyndon, 72, 77,
   190n.57
Sharpton, Al, 166
Shelton, Hilary, xxv
Sherman, Ed, xiii, xiv, 182n.12
Showden, Carisa, 186n.44
Sidoti, Linda, 87–88
Sifford, Charlie, x
Simpson, Caroline Chung, 193n.7
Slaughter, M. M., 87, 191n.5
slavery, 58; evocation of Middle
   Passage in *Beloved*, 110–11; exhibit
   of American, in Lazarre's *Beyond
   the Whiteness of Whiteness*, 115–16;

historical condition of black
   motherhood and, 61, 84; legacies
   of bodily theft and coercion from,
   31
social injustice: loss of public terrain
   for challenging, 23, 25–26, 28,
   39–40; role of multiracialism in
   challenging, 13, 14
Sollors, Werner, 35, 141, 194n.34
Somerville, Siobhan, 52–55, 188n.20
Souls of Black Folk, The (Du Bois), xi
speech, political correctness and
   misrepresentation of, 136, 152–53,
   154
Speirs, Kenneth, 7, 16, 18, 184n.5
Spencer, Jon Michael, 37
Spencer, Rainier, 25, 181n.1
Spillers, Hortense J., xx–xxi, xxiii, 69,
   76, 183n.31
spook, customary and primary
   meaning vs. historically racist
   connotation of, 136, 152–53
Squires, Catherine, 181n.1
state: Althusser's theory of, 7; desire
   to relinquish its obligation to
   redress inequality, 25–26, 82; in era
   of civil rights, xxvii; liberal theory
   of, 27; *Loving* decision endowing
   fathers with responsibility for
   family, 47–48; neutral, as ideal,
   xxvi, xxvii–xxviii; privatization of
   responsibilities for racial, sexualized, and economic redress, xxviii,
   xxix–xxx; recognition of social
   identities, gaining, 9, 12; regulation
   of family, 43–44, 45; rift between
   appearance of neutrality and overt
   interest in black family, 54–55;
   shift from politics of public
   resource distribution to politics of
   personal responsibility, 62, 82. *See*

white mother of black/multiracial children: active redressing of society's devaluation of blackness/ black children, 92; affective attachment to black children, 64, 65; challenges of parenting in interracial family, 118, 189n.46; claim to black futures, xxiv–xxvi; condition of affect between mother and child undercut by devaluation of blackness, 87–88, 92; leadership in multiracial politics, xxiv–xxv, 6, 20–24, 67–68, 118, 121, 122, 185n.29, 189n.46; personhood of white motherhood, emergence of, 20–24; potential of kinship beyond family and citizenship, 73–80; responsibility to develop analysis that puts pressure on assumed privileges of whiteness, 79; transformation of consciousness for, 115–16, 117, 121; unaccounted form of illegitimacy for, 103–5. *See also* memoirs, whiteness of maternal

whiteness: cultural differences engulfed by, at exclusion of black identity, 133; as form of privilege to be dismantled or extended to include multiracial kinship, 122; Jewish form of, 138–39; Jordan's disavowal of, in *Color of Water*, 127–28; Lazarre's exploration of, as barrier between white mother and multiracial child, 113–20; produced through logic of merit, in Roth's *Human Stain*, 145–46; as race neutrality, 127, 147; rendered racially aberrant by motherhood, 119; white normativity embattled and particularized in 1990s, 139;

white writers attempting to disassociate from, 122

whiteness studies, emergence of, 122, 139

white privilege, 28, 31, 79, 99, 134; attempts to extend, to multiracial children, 20, 121, 122; destabilization of, through having nonwhite children, 20–21, 118, 189n.46; Jewish form of whiteness and, 138–39; *Loving* case and, 59; refusal of, 111

white supremacy: ban on interracial marriage to prevent interracial children, 69–70; discrimination against interracial kinship and, 104; interracialism and renunciation of, 97, 98; racial passing and complicity in cultural politics of, 146; as rationale for antimiscegenation, Warren's *Loving* decision and, 45, 47

white women: special role in keeping bloodlines pure, 192n.2; working-class, 124–25. *See also* white mother of black/multiracial children

Wiegman, Robyn, 30, 32, 38, 186n.46

Williams, Gregory Howard, 37

Williams, Kim, xxv, 20, 21, 125, 181n.1; on potential of multiracial collectivity, 80; on white mothers' involvement in multiracial politics, 67–68, 73, 74, 78, 79–80

Williams, Patricia, 21, 185n.29, 189n.46

Williams, Sherley Anne, 106

Williams, Wendy, xxi

Wilson, William Julius, 57, 63, 189n.31

HABIBA IBRAHIM is assistant professor of English at the University of Washington.

www.ingramcontent.com/pod-product-compliance
Lightning Source LLC
Chambersburg PA
CBHW020855270326
41928CB00006B/712